Philosophical and Theological Writings

Franz Rosenzweig

Philosophical and
Theological Writings

Translated and edited,
with notes and commentary, by
Paul W. Franks and Michael L. Morgan

Hackett Publishing Company, Inc.
Indianapolis/Cambridge

For further information, please address:
Hackett Publishing Company, Inc.
P.O. Box 44937
Indianapolis, IN 46244-0937

www.hackettpublishing.com

Cover design by Listenberger Design & Associates
Interior design by Abigail Coyle

Library of Congress Cataloging-in-Publication Data

Rosenzweig, Franz, 1886–1929.
    [Selections. English. 2000]
    Philosophical and theological writings / Franz Rosenzweig ; translated and
edited with notes and commentary by Paul W. Franks and Michael L. Morgan.
        p. cm.
    Includes bibliographical references and index.
    ISBN 0-87220-473-1 (cloth)—ISBN 0-87220-472-3 (paper)
    1. Judaism. 2. Philosophy, Jewish. 3. Rosenzweig, Franz, 1886–1929.
I. Franks, Paul., W., 1964–   II. Morgan, Michael L., 1944–   III. Title

BM45.R67213 2000
181'.06 — dc21   00-032028

Contents

Preface

This small volume is intended to contribute to the recent renewed interest in the writings and thinking of Franz Rosenzweig. When Rosenzweig was imported to the North American continent in the postwar period, it was by German Jewish intellectuals involved in the study of Judaism and in Jewish theological reflection. Through the 1950s and into the 1960s, Rosenzweig was a centerpiece of Jewish theological thinking, largely along with Martin Buber as the source of a view of revelation and the divine-human encounter that seemed to be situated somewhere within the existential tradition. This view of revelation was available as part of a recovery of Biblical faith and could be used to confront the scientific orientation of American culture and the challenges of religious naturalism, which primarily arose within Jewish circles with the Reconstructionism of Mordecai Kaplan. From the late 1960s through the 1980s, Rosenzweig's star was on the wane. Revelation and faith, as central theological and theoretical notions, gave way to much more historical and often political thinking. To be sure, someone like Emil Fackenheim, whose work is deeply influenced by Rosenzweig, never failed to acknowledge his indebtedness and mark the importance of Rosenzweig, but overall his prominence among Jewish thinkers had diminished, and beyond that circle he was barely known.

That situation has changed dramatically. The emergence of the movement we now call "postmodernism" with all its dimensions and strands has brought with it a renewed interest in otherness and difference, history and memory, and the notion of the messianic. And this movement has brought with it a greater interest in Heidegger and all those who followed him—Gadamer in Germany and Foucault, Derrida, Levinas, and many others in France—and with issues that concern the political and the religious. All of this has touched religious thinking, to be sure, but its greatest impact is much broader.

Postmodern concerns, strategies, and themes permeate general culture, literature, art, music, film, and almost all academic disciplines, and the key figures hence have become part of the general cultural and intellectual world. In this context, Rosenzweig has emerged as a figure of special interest. He was a contemporary of Heidegger and, like Heidegger, an advocate of the "new thinking" and its challenge to the old philosophical tradition. He was modernist in some ways and yet seemed to point beyond modernism to something new and uncharted. Levinas, Scholem, and Benjamin knew his work and were moved and influenced by it. Furthermore, his life itself bridged the gap between intellectual thinking and real, concrete life, while his protracted illness and almost heroic encounter with it spoke powerfully to the ironies of human existence, as did his death, on the brink of the rise of Nazi fascism. Like Benjamin, Rosenzweig has emerged as a forerunner of powerful and important ideas that in the past decade have been influential and provocative.

Today, then, Rosenzweig is interesting for different reasons than he was in the immediate postwar period. Now there are philosophers, literary critics, and students of culture, politics, and ideology, as well as religious thinkers, who seek engagement with his works and his thinking. This volume is intended as a vehicle for all of these audiences to enter into the study of Rosenzweig's work, his development as a philosopher and theologian, and his importance for understanding 20th-century culture. The theological, the historical, the political, the philosophical, and the literary—all are intertwined in these essays. What emerges is a person struggling to confront the challenges of European history and culture in the years around World War I and whose thinking attempts to meet those challenges and then go on, to live a particular kind of life, for him a Jewish life, in which meaning and purpose can be grasped and acknowledged.

For nearly fifty years, the major resource for teaching Rosenzweig has been Nahum Glatzer's book, *Franz Rosenzweig: His Life and Thought*, first published by Schocken Books in 1953 and now available through Hackett Publishing. That work was the first book-length English translation of Rosenzweig available to the North American public, and notwithstanding other translations in book form, it remains the single best place to introduce students to Rosenzweig's life and career and to the range of his writings.

Other available translations and collections are less helpful. While the existing translation of Rosenzweig's major work, *The Star of Redemption*, is deeply flawed and almost impossible to use, there have been recent translations of his Biblical studies, his translation and commentary to the poems of Judah Halevi, and other shorter works. Each volume has its strengths and weaknesses, but none provides an overview of Rosenzweig's intellectual career and makes available texts central to tracing that career. Hence, we felt that a set of new translations of especially significant philosophical and theological works would be a useful addition to the translated works, especially for educational purposes.

A new translation of the *Star*, up to contemporary standards and with scholarly notes, is a current necessity. Any serious study of Rosenzweig's life and works must focus on that work. But even without having such a translation in hand, the student of Rosenzweig can understand a great deal about his intellectual development if one watches him move toward the *Star* and then beyond it. In this volume, we have attempted to chart that course. Our goals have been these: to translate several works that are significant signposts along the way, from his earliest theological essay "Atheistic Theology" to a very late review of the republication of Cohen's *Religion der Vernunft* in 1929, shortly before his death; to provide translations that are as close to Rosenzweig's German as possible, readable but reliable, enabling teacher and student to study them carefully and examine them in detail; to include notes on Rosenzweig's many allusions, quotations, and so forth; to "stitch together" these works with a narrative that situates the works, clarifies their main themes and arguments, and thereby facilitates the study of the pieces themselves; and to include a bibliography that we believe would be most useful to North American students of Rosenzweig's thought.

All of the translations are new ones. When we began this project, there was no published translation of the *"Urzelle,"* the core of the *Star* from Rosenzweig's letter to Rudolf Ehrenberg of 1917; nor was there a full published translation of "The New Thinking" or the selections from Rosenzweig's book on Hegel. An old translation of "Atheistic Theology" did exist but was difficult to find for most readers, and the volume in which a translation of "Apologetic Thinking" could be found is now out of print. A relatively inaccessible version of "Transposed Fronts" also existed. Now some of these pieces are available in new translations. But we believe that our translations, with their ample annotations, have a uniformity and faithfulness that make them especially usable for teaching purposes in ways that other translations are not.

Both of us have worked through the texts together several times and then, in some cases, separately. We take final responsibility together for the translations. We would like to acknowledge the excellent assistance of Ingo Farin, who provided us with initial versions of "The New Thinking" and "Transposed Fronts" and examined carefully our translation of the *"Urzelle"* at an early stage. Karl-Heinz Maurer did initial versions of "Atheistic Theology" and "Apologetic Thinking." It was Ingo who encouraged us to include "Transposed Fronts." We would also like to thank Graham Hammill, Diana Lobel, and Vera Profit for their help. Older existing translations were consulted, but the translations presented here are new products, indebted to the old but original.*

Paul Franks did the major work on the notes and Michael Morgan on the essays, but both reviewed everything and made comments, revisions, and modifications. The discussion of the significance of the year 1800 for Rosenzweig and the discussion of Schelling's importance for Rosenzweig were largely the work of Paul Franks. Overall, then, the volume was a completely collaborative project. More than that, it was a cooperative effort of two families, one of which, the Franks, grew in the course of the book's completion. We would like to thank Hindy Najman and Audrey Morgan for their love and support and note with special joy the role played by Marianna Bluma Najman-Franks in its final stages.

---

* In the notes we have done our best to track down references and allusions in order to assist the reader with texts that are often private and opaque. We invite the reader's assistance in furthering this task, either by correcting our errors or by identifying hints and allusions that we have failed to clarify.

Note

The translations are based on the following texts:

Franz Rosenzweig, *Der Mensch und sein Werk: Gesammelte Schriften III: Zweistromland: Kleinere Schriften zu Glauben und Denken*, ed. Reinhold and Annemarie Mayer (Dordrecht: Martinus Nijhoff, 1984).

> Apologetisches Denken: Bemerkungen zu Brod und Baeck, 677–86 [74–75 from *Kleinere Schriften* (Berlin: Schocken Verlag, 1937).]
>
> Atheistische Theologie, 687–97
>
> Das neue Denken, 139–61
>
> *"Urzelle"* des Stern der Erlösung, 125–38
>
> Vertauschte Fronten, 235–37

Franz Rosenzweig, *Hegel und der Staat* (München und Berlin: Druck und Verlag von R. Oldenbourg, 1920; Scientia Verlag, 1962).

> Vorwort, XII–XIII
>
> Schlussbemerkung, 239–46

References:

All transliterations of Hebrew are according to the *Encyclopedia Judaica*, the general system.

All references to Goethe's works are to Johann Wolfgang von Goethe, *Werke*, Hamburger Ausgabe, ed. Erich Trunk (München: Verlag C.H. Beck, 1996); cited as Goethe, *Werke*.

All quotations from the Bible are from *Tanakh* (Philadelphia: Jewish Publication Society, 1985).

N. N. Glatzer, *Franz Rosenzweig: His Life and Thought* (New York: Farrar, Straus and Young, 1953; reprint, 2nd ed., Schocken Books, 1961; Hackett Publishing, 1998); cited as Glatzer, *Franz Rosenzweig*.

Franz Rosenzweig, *Der Mensch und sein Werk: Gesammelte Schriften I.1 and I.2: Briefe und Tagebücher 1909–1918 and 1918–1929*, ed.

Rachel Rosenzweig and Edith Rosenzweig-Scheinmann in collaboration with B. Casper (The Hague: Martinus Nijhoff, 1979); cited as *Briefe* I and *Briefe* II.

Franz Rosenzweig, *Der Mensch und sein Werk: Gesammelte Schriften III: Zweistromland: Kleinere Schriften zu Glauben und Denken*, ed. Reinhold and Annemarie Mayer (Dordrecht: Martinus Nijhoff, 1984); cited as *Zweistromland*.

All translations are our own unless otherwise stated.

I
From 1908 to 1914

The letter to Rudolf Ehrenberg, which Rosenzweig later called the *"Urzelle* of the *Star of Redemption*," is dated November 18, 1917. On August 22, 1918, Rosenzweig reimmersed himself in the ideas of the letter and began to write the *Star;* he reported his activities to Gertrud Oppenheim on August 27 in these words: "I am deeply involved in developing my letter to Rudi into a book. It's going to be quite fantastic, entirely unpublishable. . . ."[1] What were these fundamental and fertile ideas which issued in the *Star?*

They were, we will see, ideas about philosophy and religion, about revelation, Judaism, and Christianity, ideas that began to take shape in Rosenzweig's mind as early as his transforming dialogue with Eugen Rosenstock in Leipzig during the night of July 7, 1913, if not earlier, in 1910.[2]

At eighteen, in 1904, Franz Rosenzweig graduated from the gymnasium in Cassel. During the summer of 1905 he began his university studies at Göttingen in medicine, moving to Munich for the next year and then to Freiburg. There he made his first formal contact with philosophy, in particular with the study of Kant's *Critique of Pure Reason;* in the fall of 1907, he decided to pursue the study of modern history and philosophy. The next fall, in 1908, he returned to Freiburg to study philosophy with Heinrich Rickert, the neo-Kantian, and history with Friedrich Meinecke, whose important work *Cosmopolitanism and the National State* had been published in 1906 and who would supervise Rosenzweig's dissertation on Hegel's political philosophy. By 1910, then, Rosenzweig had settled in as a student of modern history and philosophy under Meinecke's mentorship.[3]

Rosenzweig had first come to know of Rosenstock at Baden-Baden in January 1910.[4] There, in the southwest of Germany, west of Munich and on the Rhine, a group of young historians and philosophers, many of them students of Friedrich Meinecke, had met to call for the cultivation of a new civilization, a neo-Hegelian development of a new subjectivity and a new unity.[5] Rosenzweig and his friends acknowledged the great philosophical legacy of 1800 and sought to renew it in 1900, but not as a moment of intellectual comprehension as much as a moment of practical achievement.[6] In a letter to Hans Ehrenberg (September 26, 1910), he affirmed that history was not merely something to be contemplated but rather something to be acted upon.[7] History is the sum total of human actions and not a divine theodicy. For Rosenzweig, at this stage, this pragmatic or "existential" conception paved the way for a new conception of religion as the shape of that human action, but it was, as Altmann argues, not real religion, from which at this time Rosenzweig was still alienated.

The next step had to wait three years, when, impressed by Rosenstock, Rosenzweig had gone to Leipzig in 1913 in part to study with the young instructor of law. In 1910 Rosenzweig was a historian on the way to becoming a philosopher; by 1913 that transformation had occurred, and so when he and Rosenstock were reunited, their meeting took shape as an encounter between the young Rosenzweig as a philosopher and Rosenstock as an existential man of faith.

The transforming evening discussion of July 7, 1913, began with a "heated discussion of science and religion, inspired by a novel by Selma Logerlof, *The Miracles of the Antichrist*," and focused on the issues of faith and skepticism. "Franz, a student of philosophy and history for eight years by that time, defended the prevailing philosophical relativism of the day, whereas Eugen bore witness to prayer and worship as his prime guides to action."[8] Persuaded by Rosenstock's simple faith, forced from his relativism to a nonrelativistic position, Rosenzweig decided to convert, but, as Glatzer has argued, the experience of Yom Kippur that fall led to a recantation, a return. Already by October 23, in a letter to his mother, Rosenzweig could say, "that 'connection of the innermost heart with God' which the heathen can only reach through Jesus is something the Jew already possesses . . . he possesses it by nature, through having been born one of the Chosen People."[9] In a letter to Rudolf Ehrenberg of October 31, his reversal is stated in terms that have become famous: "after prolonged, and I believe thorough, self-examination, I have reversed my decision. It no longer seems necessary to me, and therefore, being what I am, no longer possible. I will remain a Jew."[10]

Rosenzweig describes, in two letters written to Hans Ehrenberg in December of 1913, a new view of philosophy and revelation. Philosophy is the expression of nature as created, as the locus of freedom. Revelation breaks into history and gradually absorbs philosophy, until creation expends itself and the final redemption, the All in All, is realized. Moreover, this is not mere theory; it is a historical fact. Pagan philosophy is Christianized in the West, ultimately culminating in Hegel, who is both the last of the pagan philosophers and the "first of the new

Church Fathers," initiating a period of "spiritualized Christianity."[11] This is the meaning of 1800, after which "the Greeks are no longer a power." After 1800, the monologues of the philosophers would be replaced by the dialogues of human beings with faith.[12]

This "new philosophy of faith," as Altmann calls it, gave revelation a place in history and managed, too, an understanding of philosophy and faith within a conception of Western history, with the turning point coming in 1800. It also figured the relationship between the old philosophy, culminating in German Idealism, and the new method of thinking, originating in the actions of religious life. And these actions, as Rosenzweig came to see, took two forms, those of the church and those of the synagogue. By October 1913 Rosenzweig not only had a new view of faith and philosophy and the role of revelation in history, he also had a new view of the special roles and overall compatibility of Judaism and Christianity. And with this new view came a new resignation, to immerse himself in Judaism and return to the faith of his parents and ancestors.[13]

By the spring of 1914 Rosenzweig had begun his return to Judaism. The chief intellectual markers on the road to the *Star* are easy to plot. Rosenzweig initiated a period of study and association with Hermann Cohen, then in Berlin, and whom he had met in November of 1913. In April he set out his new ideas about revelation for the first time in an essay "Atheistic Theology," which was written at the request of Martin Buber for a projected second volume of the book *Vom Judentum* [On Judaism] but was rejected by the editors of the volume and never published during Rosenzweig's lifetime. In it Rosenzweig argued against romantic tendencies in both Christianity and Judaism that located the point of orientation in life respectively as the person of Jesus and as the historic existence of the Jewish people; not these, he argued, but rather an event of revelation could give life the orientation it needed.[14] Subsequently, during the summer, while studying some Hegel manuscripts, he discovered a document that was eventually published in 1917 as the oldest program for a system of German Idealism, written in Hegel's hand but claimed by Rosenzweig to have been the work of Schelling. These, then, were the influences on his thinking—Cohen, Rosenstock, Hegel, and Schelling.

But at the same time, Rosenzweig was returning to Judaism and its sources. He lived in Berlin for one year, from the fall of 1913 to the fall of 1914, and studied at the Hochschule für die Wissenschaft des Judentums during the winter and spring of 1914. The Hochschule had been founded in 1869–70 by Abraham Geiger and Moritz Lazarus and opened its doors in 1872. When Rosenzweig attended it, the school was located at Artilleriestrasse 14, where it had moved in 1907. It was located on five floors, with a marble entry, a spiral staircase, a ceiling of panelled wood, a library, a lecture hall, and classrooms. During the last year of his life, in 1923–24, when he lived in Berlin, Franz Kafka was a student of Hebrew in the Hochschule's adult education program; he described the building fondly in a postcard to Robert Klopstock of December 19, 1923:

> To me the Academy of Jewish Studies is a refuge of peace in wild and woolly Berlin and in the wild and woolly regions of the mind. . . . A whole building of handsome lecture rooms, large library, peace, well-heated, few students, and everything free of charge . . . the school exists and is a fine place, and basically not at all fine but rather odd to the point of grotesquerie and beyond that to the point of intangible delicacy (namely, the liberal-reformist tone and scholarly aspects of the whole thing).[15]

Despite its ample accommodations, the Hochschule always suffered from lack of funds and never had many regular faculty. At about the time Rosenzweig attended classes, at the outset of the war, its faculty numbered four men, of whom three were devoted to teaching. Perhaps the central figure was the historian Ismar Elbogen; another was Eugen Taubler.[16]

For Rosenzweig, of course, the primary figure was Hermann Cohen. On the board since 1904, Cohen had begun to teach at the Hochschule in 1905. When he retired as emeritus from Marburg in 1912, he settled in Berlin and continued to teach. In 1914, he offered a lecture course, an "Introduction to Philosophy," a seminar on Maimonides's *Moreh Nevukhim*, and a course on "The Concept of Religion in the System of Philosophy." His courses never had more than a few students. The overall tone of the teaching and the school's atmosphere involved a passionate commitment to pure scholarship and a suspicion of the neoromantic teachings of Buber and Leo Baeck. Baeck had studied at the school in 1891–97, was ordained in 1897, and received a doctorate in philosophy from the University of Berlin, under Wilhelm Dilthey, for a dissertation on Spinoza's influences in Germany. When he returned to Berlin in 1912, he began to teach, as an adjunct, at the Hochschule; he was associated with the school from then until 1942, when it was closed by the Nazis. Baeck did not teach philosophy or theology but rather Midrash and homiletics, and it was not until 1919 that the Hochschule had its first full-time regular faculty appointment in philosophy when Julius Guttmann was hired to fill the philosophy position.[17]

In letters and diary entries from May to October of 1914, there is evidence of Rosenzweig's commitment to Jewish learning. Clearly, during these months, he studied Hebrew and gained some acquaintance with Jewish sources, from the Bible and Talmud to Midrashic collections such as the Sifre and Tanḥuma; he also was becoming familiar with rabbinic commentaries on the Bible. His diary entries for May 1914 include discussion of the suffering servant of Deutero-Isaiah, the notion of prophecy, and the Shabbat poem, Lecha Dodi. In June, he points out that the existence of the people of Israel is his basic belief, not the giving and receiving of the Torah at Sinai, and in the course of his notes he refers to passages from Tractate Shabbat in the Talmud Yerushalmi and from the Midrashic collections Sifre and Tanḥuma. In a diary entry for October 9, he refers to Rashi's commentary on the Shema.

"Atheistic Theology" is Rosenzweig's first theological essay. He wrote it in April 1914, following his decision to return to Judaism and during the period he was studying at the Hochschule in Berlin. It is very much a critical piece that attacks trends in 19th- and 20th-century theology that elevate the importance of the human and, in one way or another, ground the divine in it. "Atheistic theology" comes in several guises, and Rosenzweig's targets are varied. But of special significance and as a primary target is the early, mystical Judaism of Martin Buber. The fact that Rosenzweig's essay is designed as a critique of Buber is very important to understanding it. It is also a bit surprising. For an early-21st-century reader, anyone defending revelation and the separation of the divine from the human might consider as a special opponent any kind of Enlightenment rationalism, of idealism, or of naturalism or secularism. To target a mystical view of Judaism and especially Buber's variety might seem a bit peculiar. But to Rosenzweig, Buber's conception of Judaism is social-psychological and nationalistic in ways that collapse the divine-human separation; it is a classic case of misplaced emphasis and theistic denial. One of the best places to begin when trying to understand Rosenwzeig's critique is to look at Buber's *Drei Reden* [Three Addresses].

In the years before and after the war, among young Jews, there was no work nearly as influential as Buber's *Drei Reden*, delivered in Prague in 1909–11 and published in 1911.[18] In his lectures Buber characterizes Judaism as a "spiritual process" of the Jewish people, which basically realizes itself as a striving for unity in the world (39–42). The fundamental Jewish reality is the people, a "community of blood" that is "a deep-rooted nurturing force within individual man," "the deepest, most potent stratum of [the Jew's] being," and the inherited locus of the striving for unity that is characteristic of the Jewish people (14–18). Buber here uses a vocabulary that draws on Nietzsche and the popular

Lebensphilosophie of the day. He was not alone in finding these themes—blood, community, force, and so on—powerful and evocative; his teacher Georg Simmel was, in the same period, adopting the very same terminology and views. Buber's nationalism and his mysticism here converged in a conception of the people as the residence of a powerful, driving tendency toward unity.

According to the *Addresses*, the Jewish people, confronted by psychological and social division and fragmentation, seeks to bring unity to the world. Its blood harbors a drive to make whole what is riddled with duality. As Buber, in his second address, characterizes the Jewish contribution to humankind, he elaborates the many ways in which this striving to unity realizes itself. Buber points to "universal justice" as the Jewish response to "the division of the human community" and "the idea of universal love" as the response to "the division of all living matter" (28). But the claim that Rosenzweig finds the most important and objectionable is even more radical. It is the claim that "the idea of the unitary God" is conceived by the Jew as the result of striving to deal with the "division of his I" (28). As Rosenzweig read Buber's words, he clearly reacted to them as a deep and powerful attempt to ground God Himself in human needs and to make of God a human projection: "this God Himself had emerged from the striving for unity, from the dark, impassioned striving for unity. He had been disclosed not in nature but in the subject" (27).

Rosenzweig reads Buber in the tradition of Feuerbach: "Instead of trying . . . to show the human under the might of the divine, one tries, on the contrary, to understand the divine as the self-projection of the human into the heaven of myth."[19] Here is theology turned into anthropology; "the myth of the covenant with God grew out of the Jewish people itself." According to Rosenzweig, Buber's racial, biological, and psychological account of the Jewish people claims that God is part of the mythology that derives from that people. The conclusion that Rosenzweig draws is that this kind of theology rejects the separateness of the divine and the human and the momentous presence of the former to the latter. "The distinctness of God and man, this frightful scandal for all old and new paganism, seems to be removed; the offensive thought of revelation, this plunging of a higher content into an unworthy vessel, is brought to silence." What should be affirmed, however, is both of these. Judaism cannot do without the divine and the human and the orientation that comes from the radical presence of God to the people. As against the tendencies of the 19th century toward humanism, rationalism, and naturalism and against Buber's kind of nationalism and mysticism, Rosenzweig endorses a Judaism of revelation.

Endnotes

1. Glatzer, *Franz Rosenzweig*, 81.

2. In his introduction to the correspondence with Rosenstock, Altmann claims that by 1910 and the Baden-Baden conference, Rosenzweig had already accepted the basic tendency toward action and the complete human being, explicit in Nietzsche and manifest in the emerging "existentialist" thinking of figures like Barth, Husserl, Scheler, and others. See Altmann, introduction to *Judaism Despite Christianity: The Letters on Christianity and Judaism between Eugen Rosenstock-Huessy and Franz Rosenzweig* (University, Ala.: University of Alabama Press, 1969; Schocken, 1971), 27–28.

3. The editor of Rosenzweig's *Briefe* notes that according to Bernhard Casper, in his book *Das dialogische Denken* (Freiburg: Herder, 1967), Rosenzweig attended several lecture courses with Meinecke in these years, as well as courses with von Below, Vöge, and Kantorowicz. He also studied with Rickert and Cohn.

4. Altmann says that they first met in Leipzig, in his introduction to the Rosenzweig-Rosenstock correspondence, *Judaism Despite Christianity*, 27. See Rosenzweig's letter to Hans Ehrenberg, July 1913, and the editor's note: *Briefe* I, 125.

5. See Paul Mendes-Flohr, "Franz Rosenzweig and the Crisis of Historicism," in *The Philosophy of Franz Rosenzweig* (Hanover, N.H.: University Press of New England, 1988), 142–43 also reprinted in *Divided Passions* (Detroit: Wayne State University Press, 1991) 314–15. Otto Pöggeler notes that the participants, the circle of Baden-Baden, were students of Meinecke; Albert Schweitzer was to have been invited but left Europe. Rosenzweig had begun his studies with Meinecke in Freiburg in 1907, and it was under his influence that Rosenzweig and his friends were persuaded that 1900 needed to be seen as a decisive step beyond 1800. Pöggeler comments that it was Rosenzweig's Hegelianism that broke up the circle; see Pöggeler, "Between Enlightenment and Romanticism: Rosenzweig and Hegel," in *The Philosophy of Franz Rosenzweig* ed. Mendes-Flohr, 114–15; Victor von Weizsäcker recalls the events and notes what he later takes to be the antisemitic tone of the controversy; *Briefe* I, 96–97. Among the participants at Baden-Baden were Siegfried Kaehler, Edward Mayer, Hans Ehrenberg, Victor Von Weizsäcker, Richard Kroner, Ernst Robert Curtius, Werner Picht, Kurt Breysig, Walter Sohm, and Rosenzweig.

6. For discussion of the importance of the year 1800 for German Idealism and the history of modern philosophy and the modern world, see Richard Kroner, "The Year 1800 in the Development of German Idealism," *The Review of Metaphysics* 1 (4): 1–31 (1948). The year 1800 plays a very important role in the development of Rosenzweig's philosophical and theological views. We discuss it more fully later.

7. Cited by Altmann, *Judaism Despite Christianity*, 28, from *Briefe* I, 112. For general discussion of the conference at Baden-Baden, see Altmann, 28–29.

8. Eugen Rosenstock-Huessy, "Prologue" in *Judaism Despite Christianity*, 73; and generally 72–76 on their relationship in 1913.

9. Glatzer, *Franz Rosenzweig*, 27.

10. *Ibid.*, 28 and 341–44, for the continuation of this tremendously important letter, with its account of the distinctive roles and character of the church and the synagogue in history.

11. See Altmann, *Judaism Despite Christianity*, 33–35; see *Briefe* I, 144–47, *Briefe* 202 and 203.

12. See Altmann, *Judaism Despite Christianity*, 34–35.

13. Rosenzweig reflects on the crisis of 1913 in his letter to Meinecke of August 20, 1920, in which he thanks Meinecke for his kind words about his recently published Hegel book and rejects the offer of a university lectureship. He refers to the "horror" he felt of himself and his transformation from a historian to a philosopher. Finally, he describes his state in 1920 as one then ruled by a "dark drive" which he calls his "Judaism." See *Franz Rosenzweig*, 94–98.

14. See below, Chapter 2, "Atheistic Theology." Also, Franz Rosenzweig, "Atheistic Theology," trans. Robert G. Goldy and H. Frederick Holch, "Atheistic Theology: From the Old to the New Way of Thinking," *Canadian Journal of Theology* 14 (2) (1968): 79–88. See also, Otto Pöggeler, "From Enlightenment to Romanticism," 115–16. In "1914: Franz Rosenzweig writes the essay 'Atheistic Theology,' which criticizes the theology of his day," Paul Mendes-Flohr gives a general introduction to this essay and to Rosenzweig's life and thought, in Sander L. Gilman and Jack Zipes, eds., *Yale Companion to Jewish Writing and Thought in German Culture* (New Haven: Yale University Press, 1997), 322–26. For doubts that Buber rejected the essay or even saw it, see Maurice Friedman, *Martin Buber's Life and Work: The Early Years 1878–1923* (New York: E.P. Dutton, 1981), 398–400.

15. Franz Kafka, *Letters to Friends, Family, and Editors* (Schocken Books, 1977), 402–3.

16. Taubler was a historian with a specialty in Judaism of the Hellenistic and early Christian periods. He came to the Lehranstalt [Hochschule] in 1910 and was appointed to the new Ludwig Philippson Chair in Jewish History in 1912. He remained at the Hochschule until shortly after the war ended, when he gave up his position and became a lecturer in Greek and Roman history at Berlin University. But he remained active as a Jewish historian; in 1919 he was asked to develop an organizational plan for the new Academy for the Scientific Study of Judaism, a project first initiated by Rosenzweig's article of 1917, "It Is Time," and promoted by Hermann Cohen's vigorous support for the project. For discussion of Taubler, see Selma Stern-Taeubler, "Eugen Taeubler and the 'Wissenschaft des Judentums,'" *Leo Baeck Institute Yearbook* 3 (1958): 40–59; David

N. Myers, "Eugen Taubler: The Personification of Judaism as Tragic Existence," *LBIYB* 39 (1994): 131–50, especially 134.

17. For information on the Hochschule, see Michael A. Meyer's history of Reform Judaism, *Response to Modernity: A History of the Reform Movement in Judaism* (New York: Oxford University Press, 1988), the books on Leo Baeck by Albert H. Friendlander (*Leo Baeck: Teacher of Theresienstadt* [New York: Holt, Rinehart and Winston, 1968]) and Leonard Baker, (*Days of Sorrow and Pain: Leo Baeck and the Berlin Jews* [New York: Macmillan, 1978]) and Fritz Bamberger, "Julius Guttmann—Philosopher of Judaism," *LBIYB* 5 (1960): 3–34. Also see Michael Brenner, *The Renaissance of Jewish Culture in Weimar Germany* (New Haven: Yale University Press, 1996).

18. Martin Buber gave the three addresses—"Judaism and the Jews," "Judaism and Mankind," and "The Renewal of Judaism"—at the invitation of the young Zionist organization in Prague. They are translated as the first three chapters in *On Judaism*, trans. Eva Jospe, ed. Nahum Glatzer (Schocken, 1967). Page references in the text are to this edition.

19. See below, Chapter 2, "Atheistic Theology," 17.

II

"Atheistic Theology"

(1914)

The following pages are intended to describe a still young, yet apparently momentous direction in modern Judaism and to raise objections against it.[1] Let comparison serve as a means to this end. Whether it is appropriate, the execution must demonstrate.

For some years, a development remarkable even to the uninvolved spectator has been reaching its conclusion within Protestant religious thought: the end of the Life-of-Jesus theology.[2] Before Drews[3] tried,

---

1. Although never explicitly named, Rosenzweig's target appears to be the position taken by Martin Buber (1878–1965) in *Drei Reden über das Judentum* (Three addresses concerning Judaism) (Frankfurt am Main: Rutten und Löning, 1911). For an English translation, see the first three essays in Buber, *On Judaism*, ed. Nahum H. Glatzer (New York: Schocken, 1968). The essay was originally written for a yearbook, *Vom Judentum* (On Judaism), at Buber's invitation but was rejected as inappropriate because of its implicit criticism of Buber. See Rosenzweig's August 1919 letter to Buber, *Briefe II*, 643.

2. For an influential account of historical research into the life of Jesus and its theological implications, see Albert Schweitzer (1875–1965), *Von Reimarus zu Wrede: Eine Geschichte der Leben-Jesu-Forschung* (Tübingen: J. C. B. Mohr, 1906), trans. W. Montgomery as *The Quest of the Historical Jesus: A Critical Study of its Progress from Reimarus to Wrede* (London: A. and C. Black, 1910; 3rd ed. with new introduction, 1954). Schweitzer was invited to the 1910 Baden-Baden conference because of his book but apparently did not attend. See Chapter I. Rosenzweig cites Schweitzer's book in diary entries from 1914, the year in which "Atheistic Theology" was written. See Rosenzweig, *Briefe I*, 151.

3. Arthur Drews (1865–1935), author of *Die Christusmythe* (Jena: Eugen Diederichs, 1910), *The Christ Myth*, trans. C. Delisle Burns (Chicago: Open Court, 1910; reprint, Amherst, NY: Prometheus, 1998). In this sensational work, Drews sought to show that all religiously important features of the image of Jesus were entirely mythical and that no opening whatsoever existed for seeking a historical figure behind the myth.

with insufficient means, to deal it the death blow, it was already at its end internally; the battles over the historicity of Jesus have only made this widely visible; the real work had already occurred before.

The roots of this part of liberal theology, which in the 19th century had become more and more the center of German neo-Protestantism, reach back into the 18th century. Not, however, in those well-known attempts of the Wolfenbüttler Fragmentist[4] nor in related, less significant, early manifestations of the Life-of-Jesus research may the beginnings of the Life-of-Jesus theology be sought; these products of the Enlightenment are a piece of primitive-critical historical science, not of constructive-systematic theology. The preconditions of the latter lay rather in the 18th century, in the attempts of Lessing, Herder, Kant,[5] and other less significant thinkers around them to present the human life of Jesus as the life of the great Teacher, and to present Christianity as the teaching of this Teacher. To present meant to manufacture. If those attempts succeeded in showing, within the "teaching of Jesus," spiritual forces that

---

4. In 1774–78, Gotthold Ephraim Lessing (1729–81) published a series of fragments which he disingenuously claimed to have discovered in the Duke of Brunswick's library at Wolfenbüttel, where he was librarian. Controversy was aroused by the anonymously published fragments, which critically investigated the historicity of biblical narratives and Christian interpretations. It was not determined that the author was the respected and recently deceased scholar of oriental languages, Hermann Samuel Reimarus (1694–1768), until 1814, when his son presented to the University of Göttingen library the unpublished manuscript from which Lessing had extracted the fragments: *Apologie oder Schutzschrift für die vernünftige Verehrer Gottes* (Apology or writ of protection for the rational worshippers of God). The Wolfenbüttel fragments are often said to mark the beginning of critical historical research into the life of Jesus. See Reimarus, *Fragments*, trans. Ralph S. Fraser, ed. Charles H. Talbert (Chico, Calif.: Scholars Press, 1985).

5. On Lessing, see note 4 above and note 6 below. Johann Gottfried Herder (1744–1803) wrote two works on the life of Jesus: *Vom Erlöser der Menschen. Nach unsern drei ersten Evangelisten* (Concerning the redeemer of men, according to our first three Gospels) (Riga: Hartknoch, 1796) and *Von Gottes Sohn, der Welt Heiland. Nach Johannes Evangelium* (Concerning God's son, savior of the world, according to John's Gospel) (Riga: Hartknoch, 1797). See Schweitzer, *Quest*, 34–37. Immanuel Kant gives an account of Jesus as the personified idea of the good principle in *Die Religion innerhalb der Grenzen der blossen Vernunft* in *Kants gesammelte Schriften* (Berlin: De Gruyter, 1900) vol. 6, 3–202, trans. George di Giovanni as *Religion within the Boundaries of Mere Reason* in *Immanuel Kant: Religion and Rational Theology*, ed. Allen W. Wood and George di Giovanni (Cambridge: Cambridge University Press, 1996), 39–215.

were capable of infusing even the present with living content, it was
thus proven possible to possess a Christianity beyond the dogma of
Christ. Into the place of the "religion about Jesus" stepped, to speak
Lessing's words, the "religion of Jesus."[6] The Enlightenment could—
mark these words: if it was possible—make its peace with the strongest
spiritual power of the past; the true Christianity, the very Christianity of
Jesus, taught nothing other than Enlightenment itself; only the
Church, which had covered over the Christianity of Jesus with the
Christ of Christianity, was to be set aside: Christianity itself remained in
force and, indeed, only now emerged into the light once again in its
pure, original form. Instead of believing in the God-man, what counted
was allowing oneself to be taught by the Teacher.

This proved impossible. Precisely romanticism's insight that only living "individuality" was called to rule the world, and not teaching—even
if it taught the Truth itself—made the view of Jesus as the Teacher appear obsolete even before it could be fully developed. According to this
new picture, a "Teacher" could not be the one with whose appearance
"the time" was supposed to be "fulfilled." Schleiermacher found the
problem-solving formulation, that "the emergence of a revelation in an
individual person" was to be regarded as "prepared in human nature
and as the highest development of its spiritual force."[7] Thus, not
"teacher" but rather "personality" was the human essence of Jesus, from
which Christianity sprang, today as well as once eighteen hundred years
ago. "Personality"—that was no long past, no dead objective thing;

---

6. Lessing sharply distinguished "the religion of Christ," which Jesus practiced
as a man and which all men can and should share with him, from "the Christian religion," which asserts that Jesus was more than a man and makes him, as
such, the object of its worship. The former he found clearly and lucidly contained in the Gospels, whereas the latter was expressed therein with great indef-
initeness and ambiguity, and he found it inconceivable that both religions
could have existed in one and the same person. See *Lessings Werke*, ed. Karl
Lachmann and Franz Muncker (Stuttgart: G. J. Goschen, 1886–1924; reprint,
Berlin and New York: De Gruyter, 1979), vol. 6, 518–19; *Lessing's Theological
Writings*, trans. Henry Chadwick (Stanford: Stanford University Press, 1957),
106.

7. In lectures on the life of Jesus, published posthumously in 1864, Friedrich
Schleiermacher (1768–1834) sought to reconcile the divinity and humanity of
Jesus by arguing that the divine inhabits every human insofar as the divine will
is the principle of his or her actions and that Jesus' personality manifested this
principle with a maximum degree of vitality. See *Das Leben Jesu* (The life of
Jesus), ed. K. A. Rütenik, in *Friedrich Schleiermacher's sämmtliche Werke*
(Berlin: Reimer, 1864), Abtheilung I, Band 6, especially 77–128.

Goethe's contemporaries had learned to see that a human life—notwithstanding all achievements—was inhabited by a being [*ein Sein*] that eluded history's deadening power. According to this thought, so it seemed, one now could—indeed one had to—grasp the existence of Jesus, once one was determined to avoid dogma.

Strauss's[8] grand undertaking, still nourished by Hegelian spirit,[9] to grasp the origin of Christianity purely in terms of history's overpowering necessities and eternal truth, ultimately failed not because of the outrage of the watchmen of Zion[10] but rather because of the opposition of that romantic direction, which considered personality as the decisive historical force. None other than Strauss himself acknowledged this in principle, when—one generation after the first *Life of Jesus*—he published his second, in which the explanation of Christianity in terms of the essence of myth receded behind the attempt to sketch Jesus the man as an individual character.

Already at that time, this tendency was victorious all along the line. Strauss himself, as is well known, was drawn into it by the sensation caused by Renan's piece of showmanship,[11] concocted from the ingredients of

---

8. David Friedrich Strauss (1808–1874) was the author of *Das Leben Jesu, kritisch bearbeitet* (Tübingen: C. F. Osiander, 1st ed., 1835; 2nd, slightly rev. ed., 1836; 3rd, heavily rev. ed., 1838; 4th ed., returning in part to the 2nd, 1840), translated from the 4th ed. by George Eliot as *The Life of Jesus, Critically Examined*, ed. Peter C. Hodgson (Philadelphia: Fortress Press, 1972). The enormous scandal caused by the first edition, which pioneered the mythological approach to the Gospels, cost Strauss his job and academic career. After replying polemically to his critics, Strauss made some concessions to traditional views in the third edition, but largely revoked them in the fourth. He published a more popular account of his views in *Das Leben Jesu für das deutsche Volk bearbeitet* (Leipzig: F. A. Brockhaus, 1864), trans. as *The Life of Jesus for the People*, 2 vols. (London and Edinburgh: Williams and Norgate, 1879).

9. The exact nature of the relationship between Strauss's work and Hegel's philosophy is controversial. Strauss had come to Berlin in October 1831 to study under Hegel who, however, died in November. He studied under Hegel's pupils, and his book is often said to have precipitated the end of the Hegelian school, since it forced an open schism between Hegelians sympathetic to traditional religion ("right Hegelians") and those critical of it ("left Hegelians").

10. The defenders of traditional approaches to the Gospels.

11. Ernest Renan (1823–1892), author of *Vie de Jésus* (Paris: Michel Levy, 1863) translated as *The Life of Jesus* (Buffalo, N.Y.: Prometheus, 1991). In the preface to *The Life of Jesus for the People*, xvi–xvii, Strauss offered "the hand of fellowship" to Renan's work and expressed the hope that his book was as well adapted to the German people as Renan's to the French.

German historical outlook and research. For decades since then, the life of Jesus remained the hobby horse of liberal theology. The confidence with which one believed oneself able to erect the result of critical historical science within faith's holiest of holies cannot be understood if one does not keep in mind that shared assumption of the infinite worth of personality. The man who, through unprejudiced consideration of the sources, was to be made visible underneath all the tendentious and dogmatic camouflages, had to be an eternal force, for—"time and might cannot break up defined form that develops as it lives."[12] The life of Goethe was the secret presupposition of this life of Jesus which German-liberal theology hoped to make the focal point of faith. The mood of the time and detailed research were in league.

Both time and research carry within themselves the remedies against their illnesses. The feeling that no man understands the other, that strangeness is placed between neighbors as well as between those farthest apart, and that personality stays locked within the walls of its own individuality, began to rebel against that assumption according to which the life of another, grasped in its full human singularity, was supposed to be of unqualified universal validity, and that a man as mere man, indeed precisely as such, was supposed to be to mankind what the God-man of dogma had been able to be to mankind. On the other hand, research, in its growing self-criticism, found itself more and more often on paths that led far away from that originally envisaged aim: it believed that it could detect features in the human image of Jesus which, despite all personal particularity, showed him to be rooted so deeply in the spiritual ground of his time and his people that it seemed ever more difficult to overcome this "strangeness" of the scientifically achieved image of his essence by means of the appropriating feeling. Already, scruples that had never been silenced on the theological Right were also audible on the Left, in the Life-of-Jesus theology's own camp. Mere man could not tolerate the bright light of faith's focal point, in which one had sought to place him. Was it possible, perhaps even necessary, to dispense with him entirely and, after having suffered shipwreck with one half of the dogmatic paradox of true man and true God, now to take recourse in the second half? Did philosophical theology have to step into the place of historical theology, the Christ-idea into the place of the Life-of-Jesus idea? Or is it regaining courage for the entire paradox that counts? And will it be possible to move the concept of historical-superhistorical revelation into the center of science? At the present

---

12. From the first stanza of Goethe's poem, *Urworte. Orphisch. (Primal Words. Orphic.)* See von Goethe, *Werke,* I, 359.

moment, the scientific consciousness of Protestantism stands before this decision; from here the battles of the immediate future will spring forth. Jewish thought, having always been in a vital relation to Christian scholarship—sometimes, as in scholasticism, the influencing part, sometimes, as in the 19th century, the influenced part—has exhibited no immediate parallel to the described movement. The problem of personality could not, according to the essence of our dogmatics, gain for us the central significance which it naturally possessed for Christian dogmatics. Only in its general intellectual direction has our science shared the experience of the history of Christian (and in the 19th century that meant essentially: German) theology. After the first half of the century's great attempts at religiophilosophical systems, in which, however, the tradition of our classical philosophy of religion was renewed again, not in the guiding philosophical thoughts but rather in characteristic peculiarities of method, there came to us as well, just as to Christian theology, an era of flight to detailed historical research; more apologetic than independently systematic main thoughts have determined for decades the overall shape of this research work. Cohen's beginnings of a strictly rationalistic reinterpretation of the concept of revelation were at that time the most significant evidence of the "reawakening of philosophy" in our midst as well.[13] And the past few years have even made the recipient of revelation in Judaism once again the focal object of systematic consideration: the Chosen People.

Those older religiophilosophical attempts of the 19th century had tried to render this difficult concept unobjectionable; it had arrived at softenings of a sort similar to those carried out on the figure of Christ in classical German philosophy. Just as the latter had been emptied into

---

13. Beginning in 1880, Hermann Cohen (1842–1918), already established as a leading neo-Kantian philosopher, wrote numerous articles on basic concepts of Judaism, later collected in his *Jüdische Schriften* (Jewish writings), 3 vols., ed. Bruno Strauss (Berlin: C. A. Schwetske, 1924; reprint, New York, 1980). He also wrote two books on the philosophy of religion, focusing on Judaism: *Der Begriff der Religion im System der Philosophie* (The concept of religion in the system of philosophy) (Giessen: Alfred Töpelmann, 1915; reprint, Hildesheim, Zürich, New York: Georg Olms, 1996) and *Religion der Vernunft aus den Quellen des Judentums. Nach dem Manuskript des Verfassers neu durchgearbeitet und mit einem Vorwort versehen von Bruno Strauss* (Religion of reason out of the sources of Judaism. Reworked anew in accordance with the author's manuscript and provided with a foreword by Bruno Strauss) (Frankfurt am Main: Kaufmann, 1929; reprint, Wiesbaden: Fourier, 1988), trans. Simon Kaplan as *Religion of Reason out of the Sources of Judaism* (New York: Frederick Ungar, 1972; 2nd enl. ed., Atlanta: Scholars Press, 1995).

the notion of an ideal human being, the idea of nation was reinterpreted among us into the ideal community of mankind—and in both cases the hard feature, of the divine having actually entered into history and being distinct from all other actuality, was blurred. It is not difficult to guess why, already at that time, a systematic elaboration of the idea of nation as the supporting base of Judaism was not being pursued even in our midst. For that humanization of the one who was hitherto considered divine, whereby the task of a human life of Jesus recommended itself to the Christian theologian of that time, could also appear as the enticing result of a s.v.v.[14] Jewish-People theology; but while the equation of God-man and ideal human being was able to release an individual human life of Jesus as its natural completion, at that time no theologically useful illustration of the Jewish people would have grown out of the corresponding Jewish equation of God's people with the ideal community of mankind: while Jesus the man promised, on the basis of such an equation, to gain an unanticipated weight of actual existence, the Jewish people would be nothing short of theologically vaporized by the corresponding equation; it would have become the contingent bearer of a thought not bound up with its existence. The reason is readily available and has already been expressed. Alongside the "Kantian" concept of the ideal man entered, in a friendly fashion, the "Goethean" concept of the ideal individuality; in contrast, the concept of ideal humanity seemed at that time to conflict with any interlinkage to a single people's individuality. The remarkable attempts in this direction, which originated around the 18th century's turn into the 19th, in the Germany of Fichte and Hegel,[15] sought principally to unite people and humanity only in such a manner that the people had to give birth from its womb to the ideas without which humanity would "perish;" Hegel's teaching—that world-historical peoples die after fulfilling their humanity-related task—was implicit in the natural result of such a concept of people. With such a view of the relation of people to humanity, a Jewish science, for which Judaism was an eternally subsisting magnitude, could not begin. A science of this kind would have required a theory that enabled it to understand the pure existence of a people, not only its achievement, as humanity's eternal necessity; and such an analogue to the romantic idea of personality was not yet developed for the notion of peoplehood.

Here recent decades produced a change. A representation of people developed, not without contact with that older concept of peoplehood

---

14. Abbreviation for "*sit venit verbio*" ("pardon the expression").
15. Johann Gottlieb Fichte (1762–1814) and Georg Wilhelm Friedrich Hegel (1770–1831), the most influential German Idealist philosophers of their day.

of German Idealism, yet nevertheless essentially new, which granted to it the rank of an eternal existent. He who is able to see through the pseudonaturalist wrappings of the race idea, to which this idea owes its broad popularity, recognizes here the striving to transform the concept of peoplehood in such a way that the people obtain the right to exist simply from their existence, independently of their factual achievements. Precisely the naturalistic and unspiritual thrust of the new concept has given it the force to accomplish this. Carefree and without consciousness, like a product of nature, the people now lives its life; the question of the meaning of this existence seems to have lost its justification. This only seems so; in truth, it remains as justified as it was; indeed, only for its sake occurred that apparent despiritualization of the people into a race, of the "national" to the "populist" notion [*zum völkischen Gedanken*].[16] The people that, in the eye of the philosopher, no longer lives and dies for the sake of transnational purposes has its right to existence in its own character, in the rushing of its "blood;" and wherever the will to anchor this right by means of a philosophy of history breaks forth, it is no longer said of a people, as a hundred years ago, that in it the world-renewing "Idea" is carried to maturity, after which, an empty shell, it may then lie abandoned, but rather it is now grasped in such a way that through its "essence," the world will recover. Thereby, however, the "essence," the constant character of the people, acquires a tremendous significance, and now, on the basis of this concept of the "the essence of the people," the historical people becomes capable of an evaluation of its real existence that is similar to the one that had arisen for the historical man through the concept of "personality." Now an atheistic theology could also be arrived at on the Jewish side.

We see this now in our midst. Instead of trying—in the eternity of philosophical thought or in the temporality of the historical process—to show the human under the might of the divine, one tries, on the contrary, to understand the divine as the self-projection of the human into the heaven of myth. Here the people is the human actuality, which as such already recommends itself as a content of faith to a positivistically meticulous generation. Thus the Life-of-Jesus theology believed itself able to soften the hard dogma if it pointed with all its might to Jesus the

---

16. The German word *Volk* and its derivatives acquired ethnocentric and, ultimately, racist overtones in the German nationalist movement of the 19th and early 20th centuries. Thus *völkisch* (translated here as "populist") came to mean "pertaining to the racially inherited characteristics of the German people," in contrast to whatever pertains to characteristics developed in modernity, especially through the influence of Jewish and other non-Aryan cultures.

man and only to the man. The fact that the ability of such a merely human reality to be vitally believed rather than lifelessly known is something very dubitable, was at first considered as little [on the Jewish] as on the Christian side; the satisfaction of having found a straightforwardly this-worldly object of faith, "free of metaphysics," prevented doubt from increasing. Furthermore, it was strongly felt that a living people, with respect to which any proposition about its "essence" can and must at once be tested against "actuality," poses entirely different difficulties for such an undogmatic dogmatization than the life of an individual who disappeared from the earth 1900 years ago; however, this only led to all the more bold constructions of the relationship that subsists between faith and the object of faith: the thought through which occurred, in Strauss's critique of the image of traditional faith, the rational humanization of the figure of Christ into the Jesus of the Life-of-Jesus theology, became, in the Jewish-people theology, the lever of the rationalist deification of the people: in the concept of "myth" Strauss had turned the godhead of Christ into the product of the spirit of the original community; in the production of "myth" the eternity of the Jewish people proves itself to our most recent contemporaries.

Myth is, in both cases, the superhuman grasped as the offspring of the human. The fact that in Strauss the myth of Christ did not actually develop out of the figure of Jesus, but rather crystallized around it, while the myth of the covenant with God grew out of the Jewish people itself, may be a significant difference which leads back to that already mentioned distinctness of the lasting people and the individual who has perished; yet in both cases what is essential is that man's faithful comportment toward the content of faith becomes explicable, and indeed explicable in a "purely human" way. Exactly this—here as well as there—brings about the introduction of the pagan concept of the relationship between what is believed and the believer, between god and man, into the scientific study of revealed religions. Not for nothing should one have discovered this world-historical antithesis of "mythology and revelation;" it is the highest triumph of a theology hostile to revelation to sublate it entirely in favor of its first term, to show revelation to be mythology. Furthermore, while, also in both cases, the old faith is posited as obsolete insofar as one explains it, at the same time the new faith, the positive [faith] of the Life-of-Jesus theology along with that of the Jewish-people theology, is being erected precisely on the rejected stone of the old [faith] and indeed by the same builders who rejected the stone.[17] To this end, the concept of myth needed that inner weight

---

17. See Psalm 118:22: "The stone that the builders rejected has become the chief cornerstone."

that inhabits it once again since the German Romantic movement. Where myth develops, the heart of history beats. To be sure, what is thus recognized as myth ceases, in an indifferent sense, to be true; but by the same token the historical actuality, to which the crystals of myth fasten, has proven its power to be actuality for faith. If it [historical reality] is already predestined to such significance from another side—if it is, for example, personality or, recently, peoplehood—then nothing else stands in the way of its deification: myth is the light radiating from itself—it needs no glory of any Lord to make its face shine.

This is the ultimate meaning of the entire movement. The distinctness of God and man, this frightful scandal for all new and old paganism, seems to be removed; the offensive thought of revelation, this plunging of a higher content into an unworthy vessel, is brought to silence. Yet something of it remains and must remain; for, in truth, where the thought of revelation has once attached itself to a historical actuality, this actuality is so much colored by it that it is completely impossible to circumscribe it like other actualities unburdened by this weighty thought. Here atheistic theology helps itself by a peculiar schema through which it remodels the breaking in of the active divine over the sleeping human into an oppositeness that is wondrously unmediated, or mediated only by its own tension, within the human itself. Instead of asserting God's becoming human, one asserted His being human; instead of His descent to the mountain of the giving of the law, the autonomy of the moral law; in general, instead of the history of revelation, an existing human essence, within which history unfolded but which itself was not subjected to history. It was now imperative to understand this duality, which after all was undeniable although immanent to the human, in terms of the "character" or "essence" of the human in question. With respect to the life of Jesus, there was the cleavage between the "temporal" and the "transtemporal," or between the "Jewish" and the "trans-Jewish" in his character, along with the task to conceive of the evil fact of his emergence from—or at least appearance among—the Jews, as necessary according to the principle of the highest tension; and finally it was imperative to distinguish within him, again in a way [that is] apparently purely passive [with respect to the duality in the life of Jesus], between an absolutely inexplicably unique self-awareness of his calling and the humanly graspable remainder of his consciousness. Thus was created among us, correspondingly, the concept of the "polarity" of the Jewish character. The polarity is still more than the tension, displaced into man himself, between the demand of the law and the desire of the heart, even more than the discord between the enthusiastic moment and the routine of the everyday, or between "mythical" and "rationalist" Judaism; here it means the tension between the chosenness of the called-upon people and this people itself. Only this ultimate tension possesses that uniqueness which is attributed to the Jewish "polarity" in general; only it increases oppositions, such as the one that can be detected in the essence of every people and in general of every living being, into the immeasurability of a metaphysical tension; only out of this highest bifurcation can the eternal meaning of our peoplehood's existence emerge: the continually regenerated drive to reconcile the most absolute duality with the most absolute unity.

We see the will to unity, this most Jewish of all concepts, erected by our new theologians as the crowning [feature] of their image of the Jewish people. According to this intention, however, they depart most consciously from tradition at exactly this point. For, while traditional Judaism sets for the Jew the task of unity on the basis of the revealed unity of God, and lets the acknowledgment of the future kingdom of God precede the reception of a God-ordered way of life, this correlation between the human being and his God is now considered a historical subcase of the yearning for the unity of life inherent in the character of the Jewish people in all times. [For our new theologians,] the acceptance of the Kingdom of Heaven is not a precondition, but rather only a historically real yet unnecessary consequence of that which alone is necessary: the acceptance of the one law of life. Since, then, this unity of life is thought together with its now ultimate and self-sufficient bearer, the Jewish people, to be sure only as the latter's longing, not as its fulfilled essence, [the unity of life] regains the significance of something located beyond its bearer; one does not attempt to grasp this character of longing for unity as, say, a component of the "polarity" of the Jewish essence, and it cannot be attempted, because that polarity is, at its peak, precisely the proper object of that longing for unification; only through the absoluteness of the polarity can the commandment of unification become an absolute for us. Thus, although the thought of unity is regarded as the content of the people's spirit, it nonetheless shifts again into a transnational and—here, where the people is supposed to designate a religious ultimate—a supernatural context by virtue of its particular determination as an eternal longing; although, according to the intention, [the thought of unity is supposed to be the] nucleus of the "essence" [of the people], in fact it becomes a doctrine; what is uttered of the people is, as such, a task for the individual by the same token; what inheres in the object of faith, namely as demand, is still to be fulfilled by the believer. The object of faith thus loses its unqualified inner humanity while, on the other hand, it faces the individual; at a certain point, the merely human content of faith, notwithstanding its totality, becomes "dogmatically" authoritative again. It is the same when a single point is

selected from the whole of personality by the Life-of-Jesus theology as
the content of its mission, say, its "belief in God-as-Father" which according to the neo-Protestant view surely separates Christianity from Judaism, and thus the "personality" of the one who is believed in assumes
again the features of the "teacher," now, to be sure, of the teacher in the
new sense that he also "teaches" that which is the core of his personality. In this way, that which is the core of its essence in the case of the
Jewish people becomes at the same time a law for the individual. [In the
Jewish case as in the Christian,] the human is broken through, the superhuman threatens to intrude through the breach into the arena of
atheistic theology.

Such an intrusion of the embattled principle would be impossible if
the entire atheistic theology were not fully justified even against the one
attacked by it, indeed, precisely within the latter. On the Christian side,
the development of the Life-of-Jesus theology has already proved this at
the present time. In itself, the elaboration of the human personality of
the God-man was admissible even from the dogmatic standpoint; confronted with a purely rationalistic theology of the "Christ Idea," even
the Protestant right wing will again in a certain sense have to resort to
the idea of the Life-of-Jesus theology. One could demonstrate the equivalent, point for point, about the Judaism-of-the-people theology: how it
is rooted in the tradition and how, for precisely this reason, the future
development of our theology can on no account flow past it. In the case
of the thought of unity, this is obvious. To carry [that thought] from the
dogmatic into the ethical has long been customary among us. Bahya's
book about the "duties of the heart,"[18] which has become popular, is
filled with this thought; how deeply he was seized by the mystical movement, both contemporaneously and later, is a fact to which we have recently [been] directed again.[19] The introductory prayer to the daily

---

18. Bahya ben Joseph ibn Pakuda (c.1050–c.1156) wrote *Kitāb al-Hidāya ilā
Farā'iḍ al-Qulūb* (The book of direction to the duties of the heart), which was
translated into Hebrew by Judah ibn Tibbon (1120–90) as *Ḥovot ha-Levavot*
(Duties of the heart). The Arabic text was edited by A. S. Yahuda (Leiden: al-
Matbaah al-Bariliyah, 1907–12) and translated into English by Menahem Man-
soor (London: Routledge and Kegan Paul, 1973). Little is known about the
dates and location of Bahya's life, except that he was a liturgical poet and a
judge in a Jewish court in Moslem Spain. Translated into many languages, the
book is one of the most popular Jewish meditations on the foundations of faith
and the demands of piety.
19. It is unclear which discussion of mystical interest in Bahya is intended.
Moshe Idel, "Franz Rosenzweig and the Kabbalah" in *The Philosophy of Franz*

reading of the Confession of Unity, which is older than medieval scholasticism and mysticism and which, outliving both, remains vital today, rests on the reciprocal connection between the "unification" of the concept of God through man and [the "unification"] of the human heart through God.[20] To be sure, a reciprocal connection is thereby intended, and the isolation of the human-ethical from the divine-true that is attained coldly and theoretically, not, say, in a mystical paradox, would not have been conceived by those ancients.—It has already been shown, furthermore, how at bottom the concept of polarity only transposes the struggle between superhuman revelation and human lack of preparedness—which, in contradiction to any other relation between a human author and a spiritual product, characterizes the realm of reli-

---

Rosenzweig, ed. Paul Mendes-Flohr (Hanover, N.H.: University Press of New England, 1988), 243, n.11, notes that Rabbi Abraham ben David of Posquiéres (c.1120–98, an important halachist to whom kabbalistic teachings have been attributed) initiated the two translations of the book, as mentioned by Judah ibn Tibbon, and that early kabbalists were influenced by it. On the influence of Bahya on the kabbalists of Provence, see Gershom Scholem, *Ursprung und Anfänge der Kabbala* (Berlin: De Gruyter, 1962), 195, 266, 401 (cited by Idel from a later French translation).

20. The recitation of the "Confession of Unity" (the *Shema*) in the daily morning and evening services is preceded by two blessings, discussed in the Babylonian Talmud, *Berakhot*, 11b–12a. In the oldest extant Jewish liturgies, versions of the second blessing of the morning service already contain the words, "And unite our hearts to love and to fear Your name," based on Psalm 86:11: "Unite my heart to fear Your name." In 1910, Hermann Cohen had cited this liturgical connection between the unity of the heart and the unity of God, using it to explain Bachya's conception of the duties of the heart, and he had expanded his discussion in response to Wilhelm Bacher's objection that, although ibn Tibbon's Hebrew translation used the phrase *yichud ha-lev* (unity of the heart), the Arabic original was better translated as *Läuterung der Gesinnung* (purity of disposition). See Cohen, "Innere Beziehungen der Kantischen Philosophie zum Judentum" (Inner relations of the Kantian philosophy to Judaism) in *Jüdische Schriften*, I, 284–305, 291ff., and "Die Einheit des Herzens bei Bachja" (The unity of the heart in Bahya) in vol. 3, 213–20; Bacher, "Die 'Einheit des Herzens' und die 'Einheit der Handlung'" (The "Unity of the Heart" and the "Unity of Action") and "Zu Bachja ibn Pakudas 'Herzenspflichten'" (On Bachya ibn Pakuda's "Duties of the Heart"), *Monatsschrift für Geschichte und Wissenschaft des Judentums* 1910, 348–51, 730–46; Almut Sh. Bruckstein, "On Jewish Hermeneutics: Maimonides and Bachya as Vectors in Cohen's Philosophy of Origin" in Stéphane Mosès and Hartwig Wiedebach eds., *Hermann Cohen's Philosophy of Religion* (Hildesheim, Zurich, London: Georg Olms, 1997), 35–50.

gious phenomena, and only of these—into the inner-human. Here, too, the past bears witness. Awareness of what is meant by the exchange of names, "Jacob" for "Israel," has not died among us.[21] Ancient exegesis already puts its finger on the fact that the promise to be like the dust of the earth is followed by that other one, which means the same and yet sounds so different—to be like the stars of the heaven;[22] as [ancient exegesis] explains, if they rise, the one; if they fall, the other.[23] But once again: it knows what rising and falling mean and that there is no sense in speaking about rising and falling unless an absolute measure of height stands fast, outside that which rises and falls. It is the same with the schema of myth; in this theory of the monstrous birth of the divine out of the human, the new theology is consciously rooted in the old mysticism. But it is no coincidence that that famous key phrase of the master of the Kabbalah: "God speaks: if you do not bear witness to me, then I am not" is pronounced precisely as a Word of God and is projected into the written Word of God by means of an exegetical trick;[24] God himself, not human presumption, makes Himself dependent upon

---

21. In Genesis 32:29 the name "Israel" is related to the Hebrew words for striving and for the divine: "Your name shall no longer be Jacob, but Israel, for you have striven (*sarita*) with beings divine [alternatively: with God] (*elohim*) and human, and have prevailed."

22. See Genesis 13:17: "I will make your offspring as the dust of the earth, so that if one can count the dust of the earth, then your offspring too can be counted"; Genesis 22:17: "I will bestow My blessing upon you and make your descendants as numerous as the stars of the heaven and the sands on the seashore."

23. Several versions of this interpretation are found among ancient and medieval midrashic collections. See, e.g., *Sifre on Deuteronomy*, ed. S. Horovitz and L. Finkelstein (Berlin: Gesellschaft zur Förderung der Wissenschaft des Judentums, 1939; reprint, New York: Jewish Theological Seminary, 1969), *Ekev*, Piskah 47: "If they do the divine will, they are like stars, and if not, they are like the dust of the earth."

24. The "master of the kabbalah" is Rabbi Simeon bar Yohai (2nd century C.E.), to whom was ascribed the kabbalistic work, the *Zohar*, first published in the 13th century. Rosenzweig cites the same midrash in the name of "the master of the kabbalah" in *Star of Redemption*, 171. Versions of the exegesis occur in numerous midrashic collections. See, e.g., *Sifre on Deuteronomy, Berakhah*, Piskah 346: "Rabbi Simeon bar Yohai says . . . 'And you are my witnesses,' says the Lord, 'and I am God' (Isaiah 43:12): when you are my witnesses, I am God, and when you are not my witnesses, I am not God." See Moshe Idel, "Franz Rosenzweig and the Kabbalah," 163, 242, n.4, who notes that Buber cites the midrash in "Jewish Religiosity" (given as speech in 1912–14), *On Judaism*, ed. N. Glatzer (New York: Schocken, 1967), 84. The "exegetical trick" consists in

the testimony of man; according to a profound parable, He "sells him-self" to man[25]—yet He who could "sell" also has a claim to the purchase price. The conscious connection which the new theology sought here in mysticism, it could seek in "rationalism" with equal justification or lack of justification. That the light of God is the human soul and that only the rays of that light, which the soul needs for the illumination of its earthly way, are visible—this fundamental idea of our philosophy—was and is just as susceptible as its mystical parallels to an atheistic stamp.

The most recent coincidence of mystical and rationalist humaniza-tion (because, after all, it is no more than a most recent one) lends its appearance of justification to the attempt at a resolute transformation of Judaism into something this-worldly. The certainty that God and man must be inseparably thought together stands at the entrance of every way of knowing our faith, even one that God allows to emerge in man. But the cleft, which is not to be filled in, between man as thought by both mysticism and rationalism, and man as he is receiver of revelation and, as such, an object of faith, this unfillable cleft, as it persists, despite all present possibilities of interrelating the concepts of peoplehood and humanity, in our case [as a cleft] between man and Jew, must confuse anyone who might attempt to cover the whole of the religious world with half of this pair of fundamental ideas. If this half, namely man, were in himself to be simple and without inner contradiction, then the thinker, as well as the man of action, could dispense with God. But, as [the thinker] now finds man under the curse of historicity, divided within himself between first receiver and last fulfiller of the Word, be-tween the people that stands at Sinai and the Messianic humanity, he will therefore be unable to eliminate the God to whom the historicity of history is subjugated by His historical deed. Precisely in order to under-stand the Jewish people as the heart of faith, he must think the God who builds a bridge between people and humanity. Let his theology be as scientific as it wants to be and can be: it cannot circumvent the notion of revelation.

---

reading the two occurrences of the letter *waw* in Isaiah 43:12 not as conjunc-tives but rather as marking the protasis and the apodosis of a conditional. Cf., e.g., Genesis 44:22, which is understood not as "and he will leave his father and he will die," but rather as "if he were to leave his father, then he would die."

25. Rosenzweig seems to be giving his own gloss on the midrash just men-tioned—insofar as God makes Himself in some way dependent on the testi-mony of Israel, God "sells Himself" to man. More generally, he seems also to in-voke the rabbinic doctrine that the Shekhinah (divine presence) accompanies Israel even in suffering and exile.

III
From 1914 to 1917

When the war broke out in August 1914, Rosenzweig volunteered and was sent to the Balkan front. On May 29, 1916, Rosenstock, on leave in Cassel and staying in Rosenzweig's home, wrote to Rosenzweig, in part responding to having read the latter's article on the earliest program of German Idealism and in part to reinitiate discussion of the issues of revelation, Judaism, and Christianity that had taken up the evening nearly three years earlier. The correspondence would continue until the end of the year.[1]

For our purposes, the central feature of the correspondence concerns the idea of revelation. As we have seen, Rosenzweig had already, in 1913, learned the importance of revelation from Rosenstock and developed a way of understanding Western history as a history of the relationships between philosophy and revelation, culminating in the Hegelian, idealist system and its legacy, the life of religious action. He had then, in 1914, used that notion of revelation as a historical event to challenge current trends in Christian and Jewish theology. Clearly, however, Rosenzweig was still puzzled by the idea of revelation and its relation to nature; at least he was puzzled by Rosenstock's use of the notion and its relation to what he called paganism. This is the question he puts to Rosenstock in a long letter of October 1916: "explain to me your present idea of the relation between Nature and Revelation." Rosenstock answers on October 28 and 30. It is this exchange that forms the immediate foundation for Rosenzweig's later elaboration in the letter to Rudolf Ehrenberg translated here.

The crux of Rosenstock's answer is this:

> The question you put, "Nature and Revelation," I can only understand as "natural understanding" and revelation. . . . Natural Understanding, then, knows front and back, left and right, and helps itself in this enclosure with a net of analogies. It makes comparisons and thus limps from one place to the next in this vast space. . . .
>
> The resolution not to take one's own position in this quarter of space as the center of knowledge, but as conditioned from above — this renunciation of being *omphalos kosmou* [the navel of the

cosmos] — is no longer a matter of the natural human understanding but is the means within us that makes revelation to, in, and for us possible.[2]

What Rosenstock means by "natural understanding" is akin to "natural consciousness" in Hegel and to the perspective of human agency so central to Dilthey's account of the human sciences and to others like Weber and Simmel. In everyday experience, human beings position themselves with respect to past and future, to here and there, in terms of their "I," their first-person location. It is otherwise in genuine religious life. There revelation fixes the order of history; it is a point of origin in terms of which human action and experience can be oriented and understood. The religious receptivity to revelation is a "renunciation" of natural human understanding; it is a willingness, autonomous but sacrificial, to be located within an order that is given and not constructed, fixed and not movable. Revelation comes from "above," but it is made possible by a "resolve" from "below," a human decision that acknowledges one's own limitations and reaches out to the transcendent.

But this conception of revelation and its relation to natural, everyday human understanding gives rise to several problems. It makes the two modes of existence seem exclusive and radically discontinuous, like Kant's phenomenal and noumenal modes of experience and action. But in fact, if revelation is not to be arbitrary, mysterious, and wholly unjustified to human understanding, the two cannot be so decisively separated. Somehow philosophy, together with natural understanding, and revelation must be related. Or, to put it differently, one has to come to a philosophically acceptable understanding of what God, man, and the world are and then how they are interrelated, both to clarify how revelation functions as orientation and to prevent revelation from being arbitrary and groundless. It is these tasks that Rosenzweig first begins to engage in the letter to Rudolf Ehrenberg of November 18, 1917.

The letter to Ehrenberg is, in many ways, an arcane document, written by one friend and intellectual confidant to another, in a language they shared but which is not easily grasped except by such conversation partners. The key to unlocking the secrets of the *"Urzelle"* is the problem it seeks to deal with, the question it aims to answer. Rosenzweig puts it several ways. What he has discovered, he claims, is "his philosophical Archimedean point, long sought after." Since when? Since at least 1914, when he and Rudolf had formulated the challenge "whether and how one could delimit — purely philosophically or even only in general — revelation from all properly human knowledge by any demonstrable criteria whatsoever." By then he had acknowledged the centrality of the concept of revelation and its role. In 1913 Rosenstock had given him that concept: "revelation is orientation." After revelation, he recalls here, a real "heaven" and "earth" replace a relativized up and down. "In the revealed space-time world," he reminds Ehrenberg, "the middle is an invariably fixed point, which I do not displace if I change or move myself." This concept of revelation is a "thought of stupendous simplicity and fruitfulness and surely correct." What Rosenstock had provided, then, was a solution to the problems of relativism and nihilism that had arisen for Rosenzweig, at least some time prior to 1913 but after 1910, when his conception of history and culture had seemed to him firm and satisfactory.

Some time after 1910 and the Baden-Baden conference, Rosenzweig had become pessimistic about the possibility of realizing a union of spirit and history—the actuality of rational, free action—that was fulfilled and redemptive. Revelation was the answer, or at least part of the answer, to this pessimism. But the mere concept of revelation as orientation—perhaps a response of a kind to Kant's call for "thinking as orientation"—and an absolute, unconditioned directedness was not sufficient. Why not? What was lacking? Rosenzweig suggests the following: first, a philosophical account of the relation between revelation and other forms of knowledge; second, an account of the relation between revelation and the year 1800 as the historical moment of unrest; and finally, an account that is systematic. By 1917 he had seen how to make good these deficiencies, and the letter to Ehrenberg is his first attempt to do so. The reader's question must be: how does he accomplish these tasks; how does he provide a philosophically systematic account that relates revelation to the situation that demands it and the world that follows from it?

One way to expose Rosenzweig's achievement is to clarify the relationship between revelation and the year 1800, as Rosenzweig understands it. What did the year 1800 mean for him in 1917?

Early Thoughts about 1800
Rosenzweig had long been concerned with the idea symbolized by the year 1800. Before going into more detail, it is important to note both that the *nature* of that idea varied as Rosenzweig became fascinated by different thinkers of the period and that the *significance* of the idea changed as Rosenzweig developed from a philosophically minded historian into a man of faith. **Four stages** may be distinguished, associated with four great figures of classical German culture: **Goethe, Kant, Hegel, and Schelling**. The point here is not to reduce Rosenzweig's development to external influences, but rather to trace his development by marking his partners in dialogue at different stages.

Stage 1) Goethe was the first to impress himself upon Rosenzweig, as shown by his unpublished diaries, and that powerful impression is still visible in the *"Urzelle"* and the *Star*, which are full of Goethe's language. At this point, Rosenzweig seems to have had a very positive attitude towards 1800. Thus, in a diary entry from February 9, 1906, Rosenzweig wrote: "The slogan of 1900 is 'Race,' in 1800 it was 'Humanity.' Progress? At least in 1800 the scope was wider, the goal greater."[3] Looking back, on May 24, 1908, Rosenzweig saw that his entire development from 1900 until 1906, had been *"within* Goethe."[4] Goethe's language continued to haunt his own.

Stage 2) In 1906, Rosenzweig began to study **Kant**, taking a class on the *Critique of Pure Reason* with Jonas Cohn at Freiburg. Cohn was a member of the southwestern or Baden school of neo-Kantianism, whose leading figures were Wilhelm Windelband (at Heidelberg) and Heinrich Rickert (at Freiburg) and which was concerned largely with the transcendental logic of the historical or cultural sciences, in contrast with the Marburg school, led by Hermann Cohen, which was concerned largely with the transcendental logic of the natural and mathematical sciences. The southwestern neo-Kantians were primarily concerned to find a way of taking history as the primary habitat of value and rationality, without falling into the abyss of a historicism that would render value and rationality relative to historically shifting conditions. In 1916, Rosenzweig would describe himself as having "passed through" the "southwestern German" school.[5]

At this stage, Rosenzweig came to think

a) of both Goethe and Kant as synthesizing the subjective and the objective—the former by irrationalizing the rational, the latter by rationalizing the irrational—and

b) of his own destiny as the achievement of the still unnamed synthesis of Goethe's poetry and Kant's philosophy: if his development had been *"within* Goethe" from 1900 to 1906, then 1907–8 marked the "negation of this development," a passing beyond "'Goethe's' limits (i.e., in a word: *Critique of Pure Reason*) . . . Now synthesis follows the thesis Goethe and the antithesis Kant, for which I know no name—it would have, so I hope, to be my own."[6]

Stage 3) Rosenzweig studied under Friedrich *Meinecke*, who combined historical scholarship with political philosophy and was associated with the southwestern neo-Kantians, especially *Rickert*, his colleague at Freiburg, in whose seminar Rosenzweig also participated.[7] Meinecke had expressed his own commitment to the reattainment of the achievements of Kant and Goethe:

Germany . . . did not remain on the heights she had attained with
Kant and Goethe. The force of primal genius, which merged its in-
wardness with nature and human existence, which triumphed over
the paralyzing schism between the self and the world and dissolved
it in universal harmony, casting new light and warmth over individual and public life—that force ebbed and abated. The self and
world, culture and nature, again diverged, and today their conflicts
oppress us. . . .

But at least we want to regain those heights. We do not know
whether it is possible, whether we incomplete beings can again become whole; but our need for wholeness cannot be denied, and
we are not without strength to strive for it. Nor, flawed though we
are, do our efforts to develop the material world lack a certain
grandeur. The social and political transformations of our time have
created new psychic and moral challenges that fully engage us.[8]

In 1908–9, Rosenzweig came to think of **Hegel's** system, with its idea
of the state realizing reason in history, as an attractive synthesis of Kant's
rational universality and Goethe's poetic particularity. Hence his dissertation topic, inspired by the chapter on Hegel in Meinecke's *Cosmopolitanism and the National State.*

Rosenzweig's Hegel project coincided with a general **Hegel revival**
among southwestern neo-Kantians. Thus, in 1910 Windelband gave
an address to the Heidelberg Academy of Sciences entitled "Die
Erneuerung des Hegelianismus" ("The Renewal of Hegelianism")
(Heidelberg: Carl Winters Universitätsbuchhandlung, 1910). As
Windelband noted, the Hegel revival seemed very strange to the neo-
Kantians of an older generation, who had been educated in the middle
years of the 19th century. At that time, the return to Kant had been conceived in part as a reaction against the old style of metaphysics with its
extreme inattention to the other sciences (and also, one might add, as a
reaction against a new style of naturalism that paid attention only to natural sciences). The old style of metaphysics was exemplified by the old
Hegelianism that had been dominant in the 1820s and 1830s. Yet now,
Windelband claimed, the "return to Hegel" was a sign, not of regression, but of progression, even of *necessary* progression. Just as the original development from Kant, via Schelling and Fichte, to Hegel, was
necessary, so "the repetition of this process in the progression of the
most recent philosophy from neo-Kantianism to neo-Hegelianism is not
accidental, but rather possesses within itself a material necessity." (It is
also not accidental that the classic depiction of the "Kant to Hegel"

development as necessary is by Richard Kroner, a southwesterner present at Baden-Baden!) It had been necessary, in the mid-19th century, to combat interpretations of Kantianism as a theory of psychological processes. To this end, Lotze, Windelband's teacher, had turned (southwestern) philosophy's attention to the logic of values, which enabled a return to Kantianism properly (i.e., nonpsychologically) understood. Since then, history had proven to be the home of values and hence "the true organon of philosophy." Now the current generation of neo-Kantians was ready to renew Hegel's dialectical method, which would systematically interrelate historical and logical processes. But this would not be a regression to old Hegelian metaphysicians, because the neo-Hegelians would engage with the cultural sciences as earlier Hegelians never did. The legitimate enterprise of neo-Hegelianism was thus "to work the principles of reason out of the historical cosmos as presented by the experience of the cultural sciences." In short, the way to avoid historical relativism was to develop a working relationship between philosophical and historical research under the sign of Hegel.[9]

On January 9, 1910, the conference at Baden-Baden was attended by students of Windelband (including Hans Ehrenberg), students of Rickert (including Cohn), and students of Meinecke (including Rosenzweig). For some, if not all, of the participants, this conference was part of the neo-Hegelian development described and prescribed by Windelband. As his letter to Frank shows, Rosenzweig was already dissatisfied with Hegelian approaches to history before the conference.[10] Nevertheless, he was perceived as Hegelian at the conference. For according to the recollection of Viktor von Weizsäcker, Rosenzweig gave a dialectical account of the present, treating the 17th century as thesis, the 18th as antithesis, and the 19th as synthesis. This led to what von Weizsäcker called "the catastrophe." Some of Rosenzweig's fellow Meinecke students—notably Siegfried Kaehler—denounced "this sort of antihistorical abstraction" and, refusing to have anything to do with such an undertaking, they left the group.[11] To von Weizsäcker, the break signified the end of neo-Hegelianism: "neo-Hegelianism was completely unable to become foundation and direction for the problems that were set for the special sciences at that time. The crisis of science was much too encompassing and the decentralization of the sciences was much too advanced for them to have been able to be repaired by this attempt at the revival of our classical philosophy. The 'decline of the west' had just begun."[12]

Rosenzweig was now firmly convinced that the Hegelian synthesis of philosophical idea and historical actuality (represented by the collegiality of Rickert and Meinecke at Freiburg and symbolized more generally by Windelband's southwestern neo-Hegelianism) could not work: dialectical history was too philosophical to satisfy the historian, and actual history was too gross to satisfy the philosopher. Although he had already begun to think this before the Baden-Baden conference, the disappointment of his reception there must have pushed him further in this direction. As he fell out of sympathy with neo-Hegelianism, the significance of the idea of 1800 shifted. Before, the new synthesis of 1900, for which Rosenzweig was searching, was conceived primarily as *realizing* the idea of 1800—through the ethical and political mission of the German state, through the collaboration of southwestern historians and philosophers. Now the new synthesis was conceived more as *overcoming* the idea of 1800. Specifically, although one might have thought that Rosenzweig's turn to religion occurred in 1913, in 1910 he already thought of religion as the way to overcome the generation of 1800's deification of history.[13]

Stage 4) Since, in Hegelian dialectics, a synthesis is *both* the realization *and* the overcoming of prior moments, Rosenzweig's idea of struggling *against* the 1800 divinization of history does not necessarily constitute a move beyond Hegelianism, although his "struggle for religion" seems to move him beyond neo-Hegelianism as conceived by Windelband. Rosenzweig's decisive move beyond Hegel, toward the *"Urzelle"* and the *Star*, was enabled in large part by the influence of **Friedrich Wilhelm Joseph von Schelling** (1775–1854).

The move from Hegel to Schelling is brought out dramatically in Rosenzweig's treatment of his major scholarly discovery. In 1914, while working in the Hegel archives, Rosenzweig discovered unsuspected importance in a recently acquired fragment of a manuscript in Hegel's handwriting. In the fragment, Rosenzweig detected the first system-program of German Idealism—indeed, as Rosenzweig believed, the first articulation of the concept of systematicity that had dominated philosophy from the period of 1800 until the present day. But, remarkably, when he published the fragment in 1917—the same year in which he wrote the *"Urzelle"*—he argued that, although it had been *written* by Hegel, it had been *composed* by Schelling: Hegel had transcribed the crucial text from a lost letter of Schelling's. Indeed, in the article that publicized his discovery, Rosenzweig said very little about Hegel but gave a novel account of Schelling's development, emphasizing its continuity in an unprecedented fashion and arguing that, although the fragment dated from 1797 to 1798, it already contained *in nuce* elements of Schelling's *mature* philosophy (generally thought to have developed only after 1808). Rosenzweig's argument is a remarkable *tour de force*, as indicated by the fact that, although the fragment is in

Hegel's handwriting, and although no trace of the supposed original text has ever been found, the fragment's ascription to Schelling has remained a live option for scholars, and the fragment has been published in various editions of Schelling's works. However, as early as 1926, arguments were advanced for ascribing the fragment to Hölderlin (in whose collected works it has also been published) and, since 1965, it has been generally accepted that the fragment was in fact composed by Hegel himself.[14]

For our purposes, what is important is not the accuracy of Rosenzweig's Hegel and Schelling interpretations, but rather the coincidence of Rosenzweig's development of the project of the *Star* with his turn from Hegel to Schelling as the best representative of 1800 and the best precursor of 1900. For both the *"Urzelle"* and the *Star* remain explicitly under the influence of Schelling, especially of Schelling's post-1809 work, known as the *Philosophy of the World-Ages*, which Rosenzweig now regarded as the best expression of the idea of 1800, the synthesis of Goethe and Kant, of poetry and philosophy, of history and philosophy, of revelation and reason.

Schelling's philosophy in *The World-Ages* is best seen as a stage in his lifelong struggle to respond to Friedrich Heinrich Jacobi's challenge to philosophy.

Jacobi's challenge: Beginning in his famous controversy with Mendelssohn over Lessing's alleged Spinozism, Jacobi issued the followed challenge to philosophy, which he regarded as a rationalist attempt to explain everything:

a) As Spinoza had argued, philosophy could not consistently maintain the duality, demanded by traditional theism, between the world and God as its first and absolute cause; for such a duality would necessitate an explanation for the existence of a world distinct from God, entailing either that God needs the world and is therefore not absolutely self-sufficient or that the world exists for some reason not grounded with necessity in God, which is incompatible with His status as first cause. The only consistent philosophy was a *monistic* system in which finite, worldly entities were modifications of God's infinite substance.

b) However, a God who did not transcend the world was not, properly speaking, God at all. So the only consistent philosophy was *atheistic*.

c) Indeed, finite persons whose properties were necessarily grounded in God were not, properly speaking, persons capable of free agency at all. So the only consistent philosophy was *fatalistic*.

d) More generally, finite entities whose properties were necessarily grounded in God were not, properly speaking, entities at all. So the only consistent philosophy was *nihilistic*. Putting the point differently, a consistent philosophy would seek, like Spinozism, to comprehend everything in the world as fitting into a system of relations, but such a system would leave out exactly the *substantial being* that distinguishes existent entities from nonentities. Thus consistent philosophy would culminate in the demonstration that God, man, and world are each nothing. By asserting that "All is One," philosophy was also affirming that "All is Nothing." As the motto to his book on Lessing's alleged Spinozism, Jacobi chose the boast made by Archimedes, "Δός μοι ποῦ στῶ" ("Give me a place to stand [and I will move the world]"), and repeated by Descartes in his *Meditations*. His point was that philosophy left one with no firm place to stand whatsoever.

Jacobi's response: Jacobi himself recommended that, in response to this problem, one abandon the philosophical attempt to explain everything. Instead, one should return to one's "natural faith" in the "revelation" to one's physical and spiritual perceptual organs of genuine entities, personal agents, and God. The presence of external objects, other agents, and "Someone entirely Other" was a brute fact, incomprehensible and indemonstrable, yet undeniable, expressed by Jacobi in the formula, "No you, no I," which anticipates the development of dialogical philosophy.[15]

Schelling's response: Schelling agreed with Jacobi that Spinoza had shown systematic monism to be the only consistent path for philosophy. However, rather than abandoning philosophy, Schelling sought to show that this did not mean that philosophy had to be atheistic, fatalistic, or nihilistic. To show this, Schelling employed insights gleaned from Kant, Reinhold, and Fichte (in 1795–97); ideas based on developments in natural science (in 1797–1808); and notions rooted in theosophy and mythology (from 1809, in what is known as his "philosophy of the world ages," known mainly through unpublished drafts and lecture notes). His central idea was that monism could be compatible with theism, freedom, and the existence of finite entities if, unlike Spinoza's, it was a *developmental* monism.

In his early work (1795–1807), Schelling sought to interpret nature as latent mind developing towards self-expression, and mind as expressive nature developing towards self-consciousness. On the basis of these interpretations, the mind-nature whole could be viewed as developing towards self-consciousness through a series of stages that required separation into distinct natural entities, each of which had its own organic course of development, and some of which had their own organically developing personalities. Developmental monism was supposed not only to be compatible with but to give the best account of individual entities and personal freedom.

Although Schelling seemed to have reached the goal of a monistic system by 1801, in fact he saw that he had not responded fully to Jacobi's challenge as long as he had given no explanation why finitude had to arise from the absolute first cause, why the whole had to develop at all. Consequently, Schelling undertook to account for the creation of the world from God and of time from eternity, in work beginning with his 1809 *Investigations of the Essence of Human Freedom.* He realized that, in light of Spinoza and Jacobi, the relationship between the first cause and the world could not have the rational structure of relationships within the world, and this realization had significant consequences for his later work. First, God-before-creation would have to be understood not as an explanatory ground, and not properly speaking as God, but rather as "the dark ground"—a nonground (*Ungrund*), or abyss (*Abgrund*), prior to rational relationships in general, characterized as sheer will: a will that wills nothing. Without creation, this will could be All, but, for just that reason, it could not be the will of God. Second, *priority* to creation would have to be understood not as temporal or logical priority, but as priority in the sense of the mythical past explored by the myths of many cultures, as well as by kabbalists and theosophists. Like creation-myths, philosophy would have to take the form of narrative, but the "once upon a time," "before," "after," and "at the same time" of that narrative would have to be understood in its own fashion. Third, the development of the God-nature-mind whole would have to be viewed not only as development of human self-consciousness, but also as the development of God's *revelation* to man. Philosophy of history had to be understood as philosophy of revelation, as the portrayal of temporality from the viewpoint of eternity. (Although Schelling regarded himself as responding adequately to Jacobi's challenge, and although he is obviously influenced by Jacobi in his emphasis on revelation, Jacobi himself saw Schelling's work as the most extreme validation of the claim that philosophy was bound to be atheistic, fatalistic, and nihilistic, for Schelling's reinterpretations of God, freedom, and being were completely unrecognizable monstrosities.)[16] Fourth, philosophy could be saved from Jacobi's challenge only if rationalism were not the whole of philosophy. Reason itself—the intelligibility of finite things—had to be understood as arising from the nonground or primal will prior to reason, and the world of finitude would always bear the traces of this darkness. Hence the freedom to do evil was possible because the human will could will nothingness and destruction rather than revelation. But, hence too, the world could not be fully comprehended by any philosophy that portrayed *only* the rational relationships of things within the whole of creation because any such philosophy would have to neglect the primal forces at the ground of existence and would be unable to account for the possibility of freedom. It was on this basis that in 1841, ten years after Hegel's death, when Schelling was summoned to Berlin to combat the allegedly pernicious effects of Hegelianism upon religion, he gave an inaugural lecture that attacked the Hegelian system's claim to comprehend the whole conceptually or rationally. That lecture, given before an audience that included Kierkegaard (as well as Bakunin, Engels, and others), may be said to have initiated a criticism of Hegelianism—sometimes called an "existentialist" criticism—that was seminal for thought in the second half of the 19th century and that was inherited and developed by Rosenzweig.

It is important to note that Schelling did not reject the project of giving a systematic account of the intelligible structure of the world. On the contrary, he affirmed that project, which he considered himself to have pioneered before Hegel became famous for it. What he rejected was the notion, which he ascribed to Hegel, that such a system could ever be self-explanatory and self-contained. Rather, the relational system of essences ("negative philosophy") depended on living existence—ultimately on the existence of "the dark ground"—and living existence was necessarily outside the system and could never be comprehended within it. However, there could be a discourse ("positive philosophy") that dealt with this extrasystematic existence, although that discourse would have to differ radically from systematic philosophy. Thus, in lectures, Schelling developed his "philosophy of revelation" and "philosophy of mythology," in which he sought to interpret the history of the world as the history of revelation, using myths from various cultures as his data.[17]

There are several dimensions, then, to **Schelling's impact on Rosenzweig**. In "The New Thinking," Rosenzweig says that the *Star* is neither a "Jewish book" in the usual sense of the term nor "a philosophy of religion," but "merely a system of philosophy" that employs the conception of substance, transmitted by Spinoza to "the great Idealists of 1800." This description marks the influence of Schelling to whom Rosenzweig had attributed the "discovery" of system-construction as philosophy's task in his 1917 essay, "The First System-Program of German Idealism"—a task that had dominated not only German Idealism, but also neo-Kantianism and, indeed, all philosophy "until today" (presumably including neo-Hegelianism). As he explained in a 1916 letter to Rosenstock, "We recognize the problem of system in the Idealists (the way of philosophizing as the real crux of philosophy), but it doesn't control the form of our philosophy as it does theirs; we don't want to be philosophers when we are philosophizing, but human beings, and so we must bring our philosophy into the form of our humanity."[18] As he further explained in a December 1, 1917, letter to Rudolf Ehrenberg, he (along with von Weizsäcker and other members of their circle) still regarded philosophy as essentially systematic but now viewed systematicity not as an *objective* requirement for the content of philosophy, but rather as a subjective requirement for the philosopher as form of philosophy.[19] That is, after Idealism, philosophy had to fulfill Schelling's demand for systematicity insofar as it expressed a whole, thought by a living individual. Thus, when, in the *"Urzelle,"* Rosenzweig speaks of the feeling that he is achieving "the 'systematic' in Weizsäcker's sense," he is referring to a modified version of Schelling's conception of systematicity.

Not only Rosenzweig's conception of systematicity, but also his specific account in "The New Thinking" of the structure of the *Star* is indebted to Schelling. His description of the relation of volumes 1 and 2 of the *Star* is clearly reminiscent of the relation between "negative philosophy" and "positive philosophy" in Schelling's mature view. By showing, in the first volume of the *Star*, that systematic philosophy can teach us at best that each of the traditional topics of metaphysics—God, the world, and "the I" (i.e., the mind, which is constituted by its capacity for first-personal thought and expression)—is "everything and nothing," Rosenzweig intends to show that such a system is ultimately "negative" insofar as it depends upon what it cannot comprehend: the experience of actual divinity, worldliness, and humanity. This conception of experience—as revelation of the absolute—and not the conception of the British empiricists, lies behind Rosenzweig's description in "The New Thinking" of his philosophy as "absolute empiricism," a term suggesting Schelling. Already in the *"Urzelle,"* Rosenzweig had written: "'In' (or better: 'attached to') reason, there is something extrarational, something that cannot be encompassed by the concept of truth. . . . Just as there 'is' a God before all relation, whether to the world or to Himself, and *this* being of God, which is wholly unhypothetical, is the seedpoint of the actuality of God, which Schelling, on whom . . . you must naturally have perpetually thought, calls the 'dark ground,' etc., an interiorization of God, which *precedes* not merely His self-externalization, but rather even His self. . . ." As Rosenzweig explicitly notes in "The New Thinking," the second volume of the *Star* deals with this extrasystematic actuality by adopting a narrative style inspired by Schelling's "positive philosophy": "In his preface to his ingenious fragment *The Ages of the World*, Schelling has foretold a narrative philosophy. The second volume attempts to deliver that."

Schelling's approach to systematic philosophy also offered Rosenzweig a way of responding to the problem of historical relativism and to the failure of neo-Hegelianism. Schelling had argued that the Hegelian dialectic could articulate the systematically intelligible structure of the world, but only as a system of relations, incapable of comprehending living existence. If one regarded that system as self-contained and self-sufficient, one's thinking would be reduced to a game played with lifeless abstractions. Similarly, neo-Hegelian dialectics could articulate the systematically intelligible structure of the cultural data uncovered by historians, but only as a system of perspectives, each of which would have only relative validity. If one regarded that system as self-contained and self-sufficient, one would have no safeguard against relativism. The only way to avoid relativism was to view the system of history, from the absolute standpoint of eternity, as the manifold revelation of God, while acknowledging that God and revelation cannot be comprehended within the system. The neo-Hegelian, dialectical interpretation of history had to be supplemented by a neo-Schellingian, narrative philosophy of revelation.

At the end of the *"Urzelle,"* Rosenzweig writes, "The eternal occurrence in God can be understood . . . on two grounds: from the basis of the fulfilled philosophy (Schelling) and on the basis of revelation (mysticism). Thus theosophy—I am myself still astonished and resistant to this thought—is joined to *theo*logy and philo*sophy*, concluding the triangle of the sciences." At the very end of the letter, he again expresses his astonishment "about the exceptional position of mysticism *between* actual theology and actual philosophy." As explicitly noted, Schelling is the source of the idea that the system of "negative philosophy" requires a narrative history of revelation that is informed by mysticism and theosophy. This enables Rosenzweig to explore the mythological dimension of biblical, rabbinic, and kabbalistic traditions, which had been a stumbling block to various earlier attempts to philosophize about Judaism (including Hermann Cohen's).

In his *Philosophy of Revelation*, Schelling developed (using a notion derived from Joachim of Floris) a three-stage schema of the ages of the world since the birth of Christianity, associating the Petrine age with Catholicism, the Pauline with Protestantism, and the Johannine with his own time. Alluded to in the *"Urzelle,"* Rosenzweig's conception of the three ages is worked out in more detail in other letters of the period, especially in the important correspondence with Eugen Rosenstock-Huessy in 1916, and is articulated in the *Star*. Rosenzweig's conception of the significance of 1800 is now conveyed through his understanding of the time of Goethe, Kant, Hegel, and Schelling as the initiation of the Johannine age of the world.

Of course, Rosenzweig is far from being simply a follower of Schelling. Several significant differences from Schelling emerge from what, in "The New Thinking," Rosenzweig calls the "decisive influence" of Rosenstock. Some spring directly from Rosenstock, while others are formulated by Rosenzweig in his dialogue with Rosenstock. As Rosenzweig writes in the "*Urzelle*," it was Rosenstock who suggested to him that "revelation is orientation. After revelation there is an actual, no longer relativized Up and Down in nature—'heaven' and 'earth' . . . and an actually fixed Earlier and Later in time." In 1916, Rosenzweig had asked Rosenstock to explain his "present idea of the relation between nature and revelation."[20] Rosenstock had replied that, "Natural understanding . . . knows front and back, left and right, and helps itself in this enclosure with a net of analogies. It makes comparisons and limps from one place to the next in this vast space. . . . The resolution not to take one's own position in this quarter of space as the center of knowledge, but as conditioned from above—this renunciation of being ὀμφαλός κόσμου [the navel of the world]—is no longer a matter of the natural human understanding but is the means within us that makes revelation to, in, and for us possible." Without revelation, Rosenstock says, echoing Jacobi either consciously or unconsciously, knowledge would be "without any δός μοι ποῦ στῶ [Give me a place to stand]."[21] Accepting this idea, it was apparently Rosenzweig who introduced the notion of "orientation," which is taken from Kant's contribution to the controversy between Jacobi and Mendelssohn over reason and faith: "What does it mean to orient oneself in thinking?"[22] Now, the idea of a system of perspectives within which there can be absolute orientation only through revelation is certainly an inheritance of Schelling's Jacobi-inspired conception of the systematizable world as a network of relations that cannot stand on its own without an extrasystematic absolute that reveals itself in and through the world. However, Schelling does not seem to share Rosenstock's and Rosenzweig's emphasis on a specific *event* of revelation—whether in the history of the world or of an individual, whether the giving of the Torah at Sinai or the incarnation.

Schelling called for a narrative philosophy but produced only fragments. In a March 18, 1921, letter to Hans Ehrenberg, Rosenzweig remarked that, "If it [*The World Ages*] had been completed, then the *Star* would not merit anyone caring a fig about it, outside of the Jews." (Similarly, Jacobi called for a discourse that would depart from traditional philosophy by acknowledging the I-you relationship, but his writings may be said to remain monological, even when they take the form of dialogue.) Rosenzweig hopes to fulfill these unrealized hopes with the help of Rosenstock's conception of dialogical speech, originally articulated in a letter to Rosenzweig (written before the "*Urzelle*") and then published as *Die angewandte Seelenkunde*.[23] Thus, whereas Schelling's philosophy of the world-ages is an account of, among other things, the predicative structure of judgments in abstraction from their use in actual conversations, Rosenzweig's *Star* undertakes both to be and to reflect upon genuine dialogical speech in narrative form.[24]

1800 in the "*Urzelle*"

Rosenzweig does not spell out in any one place the idea of 1800 as he had developed it by the time of the composition of the "*Urzelle*." What follows is a reconstruction based on various letters to Hans Ehrenberg, Rudolf Ehrenberg, and Eugen Rosenstock between 1910 and 1918:

1) Rosenzweig thinks of history since the birth of Christianity as the story of the dialectical relations between

a) revelation, represented in the world by the Church, and

b) its "external enemies" or determining negations (i.e., the contrasting terms, difference from which makes the Church what it is); these are

i) Greek wisdom (paganism, science, philosophy) (see especially letter to Hans Ehrenberg, December 11, 1913, *Briefe* I, 145–47) and

ii) Roman imperialism (the state) (see letter to Rosenstock, November 7, 1916, and November 30, 1916, *Briefe* I, 280–89, 302–6).

2) He divides that history into three stages:

a) the Petrine (Catholicism, Church as hierarchy, beginning in 313 with the Edict of Milan; partial incorporation of the Roman Empire);

b) the Pauline (Protestantism, Church as Word, beginning in 1517 with Luther's theses; the partial incorporation of Greek wisdom, since the philosophers—Descartes, Leibniz, Spinoza—are now heretics within the Church, not pagans outside it);

c) the Johannine (beginning around 1800). Hence the idea of 1800 = the idea of the Johannine epoch of Church history.

As we pointed out above, in employing this terminology, Rosenzweig is borrowing a device taken by the Idealists—Fichte, Schelling, and Hegel—from Joachim of Floris—of course, in his own way, but under their influence, especially the influence of Schelling.

3) The Johannine period is characterized by the fact that the Church now fully incorporates its opposites. However, since (according to Spinozist and Idealist logic) all determination is negation (i.e., everything is the specific thing that it is in virtue of its contrasts with the specific things it is not, or in virtue of its position within a system of relations), the Church is now both everything and nothing. More specifically:

a) Greek wisdom (paganism, science, philosophy) is no longer distinct from the Church; hence, Hegel the philosopher is the first of the

Johannine Church fathers and Goethe the pagan is the first Christian simply speaking and as Christ wanted him, i.e., without determining negation; Freemasonry is now the organization carrying the word of the Johannine Church.[25]

b) there is no longer a State (Roman Empire) distinct from the Church, which opens the way to a nationalism in which Christianity identifies itself as a system of nations, which enables the war of 1914.[26]

4) A synthesis is achieved in the *"Urzelle."* For the following reasons, new possibilities for revelation emerge in the Johannine period, and thus the possibility of grasping revelation as orientation (as Rosenstock had done) can be situated in relation to 1800:

a) now that the duality of Greek wisdom and Jewish-Christian faith has been overcome through the construction of a single all-comprehending philosophical system, philosophy is complete, having achieved absolute self-consciousness through grasping its own history. Yet—as Schelling pointed out in criticism of Hegel—in another sense, the system cannot be self-sufficient: the living, existing, philosophizing subject remains outside the system, along with the God of revelation, uncomprehended and undigested;

b) post-Idealist philosophers, such as Schopenhauer and Nietzsche, inaugurate a new period of *Weltanschauungsphilosophie* (*Worldview-philosophy*), in which the subjectivity of the individual philosopher is the form of the system, and the lives of the philosophers are no longer merely components of the (extraneous) history of philosophy;[27]

c) so now, since:

i) (employing Rosenstock's conception) revelation involves a relation of the Absolute (God) to subjectivity that is beyond history; and

ii) (employing Rosenzweig's idea of 1800) the postphilosopher or Johannine Church father is now concerned with the transhistorical relation of the Absolute to subjectivity;

iii) it follows that the postphilosopher is prepared in a new way for revelation and is ready to hear the voice of God.[28] Thus the world is ready not only for the "negative philosophy"—the complete system of conceptual relations—already developed by Hegel, but also for the "positive philosophy" of revelation for which Schelling had called, but which Schelling himself had never adequately developed.

5) A crucial aspect of Rosenzweig's conception of the Johannine period is omitted from the *"Urzelle"* but is worked out in his 1916 correspondence with Rosenstock and is very important for the *Star*: the relationship between Christianity and Judaism, its "internal enemy," which also has a revelation-based absolute orientation within history. While differentiation from Judaism is essential to Christianity in the Petrine and

Pauline epochs, the situation shifts dramatically with the initiation of the Johannine epoch around 1800. It is a time of danger and opportunity.

As Rosenstock's letters seem to prophesy, there is danger because, during the Petrine and Pauline ages, the Jew is protected by the dogma of the stubborn Jew whose conversion comes only at the end, but now that post-Christian nationalism has emerged, this protection ceases to exist, which makes residual resentment of the stubborn Jew more destructive than ever before. "The epoch of the eternal Jew comes to an end . . . ," but in what sense?[29]

As Rosenzweig's letters suggest, there is also opportunity because both Christianity and Judaism have to "identify themselves" and, without its previous contrasts, Christian identity now depends on Judaism.[30] Some have seen here the possibility of a first genuine dialogue between Judaism and Christianity, originating in Rosenzweig's dialogues with Rosenstock and the Ehrenbergs. Although the contrast between them persists, new opportunities arise for Judaism and Christianity to clarify their different ways of testifying to revelation and to find new possibilities for dialogue.

Let us now return to the "*Urzelle*" itself. Here, for reasons we can now understand, Rosenzweig associated the year 1800 with Hegel and Goethe, with the flowering of German Idealism, with Hegel as the last philosopher and Goethe as the first Christian; it was the year that marked "the absolute self-consciousness of both." The year 1800, that is, marked the unity of spirit and nature, spirit and history, and moreover the recognition of the fact of unity by spirit as self-conscious and reflective. It was the moment when philosophy achieved its perfect realization and when the immanence of spirit in nature, exemplified by the incarnation of Jesus as the Christ, gave birth to a fully genuine Christianity. Later in the letter Rosenzweig emphasizes that the unity must be "grasped as a *Faktum*, as a world historical point." It is an "absolute end with respect to an absolute beginning," and while the end is the actual, historical realization of this "immanence thought," the beginning is the capacity for being seized by revelation. In other words, history and life have reached a point that is as fulfilled as they can be by themselves; in 1917 Rosenzweig believes that what the year 1900 shows is that nothing beyond 1800 can be achieved without some further contribution; by themselves history and nature, no matter how informed by the Absolute, are still deficient. The world and history are prepared for fulfillment but are unfulfillable by themselves. Hence, revelation is both necessary and possible. This is Rosenzweig's thinking in 1917.

It is extremely important to understand Rosenzweig's state of mind prior to 1913 and at the time of the war. German culture, politics, and history, represented by the year 1900, had not succeeded in solving the problem forecast by the flourishing of German Idealism circa 1800, the problem of realizing free, rational humanity in history, politically and spiritually at once. The eruption of war in 1914 only confirmed this failure, with its combination of political power and violence. If the individual self was to emerge as free and rational, it would have to be empowered to do so and directed by the Absolute itself, existing outside of history but engaged with persons in it, for by itself German politics was heading in a disastrous direction. The resulting theory and practice would have to be man's free response to this engagement with the Absolute. In 1914, however, Rosenzweig could see that this was needed—revelation as orientation—but not how it was possible. From 1910, if not earlier, Rosenzweig had seen history as the scene of human actions. In a sense, after 1913, he realized that genuine human actions must be performed as a response to the Absolute, to the encounter with God, but he could not yet see how the encounter of the human and the divine could take place. Why not? In part because the human agent was prohibited by philosophy and thought from receptivity to such an event of engagement and in part because the concept of the Absolute was understood in such a way that the Absolute was either wholly transcendent and inaccessible or wholly immanent and hence unsuited for such an act. The letter of 1917 is the first evidence that Rosenzweig has come to understand how revelation is possible, and the key intellectual influence on him and his solution is Schelling and his later philosophy.

For Rosenzweig, Schelling's tremendous achievement was to disclose the twin actualities of the unique individual and the actually existing Absolute that are excluded from and yet presupposed by the system of reason, the philosophy of Idealism. These gave his thinking a new foundation in the experience of the contingent, existing individual and its relation to the preconceptual, pretheoretical Absolute, the *Urgrund*, the "dark ground." As Rosenzweig puts it in the letter, "everything that happens between the Absolute and the relative 'before' it, is revelation, and everything that proceeds between the Absolute and the relative 'after' it, is nature, world, or whatever you want to call it." The relative "before" it is man, man as self-conscious I, here and now, a brute actuality, and revelation occurs when the Absolute "asks after it," as Rosenzweig puts it. Or, at a later stage of the letter, "[man's] I is dull and dumb and awaits the saving word from the mouth of God: 'Adam, where are *you*?' in order that the first half-audible timid I of shame respond to the first audible you asking after him." Revelation is a dialectic—revelation, command, shame and readiness, prayer, and salvation—which results in each I recognizing the other as a neighbor, a corecipient and corespondent beloved by the same God, drawn into the same dialectic. Rosenzweig calls this a "love . . . which ascends from the event," and he compares it to the staking out of tentpegs as "cornerposts of our worldly estate." It is, moreover, a love that brings the Absolute down to the individual and bestows the freedom whereby the individual can sacrifice to command; "through revelation, man becomes capable of his own sacrifices to the ideal." "[The pious] stands under an 'order,' an order that gives him complete power over the whole world and its ideals. . . . Revelation pushes itself into the world like a wedge; the This struggles against the This." The result is action, human response to the divine engagement, to the divine order, and to the love; it is, in effect, the creation of a community of love, of freedom, of all.

By 1917, then, Rosenzweig had come to see what modern culture required to accomplish its fulfillment. He had also come to understand philosophically how revelation was possible and what it would lead to— what fulfillment and redemption would be. In the letter to Rudolf Ehrenberg he sketches these thoughts cryptically and briefly and then, in August of 1918, begins to develop these ideas into a book for which he is justly famous.

Endnotes

1. For Rosenstock's account of the circumstances that led to the correspondence, see his *Briefe*, translated by Dorothy Emmet in Altmann, Introduction, *Judaism Despite Christianity*, 31–32, n.10. See, too, Altmann's comments, 42–43, on the correspondence and its initiation.

2. *Judaism Despite Christianity*, 119–20.

3. *Briefe* I, 25; Glatzer, *Franz Rosenzweig*, 6.

4. *Briefe* I, 81.

5. *Briefe* I, 255; *Judaism Despite Christianity*, 116.

6. *Briefe* I, 81.

7. In February 1909, e.g., he gave presentations in both seminars. See *Briefe* I, 89.

8. *The Age of German Liberation*, trans. Peter Paret and Helmut Fischer (1906; reprint, Berkeley and Los Angeles: University of California Press, 1977) 1–2.

9. See also Paul Honigsheim, "Zur Hegelsrenaissance in Vorkriegs-Heidelberg: Erkenntnissoziologische Beobachtungen" (On the Hegel renaissance in prewar Heidelberg: Observations from the perspective of the sociology of knowledge), *Hegel-Studien* 2 (1963): 291–301, who discusses Rosenzweig, as well as other southwesterners tending towards Hegelianism, such as Hans Ehrenberg, Georg Lukács, and Ernst Bloch, none of whom remained Hegelians for long, although Hegel profoundly influenced their later work.

10. *Briefe* I, 100–1.

11. "The crisis or catastrophe occurred in a session which I chaired and in which Franz Rosenzweig spoke. As I recall, Rosenzweig developed a historical construction of the present, in which, according to a Hegelian-dialectical method, the 17th, 18th, and 19th centuries were organized as thesis, antithesis, and synthesis. A split in the membership took place on that same evening. One part of the Meinecke-school, above all Siegfried Kaehler and [Edward] Meyer, interpreted this kind of historically hostile abstraction as wholly unbearable and resolved to walk out on such an undertaking." *Briefe* I, 96.

12. See von Weizsäcker's two accounts, both suggesting a hint of antisemitism in the schism, in *Begegnungen und Entscheidungen* (Encounters and decisions) (Stuttgart: K. F. Koehler, 1945), 11; *Natur und Geist* (Nature and spirit), (Göttingen, 1955), 25. See also Kaehler's August 30, 1910, letter about Rosenzweig cutting himself off from the Freiburg circle in *Siegfried A. Kaehler: Briefe 1900–1963* ed. Walter Bussmann and Günther Grünthal (Boppard an Rhein: Harald Boldt, 1993), 125.

13. See the important letter to Hans Ehrenberg, September 26, 1910, *Briefe* I,

III From 1914 to 1917

112, after Baden-Baden, where Rosenzweig quotes the following from his own diary:

The 18th century saw the practical moment of religion in its way, Kant the most deeply (also Lessing). The 19th rejected it. One sees this clearly in Schleiermacher, who does not merely polemicize against morality, but rather, insofar as he constructs religion as synthesis of the practical and the theoretical, neglects the practical, as he himself really intends; he wants to establish "feeling" as mediation of theory and practice, but it surely shifts it across to theory. Hegel's religious "intellectualism" also belongs here. Today, we stress the practical, the fall into sin, history, not, like Schleiermacher, as being laid out in time for the intuition of the beholder, but rather *as act of the agent.* Thus we also refuse to see "God in history" because we want to see history (in religious context) not as image, not as being; rather we *deny* God in *it,* in order to *restore* Him to the process whereby it *becomes.* We see God in every ethical occurrence, but not in the finished whole, in history; — for why would we need a God if history were divine, if all action, flowing in this bowl, were justified, without any further divine [aspect]. No, every act becomes sinful, if it enters into history (the agent did not want what came to be) and for that reason God must save man not through history, but rather actually — nothing else is left — as "God in religion." For Hegel, history was divine, "theodicy"; the act — as prehistorical, moral, subjective — without any further divine [aspect], "passion," "individual," "good intention," "knight of virtue." For us religion is the "uniquely authentic theodicy." The struggle against history in the sense of the 19th century is thus for us at the same time the struggle for religion in the sense of the 20th.

See also letter to Hans Ehrenberg about the consequence of Baden-Baden, November 11, 1910, *Briefe* I, 115–16, and letter to Hans Ehrenberg, February 14, 1911, *Briefe* I, 117: "What opens itself up to me as universal-history is properly speaking only the matter; the material for leaping hither and thither; neither Hegel's 'course' nor Ranke's 'fable.'"

14. For an edition of the fragment and a collection of papers, including the original paper by Rosenzweig and the 1965 paper by Otto Pöggeler, see Christoph Jamme and Helmut Schneider, eds., *Mythologie der Vernunft: Hegels "ältestes Systemprogramm" des deutschen Idealismus* (Frankfurt am Main: Suhrkamp, 1984); for a history of the debate, see Frank-Peter Hansen, *"Das älteste Systemprogramm des deutschen Idealismus": Rezeptionsgeschichte und Interpretation* (Berlin: Walter de Gruyter, 1989).

15. For Jacobi's main texts in translation, see *Friedrich Heinrich Jacobi: The Main Philosophical Writings and the Novel "Allwill,"* trans. and ed. George di Giovanni (Montreal: McGill-Queen's University Press, 1994). For further discussion, see Paul Franks, "All or Nothing: Systematicity and Nihilism in Jacobi, Reinhold, and Maimon," in *The Cambridge Companion to German Idealism,* ed. Karl Ameriks (forthcoming).

16. For their bitter dispute in 1812, see Wolfgang Weischedel, ed., *Streit um die göttlichen Dinge. Die Auseinandersetzung zwischen Jacobi und Schelling* (Darmstadt: Wissenschaftliche Buchgesellschaft, 1967).

17. Schelling wrote several incomplete drafts of *Die Weltalter*, but they remained unpublished despite numerous announcements. See Schelling, *Schellings Werke. Nachlassband. Die Weltalter. Fragmente. In den Urfassungen von 1811 und 1813* (Schelling's works. Volume of posthumous publications. The Ages of the World. Fragments. In the original versions of 1811 and 1813), ed. Manfred Schröter (München: C. H. Beck, 1946). For a translation of the 1811 version, see *The Ages of the World*, trans. Frederick de Wolfe Bolman Jr. (New York: Columbia University Press, 1942), and, for a translation of the 1813 version by Judith Norman, see Slavoj Zizek, *The Abyss of Freedom/Ages of the World* (Ann Arbor: University of Michigan Press, 1997). The distinction between "negative philosophy" and "positive philosophy" was introduced later, in 1827–54, but seems to represent a development of, rather than a departure from, the philosophy of the world ages, which Schelling was still calling the topic of his lectures on "positive philosophy in 1827–33. His ideas about the philosophy of mythology and revelation also remained unpublished. For lecture transcripts, see *Schellings Werke IV: Schriften zur Religionsphilosophie 1841–1854*, ed. Manfred Schröter (München: C. H. Beck, 1946), and for translations of extracts, see Victor C. Hayes, *Schelling's Philosophy of Mythology and Revelation* (Armidale, NSW, Australia: Australian Association for the Study of Religions, 1995).

18. *Briefe I*, 318; *Judaism Despite Christianity*, 167.

19. *Briefe I*, 484–86.

20. *Briefe I*, 256; *Judaism Despite Christianity*, 117.

21. *Briefe I*, 276; *Judaism Despite Christianity*, 119–20.

22. *Briefe I*, 317; *Judaism Despite Christianity*, 166. For Kant's essay, see *Religion and Rational Theology*, trans. and ed. Allen Wood and George di Giovanni (Cambridge: Cambridge University Press, 1996), 7–18.

23. Mark Huessy and Freya von Moltke, trans., Clinton C. Gardner, ed. *Practical Knowledge of the Soul* (Essex, Vt.: Argo, 1988).

24. On Schelling's account of predication, see Wolfram Hogrebe, *Prädikation und Genesis. Metaphysik als Fundamentalheuristik im Ausgang von Schellings "Die Weltalter"* (Predication and Genesis. Metaphysics as fundamental heuristics beginning from Schelling's "The Ages of the World") (Frankfurt am Main: Suhrkamp, 1989).

25. Letter to Rudolf Ehrenberg, February 1916, and to Hans Ehrenberg, May 9, 1918, *Briefe I*, 184–86 and 553–56; this, too, is an Idealist notion, developed notably in Fichte's 1800 *Philosophy of Freemasonry*, trans. Roscoe Pound (Seattle: Research Lodge, No. 281, F. & A. M., 1945).

26. Letter to Rosenstock, November 7, 1916, *Briefe* I, 281; *Judaism Despite Christianity*, 129–38.

27. Letter to Rudolf Ehrenberg, December 1, 1917, *Briefe* I, 484–86.

28. Ibid.

29. *Briefe* I, 298–302; *Judaism Despite Christianity*, 140.

30. *Briefe* I, 302–6; *Judaism Despite Christianity*, 160.

IV

"*Urzelle*" to the
Star of Redemption
(1917)

Dear Rudolf,[1]

Meanwhile, already a month ago now, I achieved something important, so at least it seemed to me at first; now I have become doubtful again, because the usual criterion of such discoveries—the rabbit-like fecundity of their applications—failed to appear this time, but that perhaps for external reasons. Here it is: my philosophical Archimedean point, long sought after. Perhaps you still recall: on our 1914 tour of the Harz [mountain range], we had just stepped out of a fir forest, on the first day, and spoke about whether and how one could delimit—purely philosophically or even only in general—revelation from all properly human knowledge by any demonstrable criteria whatsoever. I knew nothing further than the mark of the "reluctant," of the "*Ecce deus fortior me qui veniens dominabitur mihi,*"[2] the fact that "the prophet, a hounded beast, struggles against the gradually ascending image." The

---

1. Rudolf Ehrenberg (1884–1969), Rosenzweig's second cousin, a convert to Christianity, whose work on biology is later cited by Rosenzweig as an example of "new thinking," and Rosenzweig's frequent correspondent. For Rosenzweig's letter about his decision to remain Jewish, see *Briefe*, I, 132–7; Glatzer, *Franz Rosenzweig*, 28.

2. See Dante Alighieri (1265–1321), *La Vita Nuova* (Poems of youth), trans. Barbara Reynolds (London: Penguin, 1969), 29–30: "The moment I saw her I say in all truth that the vital spirit, which dwells in the inmost depths of the heart, began to tremble so violently that I felt the vibration alarmingly in all my pulses, even the weakest of them. As it trembled it uttered these words: *Ecce deus fortior me, qui veniens dominabitur mihi* (Behold a god more powerful than I who comes to rule over me)."

assumption, then, [is] that man[3] of his own accord follows only "his impulses" and that the voice of God calls him always in a directly opposed direction. Certainly not straightforwardly false, but much too impoverished and, besides, convincing—only for men, who already have no further genuine interest in pure philosophical criteria. I felt the inadequacy even then, but all reflection on the concept of revelation, intended and wanted as central concept (it was not my fault that at that time a programmatic announcement concerning this concept remained unprinted, in the article "Atheistic Theology,"[4] the rest of which I read to you there in the Harz), therefore all reflection, brought me insights that were only into the history of philosophy and were never purely conceptual. The previous year in correspondence with Rosenstock[5] I asked him straight out what he understood by revelation. He answered: revelation is orientation.[6] After revelation[7] there is an actual, no

---

3. *Mensch.* No gender-specific reference is intended in this or other uses of "man."

4. See Chapter 2.

5. Eugen Rosenstock-Huessy (1888–1973), a convert from Judaism to Christianity, with whom Rosenzweig had the momentous conversation of July 7, 1913. The correspondence referred to by Rosenzweig may be found (inter alia) in Rosenzweig, *Briefe* I, 191–320 and, in translation, in Rosenstock-Huessy, ed., *Judaism Despite Christianity: The "Letters on Christianity and Judaism" between Eugen Rosenstock-Huessy and Franz Rosenzweig,* trans. Dorothy Emmett (University, Ala.: University of Alabama Press, 1969). Of particular importance for Rosenzweig were Rosenstock-Huessy's letter about speech, later developed into the treatise *Angewandte Seelenkunde* (Applied psychology), in *Die Sprache des Menschengeschlechts: Eine leibhaftige Grammatik in vier Teilen* (The language of the human race: An incarnate grammar) (Heidelberg: Lambert Schneider, 1963) I, 739–810, trans. Mark Huessy and Freya von Moltke as *Practical Knowledge of the Soul* (Norwich, Vt.: Argo Books, 1988), and his idea of a "cross of actuality," in response to which Rosenzweig's idea of a "star of redemption" was conceived.

6. For Rosenzweig's question, see Rosenzweig, *Briefe* I, 256; *Judaism Despite Christianity,* 117. For Rosenstock's answer, see *Briefe* I, 276; *Judaism Despite Christianity,* 119–20. Kant introduced the concept of orientation into the 18th-century debate about faith and reason initiated by Friedrich Heinrich Jacobi (1749–1814) and Moses Mendelssohn (1729–86). See Kant, "What Does It Mean to Orient Oneself in Thinking," in *Religion and Rational Theology,* trans. and ed. Allen Wood and George di Giovanni. (Cambridge: Cambridge University Press, 1996), 7–18.

7. The ambiguous phrase *nach der Offenbarung* may also be translated as "in accordance with revelation."

longer relativized Up and Down in nature—"heaven" and "earth" (you see here how what Rosenstock calls nature is despite himself not at all the nature of natural science, but rather the nature of *poesy*; thus indeed is to be entirely understood his demands for more natural-scientific methods in the human sciences—but back to the topic again) and an actually fixed Earlier and Later in time. Thus: in "natural" space and in natural time the middle is always the point where I simply *am* (ἄνθρωπος μέτρον ἁπάντων);[8] in the revealed space-time world the middle is an immovably fixed point, which I do not displace if I change or move myself: the earth is the middle of the world, and world history lies before and after Christ (θεὸς καί λόγος αὐτου μέτρον ἁπάντων).[9] Thus approximately, not verbatim and also merely the skeleton, but a thought of stupendous simplicity and fruitfulness and surely correct (I would not trust myself if I did not *also* reach it on my own basis). Why then still not enough for me? Because although I recognized it without ado, I was still not satisfied for myself. Evidently because the place where my cognitive clockwork gets stuck is called "1800" ("Hegel" and "Goethe," namely the absolute self-consciousness of each, Hegel's as that of the last philosopher, of the last pagan brain, and Goethe's as that of—you know the Eckermann logion—the first Christian, as Christ wanted him, thus of the first "man straightforwardly"—"the great pagan" and the "decided non-Christian" mean comically nothing other than that Eckermann logion, but must first be understood from it).[10] And so I must see

---

8. Greek: Man is the measure of all things. Plato (c.427–348 B.C.E.) attributes this thesis to Protagoras (c.480–c.411 B.C.E.). See Plato, *Collected Works*, ed. John Cooper (Indianapolis: Hackett, 1997), *Cratylus*, 386a; *Theaetetus*, 152a, 160d, 161c, 166d, 167d, 170d, 178b, 183b.

9. Greek: God and His own *logos* are the measure of all things. For Hellenistic Jewish philosophers, such as Philo of Alexandria (c.20 B.C.E.–c.50 C.E.), the *logos* (literally translated as "word," "account," or "explanation") signified the intermediary rational structure whereby God created the world. In the Gospel of John, the *logos* is identified with Jesus.

10. Johann Peter Eckermann (1792–1854) acted from 1823 as the editorial assistant of Johann Wolfgang von Goethe (1749–1832) and compiled a celebrated record of his table talk. However, Rosenzweig is in fact recalling a conversation that was not recorded by Eckermann but which occurs in another collection. According to Wolfgang Herwig, ed., *Goethes Gespräche: Biedermannsche Ausgabe* (Goethe's conversations: The Biedermann edition) (Zurich: Artemis Verlag, 1965–87), III: 2, 604, Goethe said the following to Friedrich von Müller (1779–1849) on April 7, 1830: "You know how I respect Christianity, or perhaps you don't know it: who is today a Christian as Christ wanted him [to be]? I alone perhaps, although you take me for a pagan."

from this my intellectual middle point everything that is supposed to be transparent to me; on any other path my understanding runs quickly aground. Now, however, don't expect anything new. On the contrary. There is perhaps nothing new in it except my feeling that I now have a perspicuous interconnection of thoughts, where previously mere aperçus pushed one in front of the other. Thus only the "systematic" in Weizsäcker's sense.[11] And even that—well, I will see.

---

11. Viktor Freiherr von Weizsäcker (1886–1957) became a friend of Rosenzweig's while Rosenzweig was studying medicine at Freiburg in 1906, and later founded an anthropological approach to medicine. In a letter to Rudolf Ehrenberg on December 1, 1917, *Briefe* I, 484–86, Rosenzweig characterized von Weizsäcker's conception of systematicity as follows: "His [Weizsäcker's] conception of system, that is the main point for me, is in fact exactly the same as mine and indeed also Rosenstock's. I formulate it as follows: system is *not architecture*, where the stones assemble the structure and are there for the sake of the structure (and otherwise for no reason); rather, system means that every individual has the drive and will to *relation* to all other individuals; the 'whole' lies beyond its conscious field of vision, it sees only the chaos of the individuals into which it stretches out its feelers. In the Hegelian system, each individual position is anchored only in the whole and indeed (therefore) with two others, with one according to the immediately preceding and with one according to the immediately following position. It is—'said between us'—the fundamental error of my Hegel-book that I did not see that then and consequently travestied the Hegelian system unwittingly into a modern system, namely since I constantly asked: state and . . ., state and . . . (state and economy, state and history, state and people, state and culture, state and—Hegel, this latter [being] thus the chief and central error of all), questions that Hegel precisely does *not* raise. This unwitting modernization is naturally by the same token also the achievement of the book. Today we actually ask in this manner. Think about Rosenstock's letter on language. That is a persistent 'language and . . .' without one's having the feeling, as one does in Hegel's case, that language had its fixed place in a fixed system. It is made precisely into the middle point of the question-raising and indeed the question mark of the 'and' [is] thrown out in all directions. Another object—just that would be made the middle point in exactly the same way, and one of the many outstretched feelers, etc., would run to language. Thus a philosophical relativity-principle.—Where then does the Absolute remain, without which philosophy cannot do? W[eizsäcker] asks that and so do I. I say: if the 'whole' is no longer the *content* of the system, then it must be precisely the *form* of the system; or, in different terms: the totality of the system is no longer objective, but rather subjective. I myself, I the 'world-viewer,' am the limiting ether for the content of my intuited world (thus limited only from 'within,' according to its content, according to the world). The *philosopher* is the form of philosophy. (Schopenhauer is the first philosopher in the new sense; he expressed that

Thus, I say: philosophizing reason stands on its own feet, it is self-sufficient. All things are grasped in it, and ultimately it grasps itself (the only epistemological act, against which nothing can be said because it is the only one that occurs not according to the form A=B, which is the form of knowing actuality and of actuality, but rather according to the form of *logical* knowing A=A).[12] After it has thus taken up everything

clearly with the subjectivity of worldview: 'Philosophy of the impression that the world makes upon an individual subject, and the reaction to this impression' — letter to Brockhaus during the negotations over the publication of *World as Will and Representation* —, then Nietzsche, of course). Until Hegel, the lives of the philosophers were exponents of the history of philosophy; each philosopher has the life that is appropriate to the time; only at this cost does he become the voice of the thought that is appropriate to the time; from Schopenhauer on, the philosophers have *their* lives and write *their* philosophies; for the history of philosophy as objective context has ended; 'chaos' has been established; man has become the master over the subject matter (philosophy) and thus prepared to hear the voice of God (which man never hears so long as he still works behind the shield of a 'subject matter'). The Church fathers (of the new, 'third' Johannine Church) follow the philosophers; after the Idealists knew revelation as the objective content of philosophy, Schopenhauer is the first who does not, say, recognize the actual Christian content as true (as the Idealists did), but who instead philosophizes afresh about it ([although] he hardly recognizes [it] as true!). Previously, the philosopher was a Greek, who discovered Christianity; in the cases of Schopenhauer and Nietzsche, the philosopher is a Christian, who knows as little of Christianity as—most Christians, but is stuck up to the ears and beyond in Christian concepts: conversion, overcoming, change of will, the holy, rebirth, compassion, hardness. Which philosopher had taken these concepts into his mouth previously? And, to be sure, theology preoccupied itself with them since the 18th century.... And indeed, I think, Weizsäcker, too, is on this path, on the path to knowledge of subjectivity as [knowledge] of the unique, objective domain of the system."

12. According to the Idealist logical tradition which Rosenzweig is following here, "A=A" expresses the fundamental principle of logic—the principle of noncontradiction—and "A=B" expresses the form of every predication in which a property is ascribed to an object. Contemporary logicians distinguish sharply between the "is" of predication and the "is" of identity, and would not express either noncontradiction or predication in terms of identity. However, the following may help explain the thinking behind Rosenzweig's usage. First, the principle of noncontradiction is formulated by contemporary logicians in terms of propositions or contents of claims about states of affairs—"not both p and not-p"—not as an identity-statement about entities—"A=A." But traditional metaphysics takes all propositions to be ultimately about entities and thus views the principle of the noncontradiction of propositions as equivalent to the principle of the self-identity of entities. See, e.g., Leibniz's remark in *The Leibniz-Clarke*

within itself and has proclaimed its exclusive existence, man suddenly discovers that he, who has long been philosophically digested, is still there. And indeed not as man with his palmbranches—whom the whale has long since swallowed up and he can spend the time by singing psalms in the whale's belly—rather as "I, who am indeed dust and ashes."[13] I, a completely common private-subject, I fore- and surname, I dust and ashes. I am still there. And I philosophize, i.e.: I have the audacity to philosoph-ize philosophy, the sovereign mistress of all. Philosophy let it be said to me (dust and ashes), not once directly, but rather through the man with palmbranches: I fore- and surname have to be completely and generally silent, and then she has shamed the very man with his palmbranches through whom she has shamed me and has let him become quite small before a few ideals, and then she has let the ideals crawl into the Absolute—and now suddenly I come along, as if

---

Correspondence, ed. Roger Ariew (Indianapolis: Hackett, 2000), 7: "The great foundation of mathematics is the *principle of contradiction, or identity*, that is, that a proposition cannot be true or false at the same time, and that therefore A is A, and cannot be not A." Second, according to the Idealist tradition, everything is the self-identical entity it is by virtue of its differences from, and similarities to, other entities. Thus, to characterize an entity A by ascribing a property to it is *in one respect* to identify A with any other entity, B, that also has that property— "A=B"—although A must also be *in some other respect* nonidentical with B, if they are distinct entities. A third idea required to understand what Rosenzweig is saying here is that, according to Georg Friedrich Wilhelm Hegel (1770–1831), genuine knowledge always involves the identity of the knowing subject and the known object. Thus, "A=A" may express not only the logical principle of noncontradiction but also the epistemological relationship between subject and object. Rosenzweig's point may now be understood as follows. Insofar as philosophy achieves self-knowledge, it is epistemologically unproblematic because it inevitably takes the form "A=A," expressing the identity of subject and object. However, knowledge of actuality always takes the form "A=B." So, as self-knowledge, philosophy may attain the epistemologically unproblematic status of logical knowledge, a status as unproblematic as the principle of noncontradiction, but it attains that status at the cost of giving up any claim to knowledge of actuality, including any claim to knowledge of the actual philosophizing subject.

13. Genesis 18:27: "Abraham spoke up, saying, 'Here I venture to speak to my Lord, I who am but dust and ashes.'" In this verse, God has already responded affirmatively to Abraham's request to spare the city of Sodom if fifty innocent people are found there, and Abraham is about to press his requests still further, asking if God will spare the city for the sake of forty-five, then for the sake of forty, then for the sake of thirty, then for the sake of twenty, and finally for the sake of ten.

nothing had happened to me and illuminate the whole like Grabbe in the last act.[14] *Individuum ineffabile triumphans.*[15] The astonishing thing is not that it engages in "philosophy," but rather that it is still there at all, that it still dares to pant, that it "engages" [at all].

Man has a twofold relation to the Absolute, one where it has him, but still a second where he has *it*. What sort of relation is this second one? Having read this beginning again, I realize that it is grossly jubilant. Thus "the same thing once again": Not only is reason the ground of actuality, but rather there is also an actuality of reason *itself*. That reason grounds *itself* (νόησις νοήσεως,[16] principle of the Hegelian dialectic),

---

14. Christian Dieterich Grabbe (1801–36) appears as a character in the last act of his own comedy, *Scherz, Satirie, Ironie und tiefere Bedeutung.* (Jest, satire, irony, and deeper meaning), trans. Maurice Edward in Eric Bentley, ed., *From the Modern Repertoire, Series Two* (Bloomington, Ind.: Indiana University Press, 1952). Although written in 1822 and published in 1827, the comedy, which uses satire and irony to express disillusionment with reality, was not performed until 1907.

15. Latin: the ineffable individual triumphant.

16. Greek: thinking of thinking. See note 12 above for Hegel's thesis that, in every case of genuine knowledge, subject and object are identical. The thesis has Aristotelean roots, and both Aristotle (384–322 B.C.E.) and Hegel conceive the ultimate, unceasing subject and object of genuine knowledge as God. Thus, Hegel ends his *Encyclopedia of the Philosophical Sciences*, trans. Steven A. Taubeneck, ed. Ernst Behler (New York: Continuum, 1990) with the following passage on the divine first principle of nature from Aristotle, *Metaphysics*, XII, trans. W. D. Ross in *The Complete Works of Aristotle*, ed. Jonathan Barnes (Princeton: Princeton University Press, 1984), II, 1072ᵇ18: "And thought in itself deals with that which is best in itself, and that which is thought in the fullest sense with that which is best in the fullest sense. And thought thinks itself because it shares the nature of the object of thought; for it becomes an object of thought in coming into contact with and thinking its objects, so that thought and the object of thought are the same. For that which is *capable* of receiving the object of thought, i.e., the substance, is thought. And it is *active* when it *possesses* this object. Therefore, the latter rather than the former is the divine element which thought seems to contain, and the act of contemplation is what is most pleasant and best. If, then, God is always in that good state in which we sometimes are, this compels our wonder; and if in a better, this compels it yet more. And God *is* in a better state. And life also belongs to God. For the actuality of thought is life, and God is that actuality; and God's essential actuality is life most good and eternal. We say therefore that God is a living being, eternal, most good; so that life and duration continuous and eternal belong to God; for that *is* God." See also *Metaphysics* XII, 9, 1074ᵇ33–35: "[Divine knowing] must know itself, so that its knowing is a knowing of knowing [*noesis noeseos*]."

indeed explains how reason can make the claim to ground actuality (thus the Hegelian dialectic as the necessary substructure of the Kantian critique); thinking must ground itself, if it is supposed to be able to ground being; the self-grounding of thinking is thus necessary only for the sake of willing the thinkability of being; but there remains against it the suspicion that, *apart* from this relation to being, the self-grounding of thinking is a mere logical playing-around. Just as one must assume a creator, indeed a self-sufficient (almighty) one, for the sake of willing the reality of creation; but whoever believes himself able to forgo the reality of creation and intends to be able to have life in colorful reflection,[17] for him the almightiness of the creator is also a problem; from which one sees that the "being" of God must still be separated from His concept (self-sufficiency). So must the actuality of reason still be separated from its concept (self-consciousness, *noesis noeseos*,[18] Fichte's A=A).[19] "In" (or better: "attached to") reason, there is something extra-

17. See Goethe, *Faust II*, 4725–27, *Werke*, III: "The rainbow mirrors man's endeavor. Think about it and you grasp more clearly: our life consists in colorful reflection."

18. See note 16.

19. Rosenzweig is referring to the *Grundlage der gesamten Wissenschaftslehre* (Fundamental principles of the entire science of knowledge) of 1794–95, perhaps Johann Gottlieb Fichte's (1762–1814) best-known philosophical publication, although it was originally intended only as notes to accompany Fichte's first course of university lectures and although it expressed only an early stage of Fichte's philosophical development. For an English translation, see *The Science of Knowledge*, trans. Peter Heath and John Lachs (Cambridge: Cambridge University Press, 1982). In Part 1 of the *Fundamental Principles*, Fichte seeks the absolutely unconditioned first principle of all human knowledge which, following Karl Leonhard Reinhold (1757–1823), he believes is needed if Kant's revolution is to be completed and if philosophy is to become *Wissenschaftslehre* ("science of knowledge" in Heath and Lachs's translation of Fichte's neologism for scientific philosophy, or, more literally, "doctrine of science"). Fichte's procedure is to select some proposition that is universally acknowledged as valid and as absolutely certain, and then to argue that the proposition in question would be impossible if not for the absolute self-positing of some subject who thinks the proposition, which must be the first principle that is sought. Although, as Fichte says, any universally acknowledged proposition would serve his purpose, it is not without significance that he selects "A is A" or "A=A," which he takes to be equivalents. For (see note 12 above) Fichte takes "A=A" to express the fundamental law of formal logic—the law of noncontradiction—and he wants to show that the self-identity of entities ultimately presupposes the self-identity of the self. In later versions of his system, Fichte abandoned the attempt to seek the desired first principle through reflection on "A=A."

rational, something that cannot be encompassed by the concept of truth (because truth [is] always "correspondence of representation with the object" or, expressed with fewer presuppositions: agreement is of separateds, in which the "things separated" may also be different—A=B, standpoint of consciousness, critique—or even the same—A=A, standpoint of self-consciousness, dialectic). This something attached to reason beyond (said *logically*: "beyond") reason is a unity, which is *not* the unity of two: not to be formulated as equation, rather unity *aside* from duality, the equals sign in both equations, but, with respect to the difference of its application there, not as equals *sign*, rather as *actuality*, not hypothetically (*"if* a relation holds between A and B or A and A, then that of equality holds"), rather categorically (*"there is* equality 'before' all possible relation"). *Ecce realitas.*[20] Just as there "is" a God before all relation, whether to the world or to Himself, and *this* being of God, which is wholly unhypothetical, is the seed-point of the actuality of God, which Schelling, on whom (and on Hans)[21] you must naturally

---

20. Latin: behold reality.

21. Hans Ehrenberg (1883–1958), second cousin of Rosenzweig and of Rudolf Ehrenberg, whose conversion to Christianity in 1909 was a matter of dispute between Rosenzweig and his parents. See *Briefe* I, 94–95; Glatzer, *Franz Rosenzweig: His Life and Thought*, 18–19. In lectures at Heidelberg from 1910 to 1913, Ehrenberg developed a critical approach to German Idealism expressed in *Die Parteiung der Philosophie* (The philosophy faction) (Leipzig, 1911), and articulated most fully in his three-volume dialogue, *Disputation* (München: Drei Masken Verlag, 1923–25), dedicated "To the friend Franz Rosenzweig and his work, 'The Star of Redemption.'" Ehrenberg develops his own version of the line of criticism directed against Hegel by Friedrich Wilhelm Joseph von Schelling (1775–1854) and Søren Kierkegaard (1813–55): insofar as the Hegelian system achieves the systematic self-knowledge sought by philosophy as such, it does so at the cost of ignoring genuine actuality, which is different from the abstraction called "actuality" by philosophers and which is a necessary presupposition of philosophy. In *Parteiung*, 96, Ehrenberg writes, "Although . . . the absoluteness of knowledge is based on itself, it is by virtue of this that it orders itself out of inner peace, beyond itself . . . we see ourselves driven over the boundaries of this science by our self-directed logic, into the boundless-actual, see ourselves—we ourselves, the ones who are thinking, inner-logical beings— carried into the midst of the realm of the actual." Later, in *Disputation*, III, 62, he says, "To identify world and actuality is exactly the philosophical sickness of the soul." Rather, he says, using Kierkegaard's terminology (*Disputation*, III, 60), "Actuality is the moment." There is one world, according to Ehrenberg, but there are as many actualities as there are biographies, objective actualizations of life.

have perpetually thought, calls the "dark ground,"[22] etc., an interiorization of God, which *precedes* not merely His self- externalization, but
rather even His self (as the Lurianic kabbalah teaches, so far as I know;
once I told you about it).[23]

So what I'm aiming at is this: that the Absolute—I now intentionally
use this most abstract of its significations—stands between two relativi-
ties, one before it and one after it. The earth rests on the big elephant,

---

22. Schelling explained the emergence of historical finitude from eternity in
terms of God giving birth to Himself from a "dark ground," nonground (*Ungrund*), or abyss (*Abgrund*) prior to any rational ground, and then creating the
world. See, for example, Schelling, *Philosophical Inquiries into the Nature of
Human Freedom*, trans. James Gutmann (Chicago: Open Court, 1936), 35: "All
birth is a birth out of darkness into light: the seed must be buried in the earth
and die in darkness in order that the lovelier creature of light should rise and
unfold itself in the rays of the sun. Man is formed in his mother's womb; and
only out of the darkness of unreason (out of feeling, out of longing, the sublime
mother of understanding) grow clear thoughts. We must imagine the primal
longing in this way—turning towards reason, indeed, though not yet recognizing it, just as we longingly desire unknown, nameless excellence. This primal
longing moves in anticipation like a surging, billowing sea, similar to the 'matter' of Plato, following some dark, uncertain law, incapable in itself of forming
anything that can endure. But there is born in God Himself an inward, imagi-
native response, corresponding to this longing, which is the first stirring of divine Being in its still dark depths."

23. Rabbi Isaac Luria (1534–72) was one of the kabbalists of Safed, whose
ideas—communicated orally to his disciples, transcribed by a few individuals,
and at first circulated only surreptitiously—eventually attained great influence,
not only over kabbalists but also over popular Jewish practice and belief. The
doctrine of *tsimtsum* (contraction) is, in brief, that every act of divine creation
and emanation must be preceded by an act of divine withdrawal making a region of being available for creation and emanation. The Christian kabbalist,
Christian Freiherr Knorr von Rosenroth (1636–89) discussed the doctrine in
his widely-read *Kabbala denudata* (Kabbalah unveiled) (Sulzbach: Abraham
Lichtentahler, 1677–84; reprint, Hildesheim, New York: Georg Olms, 1999),
and in conversation with Jacobi, Lessing ascribed the doctrine to Leibniz. See
*Friedrich Heinrich Jacobi: The Main Philosophical Writings and the Novel "All-
will,"* trans. and ed. George di Giovanni (Montreal: McGill-Queen's University
Press, 1994), 191. Schelling certainly knew of the doctrine from these sources,
if not from elsewhere, and he was also indirectly influenced by kabbalistic traditions via his reading of Jakob Böhme (1575–1624) and his acquaintance with
Franz von Baader (1765–1841). An affinity between Schelling and Luria is also
suggested by Jürgen Habermas, *Theory and Practice*, trans. John Viertel (Boston:
Beacon Press, 1973), 215, 236.

and the big elephant on the big tortoise and so forth ad infinitum,[24] naive metaphysics taught; the earth rests on the big snake, and the big snake carries itself, for it bites itself on the tail, Hegel teaches and thereby gives at any rate an exhaustive explanation of the system earth-snake but does not explain why this system as a whole nevertheless does not fall. It does not fall, and it does not float, I say; for there is no space, "into which" it could fall, "in which" it could float; the serpent itself fills all possible space; it is *just as massive* as the earth that rests on it.

Close at hand lies the objection that it is inadmissible to call actuality "before" and "after" with the same names; the actuality of, say, God and the actuality created by God are completely two. Certainly they are two, which is precisely what I want to talk about, but how would this duality be so significant if language did not have justification and they were not *also* one. The man of philosophy and the philosophizing man are to be sure both "men"; the palmbranch must not deceive us about this.

I now assert that everything that proceeds between the Absolute and the relative "before" it is revelation, and everything [that proceeds] between the Absolute and the relative "after" it is nature, world, or whatever you want to call it. That is, of course, supposed to be only a raw first-approximation formula, nothing further. That it is no more is shown by the fact that the two relations cannot be so antithetically opposed as they seem to be; for while the Absolute definitely stands in "relation" to the relative after it, it is essential for the relative before it that the Absolute stands to begin with in *no* relation to it as such. Rather, this relative stands, for the time being, as crooked, lopsided dust and ashes,

---

24. This metaphor for an infinite regress seems to have been introduced into philosophical literature by John Locke (1632–1704), who ascribes it to an Indian philosopher and employs it to mock some ways of appealing to the notion of substance. See Locke, *An Essay Concerning Human Understanding*, ed. Kenneth Winkler (Indianapolis: Hackett, 1996), Book 2, Chapter 13, paragraph 19: "They who first ran into the notion of *accidents*, as a sort of real beings, that needed something to inhere in, were forced to find out the word *substance*, to support them. Had the poor *Indian* philosopher (who imagined that the earth also wanted something to bear it up) but thought of this word *substance*, he needed not to have been at the trouble to find an elephant to support it, and a tortoise to support his elephant: the word *substance* would have done it effectually. And he that inquired, might have taken it for as good an answer from an *Indian* philosopher, that *substance*, without knowing what it is, is that which supports the earth, as we take it for a sufficient answer, and good doctrine, from our *European* philosophers, that *substance* without knowing what it is, is that which supports *accidents*. So that of *substance*, we have no *idea* of what it is, but only a confused obscure one of what it does." See also Book 2, Chapter 13, paragraph 2.

but even so *on its own feet*; it is no B that first secures its permanence through the "=" sign, rather it has its "=" sign already in itself and asks after no A. It is B=B.[25]

But the A asks after *it*. The "dark ground" would never *give birth* to the Godhead but would rather doze along eternally in its dull B=B; but God can *produce* himself out of it and only out of it, out of this truly undivine wanting-to-be-itself B=B. The mere "interior" of God is still unfruitful; first the interiori*zation*, first the descent of God, in His own depths is "beginning." Just as the philosophizing [mind] is dead without philosophy, although philosophy comes to life, if it descends to him who is independent, condescends to him and so begins the progress of philosophizing, which concludes with the recognition of the absoluteness of philosophy and the existence-of-man-only-in-relation-to-it. A becomes active against B=B, until this, as B=A, of itself recognizes its dependence on it.

Nevertheless, no recollection of this activity of A remains for B, neither for B philosopher nor for B creation. For it is precisely the end of this progress that B is systematically digested and included. Only when B is something that itself within the system rattles the fence posts of the system, only then can the "recollection" of that presystematic life remain. Such a B is, however, only a single B among all thinkable Bs: free personality. The honest admission that freedom is "the wonder in the phenomenal world,"[26] is alone sufficient to make Kant the greatest of all philosophers as a person; all others attempt to loaf about more or less; he alone expresses it; he alone has not, through businesslike association with the truth, unlearned [how] to be a child and a fool. Once freedom is granted as that which is not capturable in "relations," thus as that which is not systematizable: *then* freedom can calmly be determined as order, devotion, etc.—provided only it stays in "memory" that it was

25. By "B=B," Rosenzweig seems here to signify a person, who is what she is and, unlike a mere B, is sufficiently self-aware to make her *logical* self-identity explicit by saying "I" but who currently has none of the genuine self-knowledge exemplified by God, who therefore does not satisfy the principle "A=A" in its *epistemological* sense, as an expression of a self-knowing subject, and who therefore also lacks awareness of divinity and revelation.

26. Kant never actually used this phrase, although he certainly regarded human freedom as a unique manifestation of the actuality of reason in the phenomenal world. See note 47 below. Rosenzweig uses the same phrase in a diary entry from August 14, 1910, published in *Briefe* I, 105, where he writes: "Kant called organism the wonder in the phenomenal world. For Hegel, that is no longer organism alone.—Is not marriage wonder in the phenomenal world? a wonder and something everyday?"

previously freedom pure and simple. And this living *anamnesis*[27] of the concept of freedom in Kant is thus the caravel,[28] upon which we can discover the new world of revelation, if only we have embarked in the harbor of the old logical world. We reach the "original ground," the "being of God," the "actuality of reason" (not in the Hegelian, rather in Hans's sense),[29] also the "one who engages in philosophy" (insofar as he is not simply "man")—we reach them all in the course of thinking only as limit-concepts; "the man" alone do we discover, in its full translogical, dull, bulky B=B-ness, in the course of thinking. Thinking *touches* upon the other B=B concepts but *knows* only this. In it alone can that prelogical process, where A "asks" after B (see above), be shown, and only by analogy with what is shown here can similar processes then first be inferred for the other B=Bs. Man, simply speaking, who "is still there," from whom I began just now, is *actually* the beginning.

This man says: I. Only insofar and because man is not merely B, but rather B=B, can he say *I*, and among all Bs he is the *only* one that can say it;[30] of all other Bs one can indeed assert by analogy that they can say it, but precisely by analogy alone; immediately they are no Is, rather He-She-It, and even man himself is merely a He-She-It, insofar as he is apprehended as B. All relation finds its foothold only between third persons; the system is the world in the form of the third person; and not merely the theoretical system, but rather just as man himself becomes object to himself, just as he wants to *make* something with or of himself, so he *enters into the third person*, ceases to be I (fore- and surname), he becomes "man" (with his palmbranch). To man as B in this theoretical-practical system of third persons, God is also only third person, only A. Although he *knows* of Him limit-conceptually, that He is essentially A=A, nevertheless only A holds for his relation to him (A=B). Of this man Spinoza writes—and Goethe underwrites—that whoever loves God should not demand that God love him in return.[31] For how could

---

27. Greek: recollection. According to a doctrine discussed in Plato's *Meno*, 70a–86d in *Complete Works*, ed. John Cooper (Indianapolis: Hackett, 1997), knowledge is not so much acquired as recalled from the soul's condition prior to birth. See also *Phaedo* 72e–78b.

28. A caravel is a kind of ship, used by Columbus in his journey to the New World.

29. That is, not the actuality of the philosopher's system, but the actuality of the philosopher's life. See note 21.

30. See note 25.

31. Spinoza, *Ethics*, trans. Samuel Shirley (Indianapolis: Hackett, 1992) Part 5, Proposition 19: "He who loves God cannot endeavor that God should love him

he?! In the heart's pure regions surges a striving to devote himself voluntarily out of gratitude to a Higher Purer Unknown[32]—it is a love in the third person, the He gives itself to the It, no You becomes audible, and therefore it is not a matter of any I, and only the I can "demand" love; and this world of the third person God is the only It, upon which there is reflected at least limit-conceptually the semblance of I-hood (A=A), as those particular comparatives, "high*er*," "pur*er*" express it: only a reflection, only an unknown is revered, the I that sticks *behind* that It (A=A next to the A of the normal equation A=B). Here all love is devotion, a devotion whose simile can be *any* giving oneself of any sort; of "such" blissful heights does he feel himself partaking when he stands before "her," and whoever possesses "art and science" "*also*" has religion.[33] Because A=A is, therefore A=B can be the ruling world-formula: all Bs interrelated, giving oneself everywhere, each can for the others take the place of A (the left side of the equation), "she" just as much as "art and science," and even man himself can place himself on the left side of the equation and make himself into A for other world-things; under the protection of A=A, *any* A=B is possible and legitimate; and only one thing can this B, that is eternally an object, *not* do: demand that God loves it in return. Since for that it would have to be able to make itself into I, equating itself to A=A, not merely to A.

But that is what man does, who has not got himself entangled in the depersonalizing thicket of relations, man outside the theoretical-practical system, man as I. He should and must demand that God love him back. Indeed, he must demand that God even love him first. For his I is dull and dumb and awaits the saving word from the mouth of God: "Adam, where are *You*?"[34] in order that the first, hesitant, timid I of

---

in return." Goethe cites this view in his autobiography *Aus meinem Leben. Dichtung und Wahrheit* (From my life: Poetry and truth), *Werke*, X, 35, saying that it had a decisive impact on his life.

32. An allusion to Goethe, *Trilogie der Leidenschaft* (Trilogy of passion), "Elegie" (Elegy), *Werke*, I, 384: "In the pure regions of our heart surges a striving to devote ourselves voluntarily, out of gratitude, to a Higher, Purer, Unknown, to the eternal Unnamed that solves its own riddle; we call it: being pious!"

33. An allusion to Goethe, *Werke*, I, 367: "Whoever possesses science and art, also has religion; whoever possesses neither, had better have religion."

34. Genesis 3:9: "The Lord God called out to the man and said to him, 'Where are you?'" This occurs after Adam and Eve have broken God's commandment by eating the fruit of the tree of knowledge, while they are hiding from God among the trees in the Garden of Eden.

shame reply to the first unhesitating You asking after him. In I and You and again I, this comportment moves like that of the ubiquitous devotion in the indeterminate He She It. In the I of revelation and in the You of conscience in its questioning, or of command, and responding in Adam's I of shame or in Abraham's readiness, and back again in the I of repentance and in the You of prayer and in the I of salvation. Between the one B, that is equal to no other B (the B that is not B1, B2, B3, etc.) — B=B — and between A=A, there is only a one-track connection, no net, no system of relations, actual and possible, where any node can become B and any can become A, more precisely: where any node *can* become and none *must* become; that is the world without determinate middle point, the world of Right and Left, of Front and Back, where everything at any instant can become Right and Left, Front and Back, and taking a little time shades the future into the past; the world whose sublime spirit teaches men to know their brothers in forest and shrub, in bush and water[35] and, nevertheless, therein and therewith enables him to realize immediately that nothing complete becomes of man. Instead of these brothers in general, who are easily and cheaply found, to whom he stands in "relation," man has only *himself* as his equal "in connection"; the word of neighborly love, over there a well-tempered banality, here becomes a trumpet blast; for it is not said to the man in whose heart's pure regions surges a striving for freely willed *devotion*, but rather to the deaf I, buried in its own I-hood, this I, of which nothing can be presupposed except this, that it loves *itself*. But just for that reason, *after* this word has for the first time opened the deaf ear, man indeed also actually recognizes in the neighbor one who is like him, recognizes him not merely as B2, B3, etc., as fellow inhabitant of the same world, fellow member of the great equation A=B, of which he knows, to be sure, only what he *sees*—for he recognizes him only as It, only as his brother in grove and rock, in bush and water; rather I recognize that he *is no He She It, but rather an I*, an I like me, no fellow inhabitant of the same space without direction and middle point, no travel acquaintance along the journey through time without beginning and without end, but rather my brother, the consort of my fate, for whom it "goes" as much as for me, who—like me—sees only the one track before him; my brother not in the world, not in forest and shrub, in bush and water, but rather

---

35. Perhaps an allusion to Goethe, "Wilhelm Tischbein's Idyllen" (Wilhelm Tischbein's idylls), *Werke* I, 375: "When in forests tree sustains itself together with trees, as brother with brother, let the wandering, let the dreaming, be unconstrained and undisturbed; yes, where individual fellows gently strive with one another, make themselves into a beautiful whole, that is joy, that is life."

in the Lord. All Bs have become fraternal, because all are substitutable for one another, every B can become A for the other. From B=B the bridge of thoughts never leads to other B=Bs, not even once; the bridge, the "=" sign, is surely altogether included in B=B itself, but it does not lead outside it. Only the fact that the word has gone out from One A=A to B=B, only that leads B=B out beyond itself, and only in this *event* that has occurred to it can it think another B=B, to which the same has occurred, a neighbor, that is like You. It discovers the other, not from its own *essence* and its heart's pure regions, but rather from the *occurrence* that has occurred to him and from his heart's deafness.

"Essence" is the concept under which the world of objects, the world of A=B, organizes itself—essence, the universal, which subsumes everything particular under itself, because it "precedes" every individual. Because he knows man in general, "all" men, or because he knows the world in general, all things, as joined in solidarity, *therefore* the Stoic "loves," the Spinozist "loves" his neighbor. Against such love, which arises from essence, from the universal, stands the other, which ascends from the event, thus from the most particular of all that is. This particular goes step by step from one particular to the next particular, from one neighbor to the next neighbor, and forgoes love for the farthest, before it can be neighborly love. So the organizing concept of this world is not the universal, neither the Arche[36] nor the Telos,[37] neither the natural nor the historical unity, but rather the particular, the event, *not beginning or end, but rather middle* of the world. The world is "infinite," both from beginning and from end, from the beginning infinite in space, toward the end infinite in time. Only from the middle arises a limited home in the unlimited world, a bit of ground between four tentpegs, which can be stuck further and further out. Viewed from this perspective, beginning and end are also transformed for the first time, from limit-concepts of infinity to cornerposts of our worldly estate, the "beginning" as creation, the "end" as salvation.

Thus revelation is capable of being a *middle* point, a fixed, middle point that cannot be displaced. And why? Because it occurs at the *point*, the rigid, deaf, immovable point, the stubborn I, that "I just am." My "freedom," and indeed not my freedom as the philosophers falsify it, since they sap away the red blood of choice and let it run into the vessel of "sensibility," of "drives," of "motives" and want to know as freedom only the bloodless residue of obedience to the law. Rather, the whole of freedom, my dull, heavy, irresponsible choice, my whole "that's just

36. Greek: origin.
37. Greek: goal or purpose.

how I am," without which that philosophers' freedom is lame from birth. For what good is all obedience to the ideal, all adoption of universally valid maxims, all Hegelian divinity, if man, from whom all these beautiful things are expected, has no forces? And even more: if he has not forces to such an extent that, in this his sinful naturalness, he knows himself master of all ideals that demand his service, and in all his point-likeness he first finds the courage to place the full stop behind each sentence of the system of ethics. But how does he attain such force and such courage?

"Ideals," "imperatives," "ideas," and *hoc genus omne*[38] say to man: devote yourself to me! Out of "gratitude," "voluntarily," so that "you become what you are,"[39] fulfill your "vocation"—but in any case, devote yourself to me! So it's a presupposition that man gives up his own. Contrariwise, revelation says: Do my will! Carry out my work! So it's a presupposition that God's own, God's will, God's work, is entrusted to man, so that he may carry it out. What a paradox is that, seen from the standpoint of the world! The highest, instead of demanding our devotion, devotes itself to our very selves; instead of raising us to its height, it lowers itself down to us; and once again, instead of promising us our Selves as payment ("become what you are"),[40] it promises us a self-abandonment, nearness to God as blessedness. Thus man, to whom God entrusts Himself, to whom He, who is both sublime and humble in one, lets himself descend—man receives, insofar as he makes room for God in himself, all that which he has given to God, even himself, man. All devotion in the world leads to God as idea of ideas, and God, insofar as He gives himself to man in revelation, brings him all worldly devotions as a dowry. Thus through revelation, man becomes capable of his own devotions to the ideal. Ideals are many. Each blocks the other's light. The law of the substitutability of all objects in the A=B-world holds for them, too; man, placed between them, knows with determinacy only that he ought to devote himself, not to which of them. Here the tragedy of the conflict of duties rules. God's command is an order, univocally called out to this man and in this situation of this man; questioning or

---

38. Latin: all things of this kind.
39. Pindar (c.518–438 B.C.E.) exhorts Hieron, tyrant of Syracuse, in Pythian Ode 2, 1.72, trans. William H. Race in Pindar, *Olympian Odes and Pythian Odes* I: "Become such as you are, having learned what that is." The phrase is sometimes translated differently, but Nietzsche invokes the same translation as Rosenzweig in the subtitle of his book, *Ecce Homo: How One Becomes What One Is*, trans. R. J. Hollingdale (New York: Penguin, 1979).
40. See note 39.

IV "Urzelle" to the Star of Redemption

switching to another strand of the system is impossible; for here there is no system consisting of lines, there is only the one double-tracked stretch; at most Lucifer's pride or Jonah's flight would be possible. After all, there is a *kingdom* of ideals (that is only systematiz*able*, thus not unifi*able*), but only a *word* of God (that *develops* itself into the manifoldness of the kingdom). For this reason, no "conflict" occurs in the world of revelation. The legend begins, where the tragedy *ceases*—with the fifth act.[41]

So no "law" is given to the pious, for he stands under an "order." An order that gives him complete authority over the whole world and its ideals. But, to be sure, an order. Silence is imposed upon his will. Not in a principled way: the "titanic struggle of duty," the quarrel between "ideal and life," etc., does not belong here; such principled distinctions are rather the peculiarity of the systematizable world, the world of A=B, regardless whether we develop this world one-dimensionally in *antitheses* with Hegel or multidimensionally in *relations* according to our contemporary striving. No such struggle—somehow comprehensible in universal concepts—is ordered to the pious. Rather, as the order itself remains as order entirely bound up with person and moment, so its articulation in the world also enters not into a general antithesis but into the particular: not, say, that "the" duty struggles against "the" love, but rather *this* duty and *this* love shoves some other duty or some other love aside. Revelation pushes itself into the world as a wedge; the This struggles against the This. Therefore the resistance of the prophet against his mission, his struggle against the gradually ascending image, cannot be confused with ethical struggles. There the higher does not battle against the lower, rather *the called against everything else which would be merely possible*, notwithstanding [the fact] that to this possible the "height" also belongs; it lacks every comparability, every suitability for organization into the system of the higher and lower. The mission disconnects the prophet from "ideal" just as much as from "life" and drives him into the *conceptless* world, into a world in which A=B has lost its validity and everything seems to him like B=B. His "nature," which rebels against the divine commission, is not in any way the "nature" in some or other antithesis to something better, but rather it is his whole man, the "better" and the "worse" in a distinctionless mixture; it is his wholeness, his secret will to *system*, that sets itself as defense against the intrusion of the ordering word; the "system" in him, the secret "life of Goethe," struggles for his self-preservation, B=A against B=B.

---

41. Classical tragedies and, under their influence, the tragedies of Shakespeare and other Renaissance dramatists, typically end with the fifth act.

What was last articulated shows that there are relations between revelation and world not merely in thinking—that would result already from the "formulae"—but also in actuality. And indeed the comportment of B=B toward A=B is an aggressive one, directed toward transformation, that from A=B toward B=B in contrast only a theoretical-skeptical (disbelieving) [comportment] that contents itself with mere reinterpretation, mere explanation of B=B as "properly" A=B. Thus it is also content in the moment, while B=B can only be content at "the end"; the "unity" of the "system" is only repaired through the "community" of "all," all might and order (A=B) through selfhood and immediacy (B=B); therefore at the "end" the problem of "brothers in forest and grove, on the rock and in the water"—solved by pantheism in every moment easily and cheaply with feeling—also becomes actual, in "the end," for revelation, and its solution, which is necessary equally for the sake of the actually feasible totality, is promised *per miraculum*.[42] Disbelief has as its justificatory ground the consciousness that B=A is only the "spiritualization," the "truth" of B=B; it intends to possess B=B in its concept of *hyle*[43]—an error; for that *hyle* concept *is* already a "spiritualization" contrasted with the presence B=B, which wholly without concept, wholly without unity, *is* therefore already A=B; nevertheless, it *may* make this error; in the chief point, namely that its B=A actually "means" B=B somehow (the man with his palmbranch *somehow* is one with the I first and last name), it is right. And this very "somehow one," that was expressed from here on through the equation of the letters in the formulae, also produces for faith the possibility of moving mountains, or more simply: for the pious the possibility of *living* his faith. If the world were not A=B but rather A=C, then such a possibility would not be intelligible. Only because the pious and life are both of one blood, only because faith is merely expected to transform the world into *its own chaos* (so to speak, to transform it back), only for that reason is revelation's work upon the world possible. But in the instant where B=B is at an end with this work, thus where *all* B=A has become B=B, and precisely because B=B has become "everything," it has lost its peculiar essence of being something that is buried in itself and undeveloped. There is no longer any being over against God: God is one and all.[44]

This amounts to the following picture: the various relations, which I discussed rhapsodically and simultaneously at the beginning, elucidat-

---

42. Latin: by means of a miracle.

43. Greek: matter.

44. The phrase "one and all" is used to express pantheism or, more generally, monism, in classical German philosophy. Jacobi made the phrase famous when

ing one by means of the other, without being able to delimit them clearly from one another, now fall into place. They are—the "man, who is still there" (despite "man with his palmbranch of ideals") as much as the "philosophizing one" (notwithstanding "philosophy"), and as much as the "original ground" (despite the "personality of God")—all concepts of *pure factuality.*[45] I might symbolize them as relations by means of the proportion mark /. Thus

---

he reported that Lessing had told him in conversation, "*Hen kai pan* (one and all)! I know of nothing else" and that Lessing had written the phrase as his motto on the garden house of the poet Gleim. See *Friedrich Heinrich Jacobi: The Main Philosophical Writings and the Novel "Allwill,"* trans. and ed. George di Giovanni (Montreal: McGill-Queen's University Press, 1994), 187, 199. Although Jacobi's exposure of Lessing's pantheism was intended to demonstrate the dire consequences of the Enlightenment, its effect was to popularize the slogan "one and all," which was adopted by members of the younger generation, such as Hegel, Schelling, and Friedrich Hölderlin (1770–1843). According to Jacobi, Lessing thought the Greek original—ἐν καὶ πᾶν—was inscribed on an ancient temple. But no source for such an inscription is known, and it has been suggested that the slogan is based on fragment 50 of the pre-Socratic Heraclitus (late sixth to early fifth century B.C.E.), recorded by Hyppolitus, trans. T. M. Robinson in *Heraclitus: Fragments* (Toronto: University of Toronto Press, 1987): "'Not after listening to me, but after listening to the account, one does wisely in agreeing that all things are one,' says Heraclitus." According to some, Lessing's slogan was in fact "ἐν ἐγω καὶ πᾶν" (I am one and all). See Altmann, *Moses Mendelssohn: A Biographical Study* (University, Ala.: University of Alabama Press, 1973), 603–21 and "Lessing und Jacobi: Das Gespräch über den Spinozismus" in Altmann, *Die Trostvolle Aufklärung: Studien zur Metaphysik und politischen Theorie Moses Mendelssohns* (The hopeful Enlightenment: Studies in the metaphysics and political theory of Moses Mendelssohn) (Stuttgart-Bad Canstatt: Frommann-Holzboog, 1982), 50–83.

45. In the original: "reine Tatsächlichkeit." In notes from November 1916, published in "Paralipomena," *Zweistromland*, 100, Rosenzweig had written, "It is the essence of revelation that it is a *matter of fact* [*Tatsache*]." Although now a common German word, *Tatsache* was introduced for theological purposes. It was coined by the Enlightenment theologian Johann Joachim Spalding (1714–1804) for his 1756 German translation of Bishop Joseph Butler's (1692–1752) *The Analogy of Religion, Natural and Revealed, to the Constitution and Course of Nature* (London: Printed for James, John, and Paul Knapton, 1736). Butler argued that Christian faith was justified by the standards of natural science because the miraculous events of Christian history were attested by respectable men, just as the experiments of the scientists were attested by respectable observers. Hence, the miracles of Christian faith were, in legal terminology, "matters of fact," and met the epistemic standards of the law-courts, on

$$A=A/A=A$$
$$A=A$$

$$B=B \text{———} A=B$$
$$A=A/ \twoheadleftarrow\text{———} \qquad A=A/$$
$$B=B \qquad\qquad B=B$$

Don't be alarmed! The symmetry is not so great as you think on first glance. Above all, I should properly have only written:

$$A=A/$$
$$B=B$$

in additional parentheses: for it goes entirely together with

$$A = A$$
$$B=B$$

of the triangle; revelation itself is exactly the relation of "pure factuality." It is entirely different on the right side of the triangle. It signifies the Idealist movement: the I=I as the key to the I=not-I, *Hegel's* concept of "spirit," Goethe's "Is not the core of the world in the hearts of men."[46] To be sure, this knowledge must itself be grasped as a *Faktum*,[47] as a

---

which Robert Boyle (1627–91) had insisted when establishing the protocols of experimental reports. See Steven Shapin and Simon Schaffer, *Leviathan and the Air-Pump: Hobbes, Boyle, and the Experimental Life* (Princeton: Princeton University Press, 1985), 22–79, especially 56–58. After Spalding, the term *Tatsache* was used by many German theologians and philosophers to signify a deed or occurrence whose actuality was well established on the basis of either one's own experience or the reliable testimony of others, despite its lack of deductive or inductive demonstration. Thus, Rosenzweig's point here is that the "man, who is still there," the "philosophizing one," and the "original ground"—as well as "revelation itself"—are actualities of this kind.

46. From one of Goethe's epigrams. See Goethe, *Werke,* I, 306.

47. The Latin word *faktum* is drawn from legal usage and originally signified a deed or occurrence of legal relevance, sometimes one whose actuality is stipulated or accepted by the court. It is sometimes used by theologians and philosophers as a synonym for *Tatsache.* See note 45. For example, in the *Critique of Practical Reason,* trans. Mary Gregor (Cambridge: Cambridge University Press, 1997), Ak. 31, Kant deduces the actuality of freedom through the "*faktum* of reason," or the actuality of our giving ourselves the moral law. In the *Critique of*

world-historical point: Hansen's discovery of "the philosopher"[48] and my concept of "1800," which likewise revolves around the philosopher as opposed to philosophy. The conception of immanence—and what else is paganism!—which Hegel theoretically and Goethe practically led to completion, is indeed itself become *Faktum* and thereby capable of becoming seized by revelation. This "pure factuality" is thus something for itself; it does not coincide with the triangle side, but rather is a philosophical *salto mortale*[49] from the philosophical corner-bastion of the triangle down—mortale: "1800" means an absolute end, i.e., an absolute beginning: as Hegel discovered in himself the last philosopher, so Goethe discovered in himself the first Christian: nothing need be added there.

What proceeds between the two base-points of the triangle, between man simply speaking and world simply speaking or between faith and unfaith or between theology and philosophy—the practical movement from left to right, the theoretical from right to left—that has already been said: that the movement from left to right is the stronger and

---

Judgment, trans. Werner Pluhar (Indianapolis: Hackett, 1987), Ak. 468, Kant writes, "Objects of concepts whose objective reality can be proved are *matters of fact [Tatsachen] (res facti)* . . . It is very remarkable . . . that even a rational idea is to be found among the matters of fact (even though it is intrinsically impossible to exhibit rational ideas in intuition, and hence also intrinsically impossible to prove theoretically that they are possible): the idea of *freedom*; the reality of this idea as a special kind of causality (the concept of which would be transcendent if we considered it theoretically), can be established though practical laws of pure reason and, [if we act] in conformity with these, in actual acts, and hence in experience."

48. "Hansen" is a diminutive for "Hans," here indicating Hans Ehrenberg. Rosenzweig is referring again to Ehrenberg's argument against Hegel, that actuality is not the world but rather the actualization of life, and that the philosopher's life is therefore a more significant work than the philosopher's system of thought.

49. Latin: life-risking leap. The phrase was made famous by Jacobi, who reported that, when he advocated, as an alternative to the rationalist obsession with explanation, "the perfect conviction that certain things admit of no explication," Lessing responded, "Good, very good! I can make use of all this too; but I myself cannot do the same with it. On the whole I don't dislike your *salto mortale*, and I see how a man can turn his head upside-down in this way, to move from it." To Jacobi's reply, "If you were to step on the elastic place that propels me, it would no sooner be said than done," Lessing responded, "But that too takes a leap that I can no longer ask of my old legs and heavy head." See Jacobi, *Main Philosophical Writings*, 193, 195.

certainly has the final victory, is reflected in the schema insofar as to the right the *salto mortale* of factuality is an addition, a unique *Faktum* in the course of history, while the left side has the factuality in its blood and at every instant makes use of it as an effective force.

The *salto mortale* on the triangle's summit is ultimately characterized as "last" insofar as the same stands above and below the proportion mark; the pure factuality is therefore without movement here, eternal. The eternal occurrence in God can be understood, as both the figure and the history of thought show, on two grounds: from the basis of the fulfilled philosophy (Schelling) and on the basis of revelation (mysticism). Thus theosophy—I am myself still astonished and resistant to this thought—is joined to *theo*logy and philo*sophy*, concluding the triangle of the sciences.

The remainder is philo-logy, i.e. silence. But seriously, what do you say to it? It has become more complete and richer than I myself expected. But in distinction from that time in the Harz, I am *myself* convinced. And I mean you, too: it is certainly only formulated for you; even if I wished to formulate it for Rosenstock, I would have to write it quite differently, and I would for that matter still not be far enough from it to write it differently. I have written it εἴς σε βλέπων[50] and possibly it even comes, since you are a "November man" and I think: second half, to you on your birthday. In any event you must keep it for yourself since in this form it is fit for your eyes only.

. . .

Now I have read through the whole thing once again today after the happy clucking yesterday that immediately followed the laid egg. A large amount of good will is required to understand it. For the terminology is still quite unstable on the first pages; in retrospect, I would now be able to improve that, but that would be to write it anew, and among other things it's too cold here for me to do that. You must try to glide along with the unstable. From a certain point on, B=B means exclusively humans: during the relatively very awkward development it still means also the translogical actuality, the transpersonal Godhead. But I think you must notice that in life, as I have also indeed noticed it in writing. Still, today the fruitfulness of the whole is really certain to me despite the many errors and remaining obscurities. But there I'm starting to cluck again, and that was only excusable yesterday.

Something else: of influences I must cite one more besides those

---

50. Greek: Looking at you.

named: Christoph Schrempf (do you know of him?),[51] with his early, apparently first work on Kant and Christ, in which he corrects the antithesis of autonomy and heteronomy by means of that of law and command. I am very astonished about the exceptional position of mysticism *between* actual theology and actual philosophy. Perhaps that is the uncoerced solution of many historical difficulties—Plotinus,[52] India, etc. Until now I really had not been able to interest myself in Steinerian theosophy[53] (I knew about it only what was in the two

51. Christoph Schrempf (1860–1944) was a controversial theologian and philosopher, influenced by Kierkegaard, some of whose works he translated into German. Schrempf was removed from his position as pastor and then left the Lutheran church after a controversy over his conscientious refusal to use the Apostolic Creed during the ceremony of baptism. In "Die christliche Weltanschauung und Kant's sittlicher Glaube: Eine religiöse Untersuchung" (The Christian worldview and Kant's ethical faith: A religious investigation), he argues that although Kantian morality and rational faith might provide a certain preparation for Christianity through subjection to unconditioned practical laws, it cannot lead to Christianity, because Christianity demands what, from a moral point of view, could only be understood as a voluntary act of love to another person; nevertheless, Christianity can supply what Kantian morality lacks because Kant's categorical imperative is merely a criterion that maxims must satisfy but does not provide content for maxims, whereas Christianity provides an unconditioned law for life. Schrempf's account emphasizes the person of Jesus, but Rosenzweig thinks a similar account may be given on the basis of Judaism, as he explains in the following passage from "Paralipomena," *Zweistromland*, 120: "Very correct in Schrempf, 'Kants sittliche Weltanschauung und christliche Glaube' ('Kant's Ethical Worldview and Christian Faith' [sic]), 50, that the decisive distinction between autonomous and theonomous ethics is that in the former ethics appears as universal law, in the latter as individual order. Just the peculiarity of Judaism! The ethical enters as 'law' but not as absolutely universal law, rather as individual, *ordered* law: qua 'law' it is a symbolic anticipation of the time when no individual orders are necessary any more because humanity is at its destination. Qua order it is trapped in time and qua *legal* order it is the oppression of the individual."

52. Plotinus (204–270), the founder of neo-Platonism, whose works were posthumously organized by his pupil Porphyry (c.234–c.305) into the *Enneads*, trans. Stephen McKenna (New York: Pantheon, 1957), and *Plotinus*, trans. A.H. Armstrong (Cambridge, Mass.: Harvard University Press, 1966ff.).

53. Rudolph Steiner (1861–1925) was a Goethe scholar who became involved with the Theosophical Society which had been founded in the United States in 1875, becoming general secretary of its German branch in 1902. In 1913, he founded the Anthroposophical Society in accordance with his own ideas, which he developed in many publications and which gave rise to a number of educa-

Meyrinck[54] novels and some time ago in the "Christian World"),[55] but perhaps I will now. But now really the end.

Your F.

---

tional initiatives. In a letter to Rudolf Ehrenberg written on September 4, 1918, Rosenzweig writes that he is currently dealing with the theosophical part of his book, "but Steiner is a lousy good-for-nothing [*ein Mistbock*], whom I don't need."

54. Gustav Meyrinck (1868–1932), an author celebrated for the uncanny atmosphere of his stories and novels, was involved in mystical societies and was a member of the Theosophical Lodge of the Blue Star in Prague in 1891. Rosenzweig is probably referring to Meyrinck's most famous novels, *Der Golem* (Munche: K. Wolff, 1915), trans. Mike Mitchell as *The Golem* (Riverside, Calif.: Ariadne, 1995) and *Das grüne Gesicht* (Leipzig: K. Wolff, 1916), trans. Mike Mitchell as *The Green Face* (Riverside, Calif.: Ariadne, 1992).

55. *Die Christliche Welt* (The Christian world), published from 1886 to 1941 and edited mainly by Paul Martin Rade (1857–1940), represented the liberal, culturally oriented wing of the Lutheran church.

V

"Foreword" and "Concluding Remark" to *Hegel and the State* (1914/1920)

Epigrams, Title Page[1]

But does there come, as the lightning-bolt comes from the clouds,
Out of thoughts perhaps, the deed, lucid and ripe?
Does the script follow as, from the orchard's
Dark leaves, the golden fruit?[2]

---

1. Both epigrams are taken from the poem "An die Deutschen" (To the Germans) by Friedrich Hölderlin (1770–1843), of which several versions exist. See Hölderlin, *Sämmtliche Werke*. "*Frankfurter Ausgabe*." *Historisch-Kritische Ausgabe* (Collected works. "Frankfurt edition." "Historical-critical edition."), ed. D. E. Sattler, (Frankfurt am Main: Stroemfeld, 1999), 5/II, 525–36. Hölderlin studied at Tübingen along with Georg Friedrich Hegel (1770–1831) and Friedrich Wilhelm Joseph von Schelling (1775–1854) and then, like them, developed his philosophical thinking at Jena, in proximity to Johann Gottlieb Fichte (1762–1814), Johann Wolfgang von Goethe (1749–1832), and Friedrich von Schiller (1759–1805). Unlike his two friends, however, Hölderlin found his calling as a poet, producing some of the most significant and original German poetry before withdrawing into the isolation of mental illness. Rosenzweig's attitude to Hölderlin as the exemplar of German language and culture is well illustrated by the following remark in a letter to Martin Buber written on October 4, 1923, *Briefe*, II, 903: "I myself rest my hopes only on a Hebrew translation [of the *Star*]. Indeed, it will come someday. May God grant that the person who undertakes it also knows German. Hölderlinisch, I mean, of course."
2. Original epigram, chosen before the First World War, 1909.

Our lifetime is narrowly limited indeed,
We see the number of our years and count them,
But the years of the peoples,
Has a mortal eye seen them?[3]

Hölderlin, *To the Germans*, 1800

Foreword

. . .[4]

The book before you, which in its earliest parts reaches back to the year 1909, was essentially ready when the war broke out. At that time I did not think that I had to give it a foreword. Today, that cannot be avoided. For, already at the threshold, the reader has a right to learn that in the year 1919 the book could only be concluded; to begin it would have no longer been possible for me today. I do not know whence one should today still draw the courage to write German history. At the time when the book developed, hope was that the Bismarckian state,[5] its breathing restricted both internally and externally, would expand itself into a free empire breathing the air of the world. This book was supposed to play its small part in preparing for that, insofar as a book can. It was supposed to decompose, so to speak, under the eyes of the reader himself, the hard and limited Hegelian conception of the state—which had come, more and more, to be the dominant conception of the past century, and out of which, "like a lightning-bolt from the clouds," sprang the world-historical deed on January 18, 1871—into its coming-to-be through the life of its thinker, in order thus to open up the prospect of a German future that would be—both inwardly and out-wardly—more spacious. Things worked out differently. A field of ruins marks the spot where the empire previously stood.

This book, which I could no longer have written today, I could just as little revise. All that remained was to publish it as it once was, thus in origin and intention a witness to the spirit of the prewar years, not to the "spirit" of 1919. Only in the addition of a second motto and several eas-ily recognizable additional sentences did I believe that I had to mark the

---

3. Epigram added after the First World War, in 1919, when the book was pub-lished.

4. Text omitted.

5. The state whose main architect was Otto von Bismarck (1815–98), who uni-fied Germany under Prussian domination.

tragic moment of its appearance. The reason why I am still publishing the book at all is essentially because the Heidelberg Academy of Sciences, by generously guaranteeing me a publication subsidy, awakened in me the confidence that a certain service might still be done by it, if no longer to German life, then nevertheless to scholarship, which still survives the life that was destroyed. . . .[6]

Concluding Remark

> ". . . out of thoughts the deed . . ."

We are at the end. We feel the extent to which we are at the end today, when the century of Bismarck, at whose gate the Hegelian life stands like the thought before the deed, has collapsed. If we envisage how this life encompasses the time in which Goethe's *Faust* came to be—1770 to 1831[7]—then it becomes clear how much more closely this [Hegelian] life itself and its work fit into the history of the 19th century than, say, the life and work of the greatest German of the epoch. It was felicitous that Hegel's Berlin disciples liked to use the calendrical coincidence to celebrate the birthdays of both in a single festival—in truth, however, the arc-of-flight of historical effect extends much more shallowly and therefore more briefly in Hegel's case than in the case of the poet who was older by two decades. That Goethe could still spread his roots deeper into the intellectual world of the 18th century—into the prerevolutionary and pre-Kantian world—is the ground of a certain independence on his part from modernity, despite all [his] devotion to it, [an independence] which has elevated him beyond the century; the fruitful regions of his life lie equally widely distributed on both sides of the great epochal divide[8] which stands for us as the classical moment of modern German intellectual history; thus, for the recollection of history and hence in the possession of the nation, this life is not one-sidedly connected, either with the ascent to that summit or with the

---

6. Text omitted.

7. The years of Georg Wilhelm Friedrich Hegel's life (1770–1831) were also roughly the years in which Goethe wrote his masterpiece, *Faust*. For Goethe wrote the so-called *Ur-Faust* (Original-Faust) in the 1770s and published *Faust I* in 1808, while *Faust II*, on which he was working at the end of his life, appeared posthumously.

8. See Chapter 3 on the significance of 1800 for Rosenzweig.

descent; not with the ascent, as are, say, the impact of Klopstock,[9] of Lessing, almost even of Kant; not with the descent, as precisely the impact of Hegel is connected. Just as [it is] with the life of Luther, so it is also with the life of Goethe: one only does it justice if one sees it in the context of a total intellectual history of the nation. Hegel should be grasped within narrower bounds—at least with respect to his national-historical significance, [even if] not with respect to his world-historical significance. In all regions of his impact—not, say, in the political alone—a leading idea of the German 19th century is expressed, along with the permanent personal statement, at the moment of liberation from the circle of the past century; but in this historical greatness of the thinker, there lies also his historical limitation, and, in particular, there lies also his limitedness with respect to this 19th century itself. For we should [not conceal from ourselves] and want not to conceal from ourselves, and have often enough hinted in the course of the book, that the whole development of the century does not accompany Hegel's thoughts, but rather that they only inaugurate its course. May the little that still remains for us to say render visible where the thoughts of the political Hegel linger behind the deeds of the century of Bismarck, and render palpable how his very lingering contained necessity, precisely the necessity of his dwelling in the fountain-chamber of the time.

The progress of the political ideas of the century did not take place—as we already said—within the Hegelian school, properly speaking. What happened to the ideas here was in many ways more their conceptual coming to a head, perhaps even their upsetting, rather than their further development. In the school properly speaking, the ideas of the master—in the majority of cases, especially in the most important of all, the case of Marx—immediately hit upon side-roads which led back to the main street of great historical life only after decades. Meanwhile, the most vigorous wanderers on this main street did not belong directly to the school; indeed, they took themselves to be in more or less sharp opposition to it and its master. Here one refers to only a few leading state-theoreticians of the time from [18]30 to [18]70,[10] which divorced

---

9. Friedrich Gottlieb Klopstock (1724–1803) was quickly recognized as a major German poet when his epic, *Der Messias* (The Messiah) began to appear in 1748. Although celebrated by the younger poets he inspired, he was soon overshadowed by them and was all but ignored in the 19th century.

10. The period from approximately Hegel's death in 1831, during a cholera epidemic, to the Franco-Prussian War, in 1870, which led to the proclamation of the second German empire.

its state-conceptions from that of Hegel, not necessarily in conceptual
opposition but in living opinion.

It is the way, which Friedrich Meinecke has shown, the way from
Hegel to Bismarck.[11] We want to follow it. It leads through the year
1848/49; Frankfurt and Berlin are the two points of transit.[12] The national liberalism of the hereditary-imperial party, the Prussian conservatism of the Gerlachs circle[13]—from both of these, both being jointly
compelling, arose the Bismarckian work. Three great treatises on the
being and essence of the state mark, in the history of German science,
these steps of national development. Dahlmann's *Politics*[14] signified the
pregnant inquiry into pre- March liberalism's education to the maturity
of statesmanlike sensibility, an inquiry of whose successes the negotia-
tions in St. Paul's Church,[15] in spite of everything, bore the first major
testimony for both following decades; Stahl's *Philosophy of Right*[16] led

---

11. Rosenzweig believed that his doctoral supervisor, Friedrich Meinecke
(1862–1953), had shown this way in the book that made him famous, *Cosmopolitanism and the National State*, trans. Robert B. Kimber (Princeton:
Princeton University Press, 1970), a ground-breaking study of the interaction of
politics and ideas in the development of the German state.

12. In February 1848, simultaneous demonstrations in various German regions
led to the "March demands" for royal cooperation in summoning a national
parliament, drawing up a national constitution, and enacting liberal reforms
such as freedom of the press. After princes found themselves compelled to meet
these demands, elected national assemblies met at both Frankfurt and Berlin
(as well as Vienna). Thus, for example, after a failed attempt to repress the popular movement by force, King Friedrich Wilhelm IV (1795–1861) of Prussia accepted the demands on March 18, and elections took place in Prussia for both
the Frankfurt and Berlin Assemblies.

13. The brothers Leopold (1790–1861) and Ludwig von Gerlach (1795–1877)
were prominent members of the court circle around Friedrich Wilhelm, who
regarded royal authority, political corporatism, and social hierarchy as matters
of divine right. After March 1848, they encouraged the king to take counterrev-
olutionary measures against the national assemblies and their liberalism.

14. Friedrich Christoph Dahlmann (1785–1860), *Die Politik: auf den Grund
und das Mass der gegebenen Zustande zurückgefuhrt* (Politics: Related to the
ground and measure of given circumstances) (Göttingen: Dieterich, 1835).
Dahlmann was a member of the Frankfurt Assembly.

15. On May 18, 1848 an elected national assembly convened at St. Paul's
Church, Frankfurt. Debates held there resulted in the proclamation of an Imperial Constitution for Germany on March 28, 1849. Friedrich Wilhelm rejected the imperial crown offered to him.

16. Friedrich Julius Stahl (1802–61), *Die Philosophie des Rechts* (Heidelberg:

the conservatism of Prussia from pre-March silence to the reverberating battlefield of the new constitutional life, thus transforming the Christian-German "circle" into a "small, yet powerful party," from which the Bismarckian deed could take its origin; finally, Treitschke[17]—himself a direct student and fiery adherent of Dahlmann, although in old age forced closer to the party of Stahl—made his appearance on the map as herald of this deed, and in his lectures on politics drew its scientific consequence. Just as the political development of the century was mirrored in the state-conceptions of these three men, so they will also help us to understand the relationship of its end to its beginning, of its deed to its thought; for the former did not spring from the latter "as the lightning bolt comes from the clouds"; the way of history was longer and more gradual than was dreamed by the longing of the poet.

The state, as Dahlmann explained, is "original," is "overwhelming, superhuman order"; he shows any attempt to reduce it to the "creation of human will" to be far from the truth. On the thought of the "ethical realm," Stahl grounds the doctrine of the state, of the ethical realm, the existence and law of whose subsistence is not merely "through the wills of the individual members." Indeed, in spite of Schelling and Hegel being the new founders of Platonic "objectivity" in the doctrine of the state, he nonetheless finds lacking in them the one thing through which the state first presents itself to him as "ethical realm": the "management of commanded orders." And he grasps the state as ethical realm precisely insofar as it is a "real and free" might of rule "but on the ground of ethically reasonable order." In correspondence to this "but," he does not hesitate to find a "double element" in its rule: "the government or state-power, i.e. the power which is exercised by men, and the law." It becomes clear, in this "and," as in that "but," what separates him from Hegel's rigorously unitary derivation of the state as law from the state as power, of the ethical order from the concept of the will. Instead of a

---

J. C. B. Mohr, 1830–37). A convert from Judaism to Christianity, Stahl was close to the Gerlachs and sought to synthesize Protestantism, monarchism, and social conservatism.

17. Heinrich von Treitschke (1834–96) was a historian and politician. At first a National Liberal who opposed Bismarck's tactics, he became an increasingly conservative supporter. He was appointed official historiographer of the Prussian state, and his lectures on politics were published as *Politik: Vorlesungen gehalten an der Universität zu Berlin von Heinrich von Treitschke*, ed. Max Cornicelius (Leipzig: S. Hirzel, 1897–98). It was Treitschke's antisemitism, expressed in the *Preussische Jahrbücher* (Prussian yearbooks) which he edited, that provoked Hermann Cohen (1842–1918), already a famous philosopher, to become a public spokesman for German Jewry and Judaism.

derivation, Stahl consciously gives a juxtaposition, which unmistakably has its ultimate cause in a religious view but, treated from a purely political point of view, permits the existential permanence of the state to emerge just as mightily as the formulations of Dahlmann cited above. Finally, Treitschke, who knew well enough that "the state is might and belongs to the world of will," was nevertheless dissatisfied with such concepts, which pointed immediately back to Hegel. He conceives the state as "the rightfully united people" or, as he initially and more robustly expressed it, "the life of the people, condensed into a might that is whole." It is evident that the two—rightfully united might and existing people—are certainly not perceived as "double element" in Stahl's sense, yet it is nonetheless evident that the will that is effective here in right and might, instead of being bound up merely in itself and its rational actualization, is bound up with an existent thing that persists outside it, namely the people. Thereby it also becomes clear in what direction the emphasis on what exists permanently, and the elimination of the will, in both Dahlmann and Stahl, is unconsciously driving: toward the grounding of the state not simply on its own will, but rather on the nation persisting outside and before it. This, however, illuminates where and how the century could and did go resolutely beyond Hegel's conceptions of the state; that derivation of the state from the will, firmly held by Hegel, was the inner reason why his idea of the state did not become the idea of the national state, and why he himself achieved a relationship to national modes of thinking at best as philosopher of history, not as philosopher of the state; the concept of the will had to be pruned from the twisted root of the idea of the state so that the idea of the state could expose its buds to the light of national modes of thinking.

It was well known to Hegel himself that the concept of the will, in the place which he gave it in the theory of the state, was a product of the 18th century, ultimately of Rousseau and the revolution.[18] Here the disciples could legitimately start, by asserting that the master's theory of the state is cast from the metal of freedom; we saw how it was precisely because of this "liberal" element that Hegel failed to make a connection with national modes of thinking. Nevertheless, this concept of the will was far removed from Rousseau and Robespierre;[19] as rational will, it had no other business than to sublate itself into the shape of contingent

---

18. That is, Hegel's concept of the will was influenced primarily by Jean-Jacques Rousseau (1712–78), *The Social Contract*, trans. and ed. Donald Cress (Indianapolis: Hackett, 1988), and by the French Revolution.

19. Maximillien Robespierre (1759–94), one of the leaders of the French Revolution, associated with the reign of fear and execution known as the Terror, until his own execution.

individual will within the whole of the state, and indeed as rational, not merely as general, will; its rationality first makes it sovereign, rather than—as for Rousseau—its sovereignty making it rational. Thus the individual man is only called forth insofar as he enters into the state. And here we grasp once again the connection that ties together Treitschke and Hegel. For both, the state is still a goal. Toward it Hegel guides the individual will, toward it Treitschke guides the nation. Both the individual as well as the nation can first fully become what they are within the state: the individual first becomes truly ethical within the state, the nation first becomes an actual people within the state; both individual man and nation are thus, in a certain sense, to be sacrificed to the state, the individual right of man as well as the totality of the nation to the deified state; the frightful schism of 1866[20] occurred in this spirit and, more relevant in the current discussion, was endured in this spirit. Only a time in which man finally seemed familiar and self-evident, after [his] having been for so long "the proper study,"[21] could subjugate him so recklessly to the distant goal of a yet-to-be-created state; only after the people had become a fluid quantity[22] through the work of the romantics could one thus surrender, almost unscrupulously and without concern, the unitary subsistence of this people for the state: the One that necessitates.

So it came about that the state that Bismarck created neither became merely something more [*ein Mehr*] than the state that Hegel conceived, nor did it become a mere fulfillment [of it]. In its national foundation, the new realm had something that was foreign or at least unnecessary for the Hegelian state-ideal, which ultimately entered with satisfaction into the haven of the Prussian particular state. But because this national

---

20. In 1866, after elections to the Prussian parliament in which conservatives won a majority of seats, the liberal German Progressive Party, formed in 1861, split into two groups: the Left Liberals maintained the Progressive Party's struggle for parliamentary liberalism, while the National Liberals (including Treitschke) compromised with Bismarck's government and supported his militaristic foreign policy. Some regarded the secession of the National Liberals as a betrayal of conviction in the face of power, while others regarded it as an act of statesmanship that enabled national unification and the continued influence of liberalism.

21. An allusion to Alexander Pope (1688–1744), *An Essay on Man*, ed. Maynard Mack (New Haven: Yale University Press, 1951), 52: "the proper study of Mankind is Man."

22. According to one terminology used in calculus, a "fluent" or "fluid quantity" is a variable mathematical quantity, and a "fluxion" is its rate of change.

foundation was indeed the life-condition of the new realm, the latter had to purchase its life-force at the cost of a destruction of the totality of this very national foundation, to be sure in accordance with historical dispensation. Already before the war one could once again gradually hear voices that did not want to recognize in Bismarck's deed simply the fulfillment of the German longing; the separation of state and nation seemed to them an indication of that other separation, which sensitive spirits had felt with anxiety immediately after 1870: the separation of state and culture. The hard necessity of external history had prevented the state of the Germans from growing out of the life of the nation with inner necessity; once again, man no longer justifiably found room within this state. And then, from the beginning of the century on, rang out the voices, both familiar and strange, of those who pursued their longing for the German state; and their longing certainly appeared more familiar to the pre-1914 generation than the fulfillment that surrounded them. Those born around 1770, confounded by the I, sought to conjure this state into existence with such passionate faith around the year 1800, but, insofar as this state was the image of that faithful yearning, it bore precisely the characteristics not of a state, but rather of a nation. Perhaps just because, as solitary man for the sake of his solitary longing, man called for the state so exclusively, and the image of the nation did not count for him at all as an independent power over and against this personal longing and seeking; perhaps for this very reason, the state could, for a time, assume for him the very face of the national communal civilization, which remained only a hope even after Bismarck's deed. Perhaps it was also for this reason that the political form of the fulfillment, as it occurred through Bismarck, could not be foreseen by anyone who at that time kept this hope fervently in his heart. Similarly, it was for this reason that Hegel was never able to succeed in guaranteeing to the nation its unconditioned, proper right: too strongly did he sense in the state itself, even in the nonnational state, the total fulfillment of that for which the individual could long, and the satisfaction of his will—too much for him still to be able to award the nation a proper place, the place of the necessary content of the state-body. Only those who came later, who denied the will of the individual even as intellectual starting point in their derivation of the state, created a place for the nation in their state-ideal, but Hegel had not.

Thus, in those years of the outgoing [i.e., the 18th] century, when the new state-ideal arose in the vicinity of Hölderlin, lie the very causes which already set boundaries to the historical impact and implications of this state-idea in the century of its development [i.e., the 19th century]. Here the intellectual history of the new empire found its beginning, even though it turned away from these origins. When 1871 became the dream's first great historical fulfillment, when "from thoughts the deed" sprang,[23] nevertheless it did not come about as the poet had hoped, not so "lucid and ripe"; certainly the hoped-for "creative genius" appeared and revealed itself mightily, but it was still not the genius of the "people"; what the Swabian youngster dreamed as immediately and tightly bound up with the appearance of this genius was not yet fulfilled: how

> our towns now
> are bright and open and awake, full of purer fire
> and the mountains of the German lands
> are mountains of the muses,
>
> As once the splendid ones were, Pindus and Helicon
> and Parnassus, and free, clear, lucid joy
> gleams under the fatherland's golden heaven.[24]

On the path from the downfall of the old realm to the foundation of the new—from Hegel to Bismarck—this dream remained unfulfilled. When this book was begun, it could nevertheless appear a veridical dream [ein Wahrtraum], one of those which stay alive just as dreams, in order one day to become what dreams can become: history-making might. Today, when the book is published, in the 150th year after Hegel's birth,[25] in the 100th since the appearance of the Philosophy of Right,[26] that dream seems to dissolve irretrievably in the foam of the waves which overflow all life. When the edifice of a world collapses, then both the thoughts that imagined it and the dreams that were woven through it are buried under the debris. What a more distant

---

23. On January 18, 1871, the second German empire was proclaimed, with Wilhelm of Prussia (1797–1888) as emperor. A new constitution, enshrining Prussian dominance, also took effect that year.

24. From Hölderlin's poem "An die Deutschen" (To the Germans). See note 1. Pindus, Helicon, and Parnassus are mountains in Greece.

25. Hegel was born in 1770.

26. Hegel's Philosophy of Right was first published in 1821, with the double title, Grundlinien der Philosophie des Rechts/Naturrecht und Staatswissenschaft im Grundrisse (Elements of the philosophy of right/Natural law and science of the state in outline) (Berlin: Nicolai, 1821). It has been translated by H. B. Nisbet, ed. Allen W. Wood, as Elements of the Philosophy of Right (Cambridge: Cambridge University Press, 1991).

future brings, whether new and unanticipated or the renewal of the lost—who would presume to predict that? Today, in the darkness that surrounds us, only a glimmer of hope falls from the once scarcely noticed conclusion of the Hölderlin verses, whose beginning we chose as the exposition's epigram in the better days of the past. A glimmer only— the prisoners in the jail still remain free to fix their gaze upon it:

Our lifetime is narrowly limited indeed,
We see the number of our years and count them,
But the years of the peoples,
Has a mortal eye seen them?[27]

---

27. Rosenzweig repeats the quotation from Hölderlin's poem used as his second epigram, to mark the condition of Germany after the First World War.

VI
From 1917 to 1925

Rosenzweig was serving on the Balkan front when, on August 22, 1918, he began to write the *Star of Redemption*, and, in a surge of intense writing, he completed the manuscript on February 16, 1919; the draft had taken but six months.[1] Shortly thereafter Rosenzweig moved to Frankfurt. On March 29, 1920, he married Edith Hahn, and in August of that year he became head of the Freies Jüdisches Lehrhaus. His dissertation on Hegel's political philosophy, *Hegel and the State*, was published in 1920 and the *Star of Redemption* in 1921. On February 8, 1922, Rosenzweig was diagnosed with amyotrophic lateral sclerosis. From 1922 to 1924 he translated the poems of Judah Halevi and wrote comments on them; in 1925 Rosenzweig began work on the translation of the Bible with Martin Buber and wrote *"Das neue Denken"* ("The New Thinking").[2]

The inspiration for the basic strategy of the *Star* came in the *"Urzelle,"* the famous letter of 1917 to Rudolf Ehrenberg. But the need had already been felt by Rosenzweig in 1913 and expressed in his first Jewish essay "Atheistic Theology," written in April 1914. In that essay, as we have seen, he pictured a similar set of developments in Christianity and Judaism; both have been "naturalized" in a sense and thus deprived of what in them can give life "orientation" and meaning. In Christianity, the 19th century had seen a quest for the historical Jesus; in Judaism, it had witnessed a focus on the historical existence of the Jewish people. Both trends eventually ran the risk of relativism and historicism; both failed to appreciate that religion requires revelation to give life meaning and direction.[3]

The facts recited above identify some, although not all, of the basic framework of Rosenzweig's career from 1917 to 1925. With the *"Urzelle"* in hand and a sense for what religion requires as expressed in "Atheistic Theology," he had begun to prepare himself to plunge into the *Star*, but before he actually did so, he added other arrows to his intellectual quiver. On a visit to Berlin, in February 1918, he and his father spent time with Hermann Cohen, in whose bathroom he came across a "discarded carbon manuscript copy (on very thin paper) of Cohen's *Religion der Vernunft aus den Quellen des Judentums (Religion of Reason Out of the Sources of Judaism)*, which he appropriated."[4] By early March he was deeply immersed in reading the book, which was making a significant impression on him. Cohen died on April 4, 1918. Stéphane Mosès, in his discussion of the *Star of Redemption*, argues that the book is importantly influenced by Rosenzweig's reading of two works. One is Schelling's *Die Weltalter* (The Ages of the World), conceived in 1810 and written and rewritten during the period between 1811 and 1815. We have discussed Rosenzweig's indebtedness to Schelling above.

The second book that Moses discusses is Hermann Cohen's posthumously published work on Judaism and the religion of reason, part of which Rosenzweig read in the spring of 1918. Mosès cites the letter to Rudolf Ehrenberg of March 5, 1918, as evidence that three chapters in particular captured Rosenzweig's attention: Chapter 10 ("The Individual as Self"), Chapter 11 ("Atonement"), and Chapter 12 ("The Day of Atonement").[5] He suggests that Rosenzweig was influenced by Cohen's treatment of atonement within the context of Yom Kippur and by his distinction between the individual and the self.[6] For Cohen, the individual is the abstract "autonomous subject who in freely submitting to the sovereignty of Law realizes his essence as a moral person." The self, on the other hand, is the concrete particular person who "discovers its true specificity through the religious experience of the *fault*" and then through *repentance* and *forgiveness*, i.e., through a reciprocal relationship with God. At a more general level, moreover, Cohen had employed the religious concepts of Creation, Revelation, Redemption, and others as "philosophical categories," which is just what Rosenzweig proceeded to do in the *Star*.

Back on the Balkan front by August, he plunged into writing the book, which he described in a letter to Rudolf Ehrenberg (September 4, 1918) as "not my 'real one' . . . but at least the prolegomena for it; my system, as I may well say. . . . It concerns you particularly for it is really nothing but the development of my letter to you of last November. It contains really everything that is in me, consequently all the influences I have undergone. I am sending you the outline. . . ." Released from the service in December 1918, Rosenzweig worked on the *Star* in Cassel and Berlin, completing it on February 16, 1919. By June he had decided to have it published.

It was thus a complex mix of sources that led to Rosenzweig's systematic thinking, from Hegel, Goethe, and Meinecke to Victor von Weizsäcker, Kierkegaard, Schelling, Eugen Rosenstock, and Cohen. Out of the *"Urzelle"* came the *Star*, the brief reflections on the significance of the Hegel book published after a decade, and the writings of the early 1920s.

Rosenzweig's *Hegel und der Staat*, which originated in his doctoral study from 1910 to 1912, was published in the summer of 1920. In a letter to Friedrich Meinecke, dated August 30, 1920, Rosenzweig described the personal crisis and change that was leading him to reject the academic life for an active Jewish life in Frankfurt. Shlomo Avineri argues, however, that in addition to this personal crisis regarding Rosenzweig's understanding of Judaism and himself as a Jew, there was another "crisis related to the fall of the German Reich and the collapse of the prewar hopes for its reformation and transformation."[7] Before the war Rosenzweig had hoped for a new era that would relieve the burden of the Bismarckian and Wilhelmian Reich. After the defeat of 1918, he lost all such hope.[8] He saw the "the tragedy of German history" in the fact that "its modern political manifestation – the Bismarckian Reich– was rooted in force, not in the rational will" and hence not in culture and spirit.[9] With the war and the defeat of 1918, Rosenzweig saw the final demise of the Hegelian dream; what Bismarck had "emasculated and perverted," the war had completely demolished.[10] As Avineri argues, moreover, this realization had a personal dimension: Rosenzweig's hopes for the future had to rest not with Germany and German Idealism, but with Judaism and specifically with a Judaism shorn of any political dimension.[11]

Once he moved to Frankfurt, he became head of the Lehrhaus and a member of the circle around Nehemiah Nobel; each morning the circle met to study Talmud. Rosenzweig also established a relationship with Martin Buber. In December he and his wife visited Buber in Heppenheim; in a letter to Rudolf Hallo, Rosenzweig reports his surprise that "Buber was no longer the mystical subjectivist that people worship, but that even intellectually he was becoming a solid and reasonable man." He invited Buber to lecture at the Lehrhaus, the ultimate outcome of which was Buber's important book, *I and Thou*. Also, in the winter semester of 1921 Rosenzweig gave a lecture course at the Lehrhaus entitled "An Introduction to Jewish Thinking," which he accompanied with a seminar on the foundations of the history of philosophy, especially German Idealism from Kant to Hegel.[12] Then, in July 1921, Rosenzweig wrote a short book on philosophy and philosophical thinking, *Understanding the Sick and the Healthy*, but withdrew the book from publication; the book was based on the lecture course and the seminar.[13]

By February 1923, the sclerosis had advanced, and by the end of the year Rosenzweig could no longer speak. The paralysis left him immobile. While Rosenzweig was invested in the project of translating and commenting on Halevi's poems, he was very keenly aware of the crisis of European culture and the role Judaism might play in its "redemption." He could write, in a letter to Rudolf Hallo, "that European culture today is on the point of collapse and can only be saved if supra-European, suprahuman powers come to its aid. I have no illusion about these powers, among which Judaism is one: they will in turn become secularized and Europeanized, especially if they succeed; indeed, I am aware that the very first gesture of help is also the first gesture toward the new secularization. The ability to secularize themselves again and again proves the eternity of these powers."[14]

Rosenzweig's project of 1922–24, translating and commenting on the poems of Judah Halevi, can be viewed as an opportunity for him to import the lessons of the *Star* into the actual life of Jewish learning and study.[15] As he puts it in "The New Thinking," "the notes to my *Jehuda Halevi* contain instructive examples of the practical application of the new thinking."[16]

In his famous comment on Halevi's poem "During the Night," for example, Rosenzweig both employs and clarifies his conception of revelation. "The longed-for event has happened," he says, "A night-vision has brought the poet the experience of the sight of God. . . . he sees God, as if his heart 'had been allowed to stand by at Sinai.' The experience of today confirms and repeats the historical revelation." This much the poem says. But Rosenzweig then asks, "what confirms revelation, and what repeats it? What is revealed?" Here he sets down these famous words:

> God reveals in revelation always only just this—revelation. In other words: he reveals always only Himself to the human, to the human only. The accusative and dative in its union is the peculiar content of revelation. Whatever does not follow immediately from this bond established here between God and human, whatever cannot verify its unmediatedness to this bond, does not belong to it. The problem has not been solved for the seer of the vision, but rather—it moves into the past. The miracle does not admonish him, but rather the vision has given to him the courage to bow down before the source of the miracle. Out of the problem of thought has arisen a strength of heart.[17]

In the poem, Halevi refers to the *problem*, "how your creation, the soul, is intertwined with me," and to his reflections that have him see the soul as a miracle come from God. This is not the revelation, Rosenzweig says, but rather its preparation. The revelation, the "vision," is an unmediated self-disclosure of the divine to the human, and the poet's response to it is "the courage to bow down before the source of the miracle." Thus, "the problem of thought" leads to "a strength of heart." As Halevi put it, "my reflections roused me from my bed, to bow down, Lord, before your magnificence." What confirms and repeats the revelation at Sinai, then, is the direct, unmediated encounter between the divine and the human; it is what thinking gives rise to and what is followed by action. Revelation itself, however, is neither thinking nor action but rather a divine disclosure and a human reception, what Rosenzweig calls, in another note, "experience and event."[18]

The notes also make clear that Rosenzweig has in mind recent developments in Christian theology and especially the emergence of Barth and radical theology.[19] In commenting on "Homecoming" he asks: "Does God or does the human being take the first step? That is a real question, not, as Protestant theologians today would like to believe, a preliminary question already solved. Nor indeed is it 'the difference between Judaism and Christianity,' as the Jewish theologians in their understandable demand for harmless 'distinctions for teaching purposes' would like to believe. Rather, it is a real question of the real heart of the human." Here Rosenzweig registers a genuine worry with Barth and his disciples, for whom every "first step" must be taken by God. Rosenzweig wants to give due respect to both the divine and the human and to the lived, temporal character of their relationship.

> The real question arises because the human always senses his own lack of power whenever he stands before God, and thus necessarily must await and request the first step from God. And yet at the same time he hears that which he cannot help but hear: that God demands the first step from him, from the human. No theory can get away from this, neither one that seeks to discredit the demanding voice of God that is heard nor one that seeks to discredit the perceived lack of power as a deception of Satan. And of course absolutely not one that might steer between such a crude alternative through clever distribution or a meticulous apportionment of roles. Instead, the matter remains an unending conversation. . . .[20]

Ultimately, of course, Rosenzweig does recognize the priority of the divine, since even a first human step is grounded in a divine demand and more, in the divine love that makes such a first step, freely taken, possible. But in any given case, as the "conversation" develops, the first step may be God's or a human one.

Rosenzweig's differences with Christian theology, however, are even more pronounced in his note on "The Far-and-Near One." What lies behind this poem, he claims, is a single, powerful thought: "that the far-away God is none other than the near God, the unknown God none other than the revealed one, the Creator none other than the Redeemer." It is a thought, he says, that has been rediscovered and forgotten again and again, and he mentions Harnack and Barth among those recent theologians who have forgotten it.

> For what people discover, the theologians forget. And the more they do so, the better theologians they are. The most accurate theology is the most dangerous. After a long drought, today we have a theology, mostly Protestant, that leaves nothing to be desired as to accuracy. We have it now: that God is Wholly Other, that to talk about Him is to talk Him away, that we can only say what He does to us.[21]

In one sense, then, Rosenzweig finds some truth in Barth and radical theology; in another, he clearly does not. Theologians overextend themselves and claim too much.

> We theologians cannot help but make prescriptions for God's conduct out of our knowledge. We know that God can be known only in His presence, and at once we make out of this a law for Him: that He does not permit Himself to be known in His absence. In truth, however, we could easily leave it to Him as to when and how and what of Himself He wants to be known. And we have to say only what we know in utter calm or in utter unrest—but whether in calm or in unrest is not up to us; that is as accurately as we can—and this accuracy *is* up to us.[22]

Rosenzweig does not forbid natural theology and proofs for God's existence; these are human ways of dealing with a God who can be, for whatever reason, distant from us. He calls this "honest knowledge" that signifies that at the moment of its acquisition the distance between God and the seeker was great. In the spirit of Kierkegaard, Rosenzweig notes that the "objectivity" of a person's knowledge of God does not entail the mode of its "subjectivity." "Even in the most dreadful nearness the human can look away and then does not know in the least what has happened to him. And in the farthest distance the glance of God and of the human can burn into one another, so that the coldest abstractions become warm in the mouth of Maimonides or Hermann Cohen—more than all our distressed prattle."[23]

In 1923 Rosenzweig completed the Halevi book and wrote "The Builders," a letter to Martin Buber on their differences over Jewish law and practice, and his introduction to the *Collected Jewish Writings* of Hermann Cohen. In the spring of 1923, Rosenzweig dictated "Sermonic Judaism" and then, shortly thereafter, wrote "Apologetic Thinking," a review of books by Max Brod and Leo Baeck, published in *Der Jude*, which he would later describe as "much more substantial, but restrained in tone."[24] But it was a difficult year; his illness progressed, and by year's end he was unable to speak or move.

"Apologetic Thinking" was in part a response to two recently published books, Max Brod's *Paganism, Christianity, Judaism: A Confession of Faith* (1921) and the second edition of Leo Baeck's *The Essence of Judaism* (1921). Brod, the friend of Kafka and prominent Prague Zionist and literary figure, and Baeck, the chief liberal rabbi of Berlin, were both significant Jewish intellectuals. Rosenzweig treats the two works as examples of apologetic thinking. He introduces his comments with an account of why apologetic thinking is natural to Judaism and concludes with a defense of its integrity and the integrity of the thinking that lies beyond it.

Rosenzweig describes apologetic thinking as, in a sense, a mode of the "new thinking." It is situated reflection on Judaism, thinking that occurs at the "border" of Judaism and what lies beyond it, occasioned by an attack from the outside. Within Judaism, thinking is legal and systematic. But "thought reacting to the occasion" depends upon its "adversary" and can take many forms. It is always, however, engaged, which can lead both to clarity in some cases and to confusion in others.

In the case of Brod's book, Rosenzweig finds its idealized picture of Christianity too estranged from actual Christian life and existence, and although its portrayal of Judaism is narrow and idiosyncratic, it has a novelty and liveliness born out of Brod's attempt to read aggadic texts in a different way. In substance, Rosenzweig finds Brod in error—he fails to see how action in the world for Jews should be tied to the *halakhah*. Nonetheless, Rosenzweig lauds Brod's insightful and novel reading of Talmudic texts.

Similarly, he expresses both respect for Baeck's famous work and reservations about it. He notes that it, too, is an apologetic book, originally written in 1906 to defend Judaism against the portrait of it given in Adolf von Harnack's *The Essence of Christianity* of 1900. Baeck's disciplined control of sources and his depiction of Judaism as a dialectic of mystery and commandment are unlike Brod's very selective, more impassioned portrayal. But, as Rosenzweig sees it, Baeck understands more, although, like Brod, he, too, treats the *halakhah* inadequately. Still, the liberal rabbi and the Zionist poet, as he calls them, share the apologetic stance, with its strengths as well as its shortcomings. Among those strengths is the capacity to see beyond itself and to move beyond mere self-aggrandizement and self-righteousness into the arena of integrity. When accomplished properly and fully, apologetics can become something else that "goes to the very ground of things" and becomes "a candid exposition of one's own [self]." This, too, is a mode of the "new thinking" but one that is not apologetic. It is what he calls "*knowledge* or real understanding."

During February of 1925, just prior to embarking on the Bible project with Buber, Rosenzweig wrote "The New Thinking" as an introduction to the *Star* and its philosophic background, "addressed," as he later said, "to the Jewish reader."[25] When Rosenzweig turned to writing "The New Thinking," then, it was within a context shaped by his investment in translation, several years of extending the teaching of the *Star* into the concrete task of recovering traditional texts, his commitment to the Lehrhaus and its role in Jewish education, and his rejection of German Idealism and philosophy in favor of a full Jewish life, albeit one hampered by his progressive illness. In many ways, the book on Halevi, the Bible translation project, and these other essays can be viewed as applications of the thinking of the *Star* and as commentaries on it, products of it, and introductions to it. All either lead into life or take place within it. This judgment even applies to "The New Thinking."

The *Star of Redemption* had fallen on deaf ears; it was a book known by some but read by virtually no one. This neglect is not surprising, given the notorious difficulty of the work, which Rosenzweig once called "my armor, the dangerous book."[26] Hence, he wrote the essay as a kind of introduction, to help the "Jewish reader" to understand its structure, its argument, and its method.

Endnotes

1. Rosenzweig was anything but enthusiastic about the war. He joined strictly for personal reasons, as a kind of test, and felt quite alien to the German cause and repelled by the horrors of the war. Nonetheless, he took the war to be neither good nor bad. For discussion, see Stefan Meineke, "A Life of Contradiction: The Philosopher Franz Rosenzweig and his Relationship to History and Politics," *Leo Baeck Institute Yearbook* 36 (1991): 467–70.

2. For a brief sketch of Rosenzweig's career which refers to the influences on him, from Schelling to Rosenstock and Cohen, see Paul Mendes-Flohr, introduction to *The Philosophy of Franz Rosenzweig*, (Hanover, N.H.: University Press of New England, 1988), 1–14.

3. For brief comment, see Otto Pöggeler, "Between Enlightenment and Romanticism: Rosenzweig and Hegel," in *The Philosophy of Franz Rosenzweig*, 115–16. See also Paul Mendes-Flohr, "Franz Rosenzweig and the Crisis of Historicism," in *The Philosophy of Franz Rosenzweig*, 145. The essay is also reprinted in Mendes-Flohr, *Divided Passions* (Detroit: Wayne State University Press, 1991), 311–37, 316–17. One might mention the similarity of Rosenzweig's theme and the motives that led Karl Barth and Rudolf Bultmann to a radical revision of theology and a rejection of 19th-century liberal theology; see Barth's reflections in *The Humanity of God* (Richmond, Va.: John Knox Press, 1960) (orig. 1956) and Bultmann's discussion in the famous lecture of 1924, "Liberal Theology and the Latest Theological Movement" in *Faith and Understanding* (Philadelphia: Fortress Press, 1969) 28–52. Also, see Mendes-Flohr's comments on the essay in Gilman and Zipes, eds., *Yale Companion to Jewish Writing and Thought in German Culture* (New Haven: Yale University Press, 1997), 322–26.

4. Glatzer, ed., *Franz Rosenzweig: His Life and Thought*, 65.

5. Ibid., 47 and 297, n.63.

6. Ibid., 47–48.

7. Shlomo Avineri, "Rosenzweig's Hegel Interpretation: Its Relationship to the Development of His Jewish Reawakening," in Wolfdietrich Schmied-Kowarzik, ed., *Der Philosoph Franz Rosenzweig (1886–1929): Internationaler Kongress— Kassel 1986*, Bd.II, Das neue Denken und seine Dimensionnen (Freiburg/ Munchen: Verlag Karl Alber, 1988), 831–38, 832.

8. For a detailed discussion of Rosenzweig's swings of mood and ultimate despair at the culmination of the war in 1918, see Meineke, "A Life of Contradiction," 476–83.

9. Ibid., 834.

10. In a letter to Meinecke in 1923, Rosenzweig reminds his teacher about the preface that he had written in 1918 and the fact that he, in 1919, "expected not

a perfection of history, but a new Deluge." See Otto Pöggeler, "Between En-lightenment and Romanticism: Rosenzweig and Hegel," in *The Philosophy of Franz Rosenzweig*, 108–9. From 1917–18 Rosenzweig published and wrote several pieces on the war, world history, and the current situation; for discussion, see Mendes-Flohr, "Franz Rosenzweig and the Crisis of Historicism," in *The Philosophy of Franz Rosenzweig*, 147–55.

11. Ibid., 835–38; Avineri focuses on Rosenzweig's negative view of Zionism and ascribes his opposition in part to his judgment of Germany, politics, and the destruction of the Hegelian dream of a rational and free state. Meineke elaborates a similar point in much greater detail, treating not only the *Star* and Rosenzweig's opposition to Zionism but also his role in directing the Lehrhaus; see "A Life of Contradiction," 483–88. Stéphane Mosès has argued for a more political turn in Rosenzweig's thinking, after the *Star*, and a move towards Zionism; see Mosès, "Franz Rosenzweig in Perspective: Reflections on His Last Diaries," in *The Philosophy of Franz Rosenzweig*, 191–95, and "Politik und Religion. Zur Aktualität Franz Rosenzweigs," in *Der Philosoph Franz Rosenzweig*, Band II, 855–75.

12. Otto Pöggeler refers to these courses in "Between Enlightenment and Romanticism," 118. For Nobel, see below, Chapter 10, note 3.

13. For brief comments, see N. N. Glatzer, introduction to *Franz Rosenzweig: Understanding the Sick and the Healthy* (New York: Noonday Press, 1953), 9–21.

14. Glatzer, ed., *Franz Rosenzweig: His Life and Thought*, 129.

15. We have in English a translation of Rosenzweig's book, together with extensive discussion of the work, his views on translation, and much else. See Barbara Ellen Galli, *Franz Rosenzweig and Jehuda Halevi: Translating, Translations, and Translators* (Montreal & Kingston: McGill-Queen's University Press, 1995), especially Part 2, Chapter 1: "Placing the Halevi Book, Rosenzweig, and the *Star*," 289–303.

16. Cited by Galli, 289; see Chapter VIII, 128 below. In the case of the translation of the poems of Halevi, a significant aspect of this application is the method of translation and the role of the translator. As Rosenzweig says, "The translator makes himself the mouthpiece of the foreign voice, which he makes audible over the gulf of space or time. If the foreign voice has something to say, then the language must afterward appear different from before." (Galli, 171; Afterword)

17. Galli, 187–88; the poem is on 20–21. For Galli's comments, see 446–49.

18. Galli, 188; note on the poem "Event."

19. In addition, see two letters to Martin Buber, Letter 841, December 20, 1922 (875–76) and Letter 852, dated February 14, 1923 (893), in *Briefe* I.

20. Galli, 194–95; note on the poem "Homecoming."

21. Galli, 204–5; note on the poem "The Far-and-Near One."

22. Ibid.

23. Ibid., 206.

24. Ibid., 133; letter to Martin Buber, June 17, 1924.

25. Ibid., 145; letter to Hans Ehrenberg, March 11, 1925. Published October 1925 in *Der Morgen.*

26. He uses this expression (*meine Rustung, das gefahrliche Buch*) in a letter to Joseph Prager, at the end of January 1922, during reflections on Nehemiah Nobel's recent death on January 22. See *Briefe* I, 747. The judgment that the book is owned by only a small number and virtually unread is Rosenzweig's own; see the letter of March 11, 1925, to Hans Ehrenberg, after he had written "Das neue Denken," *Briefe* I, 1025–26.

VII
"Apologetic Thinking"
(1923)

I

It has often been said, and even more often repeated, that Judaism has no dogmas. As little as that may be correct—a superficial glance at Jewish history or into the Jewish prayerbook already teaches the opposite— something very correct is nevertheless meant by it. Namely, Judaism indeed has dogmas, but no dogmatics. Already noteworthy in this respect is the point at which the Talmudic literature enters the discussions, to which later attempts at ascertaining Jewish dogmas had to revert. In the context of the regulations concerning criminal procedure and criminal law appears also the problem of punishment in the hereafter; and here the things are listed whose denial causes the Jew to lose his "portion of the world to come."[1] It was here that Maimonides and others were able to find a starting point. It is thus a legal context in which the problems of religious metaphysics appear. This is surely noteworthy if one thinks of the often-cited metaphysical inclination of our stock [*unsres Stammes*], which can be established for the present with certainty.

The matter becomes even more noteworthy if one considers the content of these dogmas. They deal with God, with the revealed law, with Messianic redemption, and with that which is connected with it: missing is the thought that wholly permeates Judaism, which alone can make the law comprehensible and which alone can explain the

---

1. In the tractate of the Mishnah (rabbinic legal compilation, completed in the third century C.E.) entitled Sanhedrin, which deals with the regulations of the judicial system, the tenth chapter, Perek Helek (The Chapter of the Portion), lists those who have no portion of the world to come, including those who *deny* certain beliefs. In his commentary on the Mishnah, *Kitab al-Siraj*, (Book of the lamp, completed in 1168), Moses Maimonides (1138–1204) takes this chapter as an occasion to discuss the beliefs *required* by Jewish law, which are not listed in the Mishnah.

preservation of the Jewish people, the thought of the chosenness of Israel. This truly central thought of Judaism, which, say, a Christian scholar, coming from Christology, would expect to find perhaps in first or, at least, immediately after the doctrine of God, in second place, in Jewish dogmatics, does not occur at all in, for example, Maimonides's "Thirteen Articles of Faith"[2] or in his philosophical work,[3] which after all was supposed to be a guide to those perplexed about the basic truths of Judaism. Here, too, as everywhere, the thought of chosenness of the Jewish people is a prerequisite for thought as well as life; yet it is never articulated; it is self-evident. Never do prayer and poetry tire of clothing it again and again in new words; the exegetical legends mirror it in myriad facets; mysticism sinks deep into it to the point of mythological hypostasis: it becomes word, meaning, form, but never a dogmatic formula, never – with the one great exception, nourished, to be sure, by all those other forces, of Yehuda Halevi's *Kuzari*[4] – a philosophical topic. Existence is filled with it and borne by it, all immediate utterance of existence is moved by it—however, when consciousness seeks to soar beyond mere existence, it denies it.

That has deep reasons and far-reaching consequences. A spiritual community withdraws its innermost essence here from spiritual exposure. This means that the community does not wish to be only a spiritual community, but wants rather to be what it actually is in contrast to other communities connected by spirit/intellect alone: a natural community, a people. The monstrous actuality of Jewish being has created for itself a self-protection. But what here has a protective and actuality-preserving effect, the deflection of consciousness from the secret source of life, would have had to have a paralyzing effect on life in a community which in its essence is purely spiritual, such as, for example, the Christian church. In the latter, the continually renewed lifting into consciousness of the foundation of existence, in this case the constant reformulating of Christological dogma, again and again, becomes the inner condition for the external continuation of the community.

---

2. In his commentary to Perek Helek, Maimonides lists thirteen required beliefs. Some Jews recite them daily, and a poetic version of the list, known after its first word as "Yigdal," is a regular part of Jewish liturgy.

3. *Dalālat al-ḥā'irīn* (Guide of the perplexed, completed around 1200), trans. S. Pines (Chicago: University of Chicago Press, 1963).

4. Judah Halevi (c.1105–41), *Kitāb al-Ḥujja waal-Dalil fī Naṣr al-Dīn al-Dhalīl* (Book of argument and proof in defense of the despised faith, completed in 1140), translated by Hartwig Hirschfeld as *Book of Kuzari* (New York: Dutton, 1905; reprint, New York: Pardes, 1946).

Inaccessible mystery stands opposed to inexhaustible mystery, substantiality to spirituality.

But this has an effect also on the direction and the reach of scholarly thought in general. Not only has Jewish patristics never produced an Augustine,[5] a thinker who, in almost corporeal vision, set the stage for the history of the coming millennium, producing instead of him the powerful swimmers through the "sea of the Talmud," but Jewish scholasticism also never brought forth a Thomas.[6] The *Summa* of Aquinas, that mighty system of a comprehensive Christian science, whose great and truly systematic intention could not, however, overcome the historical birth defect of scholasticism's apologetic-dialectical method and was therefore not able to realize itself, has on our side no counterpart in Maimonides's philosophical work, the *Guide of the Perplexed*, but rather in *his* "Great Ḥibbur,"[7] as he himself calls his giant halakhic opus, which actually snaps up the entire universe as well, but in the sieve of Jewish law. Here, in a different way, is the same immediate totality as was intended there, the same will to make the heart of one's own religious life the center of a spiritual cosmos; one was justified—starting out from considerations different from those developed here—in interpreting "my great Ḥibbur" in Maimonides's mouth as meaning "my summa." The *Guide of the Perplexed*, however, would disappoint one who approaches it in the expectation of finding a system. Just as it starts with a lengthy treatise, which unfolds all the material on the problem of biblical anthropomorphism, so it is thereafter the apologetic thread on which the individual treatises making up the work are strung. The defense is directed against the attacks of philosophy, not or only peripherally against other religions, by which the defense could therefore have been taken over. The apologetic nature of the fundamental attitude yields the completely unpedantic character, which still today is a fresh breeze for the reader and strikes him as in no way

---

5. Augustine, Bishop of Hippo (354–430).

6. Thomas Aquinas (1225/7–74), author of the *Summa Theológica* (Theological summation), a systematic exposition of Christian theology, trans. and eds., the Dominicans of Blackfriars (Blackfriars, Cambridge, London, and New York; Eyre and Spottiswerk, and McGraw-Hill, 1964–).

7. Maimonides composed an encyclopedic code of Jewish law, entitled *Mishneh Torah* (Repetition of the law, completed in 1180), translated as *The Code of Maimonides* (New Haven: Yale University Press, 1949–). Elsewhere, Maimonides frequently referred to this work as his *ḥibbur ha-gadol* (great compilation). See Isadore Twersky, *Introduction to Maimonides' Code* (New Haven: Yale University Press, 1980), 18 note 25, 33.

"scholastic"; this thinking has what systematic thinking cannot have so easily: the fascination—and the truthfulness—of thought reacting to the occasion; but therefore a limit is also set for it which only systematic thinking removes: exactly the limit of the occasional; only systematic thinking determines the circle of its objects itself; apologetic thinking remains dependent on the cause, the adversary.

And in this sense Jewish thinking remains apologetic thinking. It is characteristic that here it does not arrive at the phenomenon in which the self-sufficiency of thinking usually manifests itself within a culture, the struggle of schools within the common thinking. With us, the conflict between nominalism and realism has its counterpart in the Maimonidean controversy,[8] with its labor pains and after-pains and its own two phases, separated by a century—thus not the struggle within thinking, but rather the cultural struggle over thinking itself, the struggle between those who heeded the call of the occasion and those who themselves denied it. Neither did it become different in the 19th century, when after a fallow period of nearly four hundred years once again—in Germany since the [18]20s[9]—a Jewish philosophy developed, which until today has not been appreciated in a way commensurate with the quality of its achievements. All reservation about apologetics has not been able to prevent the fact that the legitimate method of thinking itself remained apologetic. One did not become a Jewish thinker in the undisturbed circle of Judaism. Here, thinking did not become a thinking about Judaism, which was simply the most self-evident thing of all, more a being than an "ism," but rather it became a thinking within

---

8. The Maimonidean controversy was a conflict over the compatibility of Maimonides's philosophically influenced views with traditional Jewish beliefs and over the role of philosophy in the educational curriculum. Maimonides defended himself against the criticism that his Aristotelian view of spiritual immortality was incompatible with traditional belief in corporeal resurrection. However, the two main phases of the controversy occurred after Maimonides's death. The first culminated in 1232, when Jewish denunciation of Maimonides's *Guide* and the book of his *Mishneh Torah* dealing with dogma led to their being burned by the Church at Montpellier. The second occurred around 1305 when, during heated debates, a leading halakhic authority, Rabbi Solomon ben Adreth (1235–1310), banned those under the age of thirty (according to some texts, twenty-five) from studying philosophical books written by non-Jews.

9. Perhaps an allusion to the *Wissenschaft des Judentums* (science of Judaism) movement, which introduced critical, historical methods into the study of Judaism. The groundbreaking *Zeitschrift für das Wissenschaft des Judentums* (Periodical for the science of Judaism), 1 vol., was published in 1823.

Judaism, a learning; thus ultimately not a fundamental but rather an ornamental thinking. Anyone who was supposed to reflect on Judaism had somehow, if not psychologically then at least spiritually, to be torn at the border of Judaism. Therefore, however, his thinking was then determined by the power which had led him to the border, and the depth horizon of his gaze was determined by the degree to which he had been carried to, on, or across the border. The apologetic is the legitimate force of this thinking but also its danger. Two significant works of the recent time are to be considered from this double perspective in what follows.[10]

II

Gustav Landauer reacted to the publication of the nucleus of Brod's confessional book with a reply that was moved by an injured sense of justice: he saw it as yet another attempt to comprehend one's own domain in its ideality and the foreign one in the entire breadth of its historical and historically tainted actuality.[11] I would think that this danger belongs among those that, just because they are so obvious, can be easily avoided. Quite on the contrary, it seems to me that the danger of all apologetics lies much more in the fact that one takes one's own, which, after all, one knows oneself, in its full breadth and depth of actuality, while the foreign, of which one has only "taken notice," for the most part only as it occurs in a book, i.e., therefore precisely as an—ideal. For every actual observer of human nature knows that personal statements

10. Max Brod (1884–1968), *Heidentum, Christentum, Judentum: Ein Bekenntnisbuch* (Munich: Kurt Wolff, 1921); *Paganism, Christianity, Judaism: A Confession of Faith*, trans William Wolf, revised with an author's preface (University, Ala.: University of Alabama Press, 1970). Leo Baeck (1873–1956), *Das Wesen des Judentums*, (1st ed. Berlin: Nathansen and Lamm, 1905; 2nd rev. and aug. ed., Frankfurt am Main: Kaufmann, 1922); *The Essence of Judaism*, trans. Victor Grubwieser and Leonard Pearl, revised by Irving Howe (New York: Schocken, 1961).

11. The nucleus of Brod's book was published as "Franz Werfels 'Christliche Sendung'" ("Franz Werfel's 'Christian Mission'"), *Der Jude*, Jahrgang I, Heft 11, (1916–17) 717–24. In response, Gustav Landauer (1870–1919) wrote "Christlich und christlich, jüdisch und jüdisch" ("Christian and Christian, Jewish and Jewish") *Der Jude*, Jahrgang I, Heft 12, (1916–17) 851–52. Landauer was assassinated in 1919 during his participation in the socialist revolution in Munich.

‍‌‍‍‌‌

can be used as sources only with much caution. And this is by no means because, on account of natural bias, they create in general too favorable a picture, but rather on the contrary, because they tend to come out too theoretical, too absolute, too bony, and to lack the correction of theory by practice, the flesh covering the bones. The well-known utterance by a man who ought to know—"Give me two written words by anyone, and I'll bring him to the gallows"—is valid also for spiritual movements.[12] We all know what a tragicomic caricature of Judaism results if, apparently with complete objectivity, one strings a series of quotations together; and in doing so, it hardly matters whether the assembling is done by the Jewish or antisemitic side; on the contrary, the things that Eisenmenger[13] and his predecessors produce as "fiery Satanic bullets" from the arsenal of the Talmud could more truly lure one to this book than many a recent collection of carefully filtered "rays of light."[14] This is certainly connected with the peculiar lack of self-consciousness in Judaism, which is discussed in the first part of these remarks; it is indeed impossible to make a Talmudic passage comprehensible to someone who does not already understand it; for this purpose one would have to be able to open, so to speak, each time a whole complete pictorial atlas of Jewish history, Jewish faces, Jewish life, which of course cannot exist. Yet, one could not do a greater injustice even to Christianity, which points to self-consciousness so intensely, one could not do a greater injustice than to present it in terms of its own catechism. It is the first duty of theoretical neighborly love (which among us creatures committed to mutual peeping and judging is no less important than the practical one—because being perceived wrongly hurts no less than being treated wrongly) that we never forget to ask ourselves about each opinion that we form about another person: can the other, if he is as I here depict him, still—live? For that is what he wishes and ought to do—"like

---

12. The saying is attributed to Cardinal Richelieu (1585–1642).

13. Johann Andreas Eisenmenger (1654–1704), author of *Entdecktes Judentum* (Judaism uncovered) (Frankfurt am Main, 1700), a notoriously hostile portrayal of Judaism based on quotations, often taken out of context or distorted, from rabbinic works. Eisenmenger's predecessors are those who compiled such quotations for use in Christian anti-Jewish polemics during the Middle Ages, such as, e.g., *Pugio Fidei* (Dagger of faith) completed circa 1280 by Raymond Martini (1220–85).

14. An allusion to Artur Dinter (1876–?), *Lichtstrahlen aus dem Talmud* (Rays of light from the Talmud) (Berlin, 1919).

myself."[15] These legalistic machines, lacking humor and soul, whom the Christian so gladly represents under the [name] "Pharisees," would be incapable of living; just as little as those pale lilies of heaven, whom the Jew, on the basis of a reading of the Sermon on the Mount, would recognize as the only "true Christians." If one wants to understand a spirit, then one must not abstract it from the body that belongs to it. As little as the body is a decayed manifestation of the spirit, as little is that in the historical image of a community which does not fit its classical records to be judged without further ado as decay, as an "amalgam"; perhaps it is, quite on the contrary, the necessary and, in a certain sense, even the originally "intended" correction of those origins. An adult may long all his life for the purity of childhood, but he is by no means merely a decayed manifestation of the child because of this. Quite on the contrary, one may perhaps even recognize the traits of the child in their whole significance, only if one tries to fathom them in retrospect from the known face of the man.

And just here lies the weakness of Brod's book. An actual weakness, because an unnecessary one, not one of those that are only the shadow of a strength. That he also improperly schematizes "paganism" matters little in comparison, because paganism, despite the three-tiered title and the basic thought constructed in three parts, does not fall within the book's core, through which the bloodstream of experience pulses. But the depiction of Christianity, precisely because it lies near the heart of the book, suffers greatly from that method of "unfair idealizing," whereby he lends more credence to schoolmasters and theology professors than to saints and knights. It is very characteristic that the two vital Christians who have not sprung from the catechism and who have been admitted into his book because they were too close to the author to be able to remain outside—Dante and Kierkegaard—are not treated as Christians, but rather, comical as it may sound, as—Jews dispersed within Christianity. If only, even here, he had also trusted his experience more than theory, even if it was his own theory.

For his strength is that he does so in the core of the book. The book is, in a good sense of the word, what its subtitle states: a confessional book. It does not burden the reader with the private affairs of the author, as one might well fear because of the title; rather it narrates the life's journey of a way of knowing; and because this life's journey was, at the same time, the life's journey of a generation, the goal he achieves is of more

---

15. Rosenzweig is interpreting Leviticus 19:18: "You shall love your neighbor like yourself."

than private significance. Brod, in his own manner, has worked his way through the fog of theories to the actuality of historical Judaism. He succeeded in this because he did not allow himself to be led on this journey by the theoretical question about which is the correct Judaism, but rather was propelled by the practical question about which is the right life. This book answers the question of the essence of war with the essence of Judaism. It became a good theological book because it is—oh, strangest, easiest, and most difficult of all sciences!—not a theological book, but rather in its origin and its organization a war book. And it became a bad theological book when in the end it still wanted to be a theological book and to the degree that it wanted to become that.

With magnificent verve, the book's thought is refracted from the concepts of "noble" and "ignoble misfortune," which were discovered wholly personally and wholly unscholastically in war (and probably also already in prewar),[16] across the elevated viewpoints of the "incompatibility of things belonging together" and the "earthly miracle,"[17] on a path into the middle of the aggadah.[18] The concepts with which the wisdom of religion teachers of the past century had dragged this matter down to its own level remain unused by the side; this is self-explanatory; the internal apologetics of the book take to task just those concepts, which had desiccated Judaism to a mummy in the foolish belief that this would make it more "adequate to the times." Yet the intensity with

---

16. Brod distinguishes the "noble misfortune" of inescapable, human finitude from the "ignoble misfortune" of escapable limitations. See *Paganism, Christianity, Judaism*, chap. 2.

17. According to Brod, paganism unconditionally affirms this world and lacks any sense of the infinite, while Christianity unconditionally denies this world, regarding all misfortune as noble and making salvation depend entirely on miraculous grace; however, Judaism recognizes the realms of both noble and ignoble misfortune and is thus capable, unlike Christianity, of acknowledging the possibility of human deeds that are attended by divine grace and are intended to improve the world. Judaism can negotiate the ultimately insuperable "incompatibility of the correlated" realms of noble and ignoble misfortune only through the concept of the "this-worldly miracle": the divine grace that enables humans to engage in politics for the sake of heaven. See *Paganism, Christianity, Judaism*, chaps. 5–6.

18. Rabbinic literature is often distinguished into *halakhah*, which deals with legal topics, and *aggadah*, which deals with nonlegal topics. In some schools of traditional talmudic scholarship, rigorous methods are applied only to halakhic passages of the Talmud, while aggadic passages are considered worthy of study by the unlearned.

which the aggadic is thoroughly investigated here is completely new. Only very few talmudic passages are dealt with by Brod; but these passages are examined in respect to their content with a methodical seriousness that to the Talmud reader of the old school is totally alien, even incomprehensible, when applied to the "merely aggadic." In all modesty, the *am ha-aretz*[19] Brod becomes here a pioneer of a new method in the ancient domain of talmudic studies. Issues that hitherto only the preacher, and in more recent times at best the historian, had considered worthy of detailed attention are now taken completely seriously with regard to their content, one is almost tempted to say: with halakhic seriousness. Before the eyes of a generation returning home to the old book with a new attitude, there now lies not simply the old book, but also a renewed, rejuvenated one.

Manifest here is the strength of apologetic thinking, which brings about what naive thinking never could. Yet, here also the danger takes effect. As Brod discovers in Judaism the things that lift him beyond the living needs of his thinking, he is similarly, all-too-similarly prepared to discover in them the "specifically Jewish," and he does not pose to himself the question whether the remedy that he discovers for his human need is not just—as human as the need, and whether Judaism has a part in it only by virtue of its participation in—the human. Should not the restriction of the human to that which is specific to us, which is certainly necessary and blessed, and the restriction of the universal to that which is proper to us, not have more easily led to a coloration, which is certainly likewise necessary and also likewise blessed, of that light which, dazzlingly encompassing all colors, has risen for the human species? In Christianity, Brod himself sees very clearly where the point of this restriction is located: in the narrowing of divine grace's unlimited possibility of finding its way to the human, by means of the one dogmatically correct way of the experience of Christ. This is indeed correct; and in the fact that Judaism does not know, is not allowed to know, such a binding of divine grace—even if it is, as for the Christian, a binding to its own greatest deed—lies the greatest strength of Judaism; here it was permitted to preserve for its children the heavenly wine it pressed, unadulterated in the most primordial fire. Yet Brod misses the point which he could already have noticed in his story of Simeon ben Yoḥai[20]

---

19. In rabbinic literature, *am ha-aretz* (literally: people of the land) at first signifies someone whose observance of tithing laws is unreliable and later comes to signify an ignoramus with respect to Jewish law.

20. Simeon bar Yoḥai, rabbi of the mid-second century C.E.

and the remarkable "institution"[21] which he finally establishes: where this point of restriction lies for Judaism. In faith, we may be unconditioned; God does not prescribe the way of miracles for Judaism; but He does prescribe the way of His action to the human being; here, Judaism is not unconditioned but rather restricted to the one condition of the law. That the circle of this condition is cast so enormously wide that it hardly intersects with any conceivable circles of the world and its actions, changes the fact that it is a restriction of action as little as the enormous bearing of the Christian experience of Christ, which potentially can touch all human experiences, changes the fact that it is a narrowing of faith. And actually what Brod has to say about the law remains completely at the nationalistically agitated surface of the problem, although his attitude toward it is well-meaning and receptive, because of the general antiliberal atmosphere of today's generation of intellectuals. And thus it is that exactly where his book descends into the depths, it reaches a central point to which the title question with its oppositions can no longer follow and where what he pronounces in the name of his and our Judaism is true only in an ultimate sense, but not in a penultimate sense.

III

In one passage of his book, Brod sweeps "the humane mediocrities of a Baeck and a Lazarus" from his table with one of those broad gestures for which a confessional book may allow.[22] One senses that, under the

---

21. Brod, *Paganism*, 97–104, tells the story of Simeon bar Yoḥai, based on Babylonian Talmud, Shabbat, 33b–34a. Bar Yoḥai disparaged Roman contributions to everyday life, was denounced to the Roman government, and hid in a cave with his son for twelve years. Informed by the prophet Elijah of the emperor's death, they emerged, but when they saw people engaged in everyday activities, they burned them with their gaze and were divinely commanded to return to the cave. One year later, they reemerged, and this time bar Yoḥai undertook to make an improvement to everyday life in gratitude for his miraculous salvation. For Brod, this story is the illustration *par excellence* of Judaism's character, for bar Yoḥai transcended the world-denial of the Christian saint and achieved the level of the Jewish saint who perceives the miraculous possibility of politics.

22. Moritz Lazarus (1824–1903), author of *Ethik des Judentums* (Ethics of Judaism), 2 vols., (Frankfurt am Main: Kauffmann, 1898–1911), partially trans. Henrietta Szold (Philadelphia: Jewish Publication Society of America, 1900–1).

pressure of his own thinking, he has not found the quiet to read what has been thought before him. Even of Lazarus the harsh judgment—or may I speak for once for our, my own as well as Brod's, generation: the harsh prejudice?—does not hold true; his book is, as by the way was already shown by the vigorous attack that Hermann Cohen had directed against it when his Kantianism was in full bloom,[23] better than its reputation, which is perpetuated here by Brod, too. But with respect to what concerns Baeck completely, I might apply to Brod—and again, in memory of a former prejudice, to myself—here the Goethean sarcastic aphorism: *"Pereant, qui ante nos nostra dixerunt."*[24] For, on the one hand, in outer as well as inner form, a greater contrast can hardly be imagined than between Brod's confessional book and Baeck's *The Essence of Judaism*. While in the former one sees throughout the path that has led to the goal, and the attractiveness of the book depends not least on the way it obliges its reader to accompany it on this road, in the latter the scaffolds have been dismantled without a trace, and only the completed building offers itself to the gaze.

So much for the form. In content, on the other hand, the two books are as similar as two books of such different form can possibly be. Baeck's book too is, after all, apologetically occasioned. The part that Christian speech and communication in his social circle and his circle of friends have obviously played for Brod was assumed for Baeck, in a significant way, by a literary event: Harnack's *What is Christianity?*[25] This book, which with the usual learned lack of misgivings depicts a Judaism whose only possibility of existence is that it forms the dark

---

23. Cohen criticized Lazarus in "Das Problem der jüdischen Sittenlehre: Eine Kritik von Lazarus' Ethik des Judentums" ("The Problem of the Jewish Doctrine of Ethics: A Critique of Lazarus' *Ethics of Judaism*"), *Monatschrift für Geschichte und Wissenschaft des Judentums* 43 (1899): 385–400, 433–49, reprinted in *Hermann Cohens Jüdische Schriften* (*Hermann Cohen's Jewish Writings*), III (Berlin: Schwetske, 1924; reprint, New York: Arno, 1980), 1–35.

24. Von Goethe, *Werke*, XII, 480: "Let those perish who have said what is ours before us."

25. In 1899–1900, Adolf von Harnack (1851–1930), an influential Christian theologian, delivered a series of lectures at the University of Berlin, published as *Das Wesen des Christentums* (The essence of Christianity) (Leipzig: Hinrichs, 1900) and translated by Thomas Bailey Saunders as *What is Christianity?* (New York: Putnam, 1901). For Baeck's initial response, see "Harnack's Lectures on the Essence of Christianity" in *Jewish Perspectives on Christianity*, ed. Fritz A. Rothschild (New York: Crossroad, 1990), 42–45. *Das Wesen des Judentums*, published four years later, was still in part a response to Harnack.

background for the Christian light, and which without this function would have to crumble with a rattle because of the inherent improbability of its life, has caused Baeck, not, however, against Harnack, but for itself and for us, to depict Judaism, as it is, not as a foil for something else but rather in itself, in its own roundedness and fullness. And what he depicts, not with the passion of the discoverer and confessor but rather—especially in the second edition, in which the book has first grown to its full inner and outer weight—with the deep calm love of the intimate servant at home in the whole wide mansion of Judaism, is exactly what has shaken Brod: freedom's origination from grace, or, put in Baeck-like terms: the origination of the commandment from mystery, the earthly miracle, or, again put in Baeck-like terms, the great paradox.[26] Brod depicts this paradox in the strong spare dramatics of his book of confession and life; Baeck depicts this in the tireless and never tiring dialectics of his book of knowing and essence, which collects manifold material within a narrow space. It will remain a matter of taste whether one prefers the content to be mediated to oneself in the purely ecstatic form of the former or in the purely classical form of the latter— perhaps even a matter of the maturity of one's own way of knowing; in the life of knowing, after all, the time of blossoming is certainly no more worthless than the time of fruition.

As the two books are similar in what they deliver, they are also remarkably similar in their weaknesses. What has been said above about Brod's treatment of Christianity could be repeated almost verbatim for Baeck, too. If this does not come to the fore in *The Essence of Judaism*, with its only incidental treatment of Christianity, as clearly as in Brod, then it does so all the more in the more recent publication *Romantic Religion*,[27] where at best it is mitigated by a certain methodological

---

26. Baeck emphasizes the paradoxical unity of divine revelation and human deed as characteristic of Judaism. See, e.g., Baeck, *Essence of Judaism*, 124.

27. Baeck's "Romantische Religion" (Romantic Religion) was first published in *Festschrift zum 50 jahrigen Bestehen der Hochschule für die Wissenschaft des Judentums in Berlin* (*Volume in Celebration of 50 Years of Existence of the Academy for the Science of Judaism in Berlin*) (Berlin: Philo, 1922) and was then revised as part of Baeck, *Aus drei Jahrtausenden: Wissenschaftliche Untersuchungen und Abhandlungen zur Geschichte der jüdischen Glauben* (*From Three Millennia: Scientific Investigations and Treatises on the History of the Jewish Faith*) (Tübingen: Mohr, 1958). See "Romantic Religion" in *Judaism and Christianity: Essays by Leo Baeck*, trans. Walter Kaufmann (Philadelphia: Jewish Publication Society, 1958), 189–292, and in *Jewish Perspectives on Christianity*, 56–91.

awareness which deliberately poses the problem as a definite abstraction, whereby the danger for the reader does not, of course, become smaller.

It follows likewise from the related fundamental constellation of both books that both must break down before the problem of the Law. Again it seems to me, however, that the superior consciousness of the problem is under Baeck's control. Yet Baeck sees, as little as Brod, that the critical point lies here, where the essence of Judaism recognized by him is more *essence* of Judaism than essence of *Judaism*. And it will perhaps happen to him, as happened to Brod at this point where the acting emerges from the believing, that the Christian reader follows him here completely without hesitation, while the Jewish reader comes to a standstill. The fact that nearby, although by the way and not with central weight, very fine things are said by Baeck about the Law, is just as much to be noted as the fact that the liberal rabbi, especially in the second edition, has said things about the Jewish people and Jewish history of a profundity hardly ever reached by what the Zionist poet says about it. Perhaps the Jewish present shows no symptom richer in hope than this exchange of roles.

IV

Why is the word "apologetics" particularly afflicted with such a bad odor? In this regard, it is probably similar to the apologetic profession *par excellence*, that of the lawyer. Against him, too, exists widely the prejudice that considers lying, as it were, his legitimate task. It may be that a certain professional routine appears to justify this prejudice. And yet, defending can be one of the noblest human occupations. Namely, if it goes to the very ground of things and souls and, renouncing the petty devices of a lie, ex-culpates[28] with the truth, nothing but the truth. In this broad sense, literary apologetics can also defend. It would then embellish nothing, still less evade a vulnerable point, but would rather make precisely the most endangered points the basis of the defense. In a word: it would defend the whole, not this or that particular. It would not at all be a defense in the usual sense, but rather a candid exposition, yet not of some cause, but rather of one's own [self]. To what degree the two

---

28. Rosenzweig hyphenates *ent-schuldigt* (ex-culpates), perhaps to indicate that the noble sort of defense with which he is concerned does not merely fend off attacks but removes guilt or culpability.

reviewed books approximate this lofty concept of apologetics may well be gathered from what has been said.

They are both answers to attacks. They have let their theme be determined by the attack. The theme is the very essence. One could think that it would now come to its highest awareness. But precisely the apologetic character of the thinking prevents that. Insofar as the thinker looks into his innermost [being], he indeed sees this innermost, but for this reason he is still far from seeing—himself. For he himself is not his innermost but is to the same extent also his outermost, and above all the bond that binds his innermost to his outermost, the street on which both associate reciprocally with each other. Yet, without further circumspection, he equates his innermost with his self and does not sense that his innermost, the more it is innermost, is the innermost of *every* human being. Thus, although he means himself, he speaks of the human being, of all [human beings]. And thus his self, the binding of the elements of humankind into the bundle that he himself is, remains a mystery to him. Apologetic thinking does not cross this barrier. He is denied the ultimate strength of knowing as he is spared the ultimate suffering of knowing. For ultimate knowing no longer defends, ultimate knowing adjudicates.

VIII
"The New Thinking"
(1925)

At its time [of publication], I released the *Star of Redemption* without a foreword. I was alarmed by the traces of the customary philosophers' forewords with their cackling after the laid egg and their impolite lampooning of the reader, who had not yet perpetrated anything—who indeed could not have read the book yet. Even the placid Kant did not escape this danger, let alone his loud successors up to Schopenhauer. The following pages are not meant to make up for the mistake that was at that time luckily circumvented, nor should they ever be reprinted at the beginning or end of future editions of the book. They are the response to the echo which the book has aroused in the four years since its publication. Not [a response] to its rejection; that would not be my concern. But rather, precisely to the acceptance it has found. Where no door has been opened at all, one has lost nothing. But where one has been received kindly and with respect, after one has enjoyed hospitality for a while, as prescribed by a conventional introduction and, accordingly, in the forms of a conventional courtesy, one may, nay, with all decency one must, unmask one's face some day, at an opportune hour, and thus call upon the critical instant where the conventional relation becomes the personal—or not. In the full consciousness that, with this occasionally necessary act of truth, one risks, of course, amenities of social relations that one has hitherto enjoyed.

Actually the book owes the acceptance it has received until now—if I abstract from the small circle of those who could have written the book just as well or even better than I—entirely to such a "social confusion": it was bought, and—more seriously—read, as a "Jewish book."[1] It is

---

1. The Jewish character of the *Star* was a delicate matter for Rosenzweig. He insisted on it but also found that it exposed him to uncomfortable misunderstandings. In a letter to Hans Ehrenberg (1883–1958) in 1919, *Briefe* II, 637, he wrote, "I would have to let the *Star* appear as a Jewish book, *even if* it were 'just as Christian as Jewish' — which it actually is not." Similarly, in a letter to Mar-

109

considered—when it is not read and, even worse, as has been said, when it has been read—as a book of that part of the Jewish youth which by various paths seeks to find its way back to the old law. That may very well be right about me personally. What the Pharisees of the Talmud and the saints of the Church have known—that man's understanding reaches as far as his doings—apparently, to the honor of mankind, also applies to becoming understood. But, from this prejudgment on the part of the readers, the book encounters a number of—unnecessary—difficulties and the buyers [encounter] a—very necessary—disappointment. The following pages would like to try, on the one hand, to lessen those difficulties for the readers a little, and on the other hand, to assuage the disappointment of the buyers, who believed [themselves] to have purchased a nice Jewish book and afterward had to discover, like one of the earliest critics, that it was by no means meant "for the daily use of every member in every family."

I cannot describe the *Star of Redemption* any more accurately than this critic has done with pregnant brevity: it is indeed not meant for the daily use of every member of every family. It is in general not a "Jewish book," at least not in the sense that the buyers, who were so angry with me, think of a Jewish book; for while it deals with Judaism, it deals with it no more comprehensively than it deals with Christianity, and barely more comprehensively than it deals with Islam. Nor does it claim to be a philosophy of religion. How could it do this, given that the word "religion" does not even occur in it! Rather, it is merely a system of philosophy.

Nevertheless, [it is] a system of a philosophy that gives the reader, the expert as well as the lay reader, the fullest right to be displeased— namely, a philosophy which does not want to bring about a mere "Copernican Revolution" of thinking, after which he who has performed it sees all things upside down, although they are still the same things he had seen before, rather a philosophy which wants to bring about the total renewal of thinking.[2] I would not say this if I had to say it

---

tin Buber (1878–1965) in August 1919, *Briefe* II, 644, he expressed his desire to publish the book through a press that would mark the book "externally as that which it ought to be, according to my intention, and [as that which it] has also hopefully become: a Jewish book." However, in a letter to Hans Ehrenberg in September 1921, *Briefe* II, 720, he protested that, "I am as little a specialist in Judaica as Max Weber (what is Jewish is my *method*, not my object)."

2. Immanuel Kant (1726–1804) is often said to have proposed a "Copernican revolution or turn" in philosophy. He did not himself use that phrase, but others have used it on the basis of the analogy Kant drew between his own proposal for setting philosophy on the secure path of a science not by assuming, like previ-

only of my book and not of the thinking, which I do not imagine myself to have invented or even to be its sole teacher in the present. Rather, healthy human understanding[3] has always thought in this way, and among contemporary thinkers there are more who think in this manner than Überweg-Heintze[4] can dream of. What is said here is certainly not a recommendation for the book but, rather, more likely the opposite. For neither the expert nor the lay person wants novelties. The former is glad if he can continue in the way that he has learned—otherwise he would not be an expert; the latter does not want, if some day he "takes an interest in philosophy," to be served a new and revolutionary philosophy, but rather the "right" one, the "philosophy of the present"—otherwise he wouldn't be a lay person. And since the reading public consists of these two human groups, I am permitted to say what I said without fear of having recommended my own book.

According to a hallowed custom, a system of philosophy consists of a logic, an ethics, an aesthetics, and a philosophy of religion.[5] The *Star of*

---

ous philosophers, that our cognition must conform to its objects, but rather by assuming that the objects must conform to our cognition, and Copernicus' proposal to solve the ancient problems of astronomy not by assuming that the celestial bodies revolve around the observer, but rather by assuming that the observer revolves around the celestial bodies. See Kant, *Critique of Pure Reason*, trans. Werner Pluhar (Indianapolis: Hackett, 1996), Bxvi. Georg Wilhelm Friedrich Hegel (1770–1831), in the second chapter of his *Phenomenology of Spirit*, trans. A. V. Miller (Oxford: Oxford University Press, 1977), criticized philosophical views that supplement the world of healthy human understanding with an inverted world or world turned upside down.

3. The German phrase, *der gesunde Menschenverstand*, is sometimes translated as "sound common sense." Here it has been translated literally so that the resonances of "healthy" and "sick" in Rosenzweig's writing may be appreciated.

4. Friedrich Überweg (1826–71) was the author of a standard textbook on the history of philosophy, *Grundriss der Geschichte der Philosophie* (Outline of the history of philosophy) (Berlin: E. S. Mittler, 1867–68), which went through many editions. Editions published after Überweg's death were indexed, reworked, and edited by Max Heinze (1835–1909), and the book continued to be updated after Heinze's death. Thus, Rosenzweig is referring to what was, at the time, well established as the standard German work on the history of philosophy, including the present day.

5. Thus, for example, the system of Hermann Cohen (1842–1918) comprised, in order of publication, a logic, an ethics, an aesthetics, and, finally, a philosophy of religion. See Cohen, *System der Philosophie: Erster Teil: Logik der reinen Erkenntnis* (System of philosophy: First part: Logic of pure cognition); *System der Philosophie: Zweiter Teil: Ethik des reinen Willen* (System of philosophy:

Redemption breaks with this custom, despite its three volumes—the joint publication in one volume occurred only because of difficulties at the publisher at that time, and, according to the publisher's explicit promise, this will give way again to the original three volumes from the second edition on. However, with the exception of the fourth ingredient of a system of ordered punches, the *Star of Redemption* contains all the others: the logic primarily in Volume 1, Book 2, in Volume 2, Book 1, and in Volume 3, Book 3; the ethics in Volume 1, Book 3, in Volume 2, Books 2 and 3, and in Volume 3, Book 1; the aesthetics in all books of the first and second [volumes] and in Volume 3, Book 2. But, as is evident from the curious distribution, the systematic principle of this philosophy is another one. Even the title attempts to hint at precisely this principle by combining the astronomical images of the three volume headings—elements [*Elemente*], course [*Bahn*], form [*Gestalt*]. And just this transition from the customary to the new way of posing the question is effected by the formulations in the first volume, which quickly gained notoriety. To these [formulations] and to this [volume], I now turn.

The first pages of philosophical books are met by the reader with special reverence. He believes that they are to be the basis for all that follows. Therefore, he also thinks that it would suffice to refute them, in order to have refuted the whole. Hence the enormous interest in Kant's doctrine of space and time in the form in which he developed it at the beginning of the *Critique*;[6] hence the comical attempts to "refute"

Second part: Ethics of pure will); *System der Philosophie: Dritter Teil: Ästhetik des reinen Gefühls* (System of philosophy: Third part: Aesthetics of pure feeling) (Berlin: Bruno Cassirer, 1902–12; reprinted in *Hermann Cohen: Werke* VI–IX, Hildesheim: Georg Olms, 1977–); *Der Begriff der Religion im System der Philosophie* (The concept of religion in the system of philosophy) (Giessen: Töpelman, 1915; reprinted in *Werke* X); and *Die Religion der Vernunft aus den Quellen des Judentums* (The religion of reason out of the sources of Judaism) (Leipzig: G. Fock, 1919), re-edited by Bruno Strauss as *Religion der Vernunft aus den Quellen des Judentums* (Religion of reason out of the sources of Judaism) (Frankfurt am Main: Kaufmann, 1929; reprint, Wiesbaden: Fourier, 1988). Rosenzweig addresses the significance of the change of title in "Transposed Fronts," translated in this volume, Chapter 10.

6. Kant's *Critique of Pure Reason* is divided into two units, the Transcendental Doctrine of Elements and the Transcendental Doctrine of Method. His doctrine of space and time is given primarily in the Transcendental Aesthetic, Part 1 of the Transcendental Doctrine of Elements.

Hegel with reference to the first triple-step of his *Logic*,[7] and Spinoza with reference to his definitions.[8] And hence the helplessness of the *general reader* before philosophical books.[9] He thinks they must be "especially logical," by which he means the dependence of each subsequent sentence on each preceding one, such that when the famous one stone is pulled out, "the whole comes tumbling down." In truth, this is nowhere less the case than in philosophical books. Here, a sentence does not follow from its predecessor, but, much more likely, from its successor. It will be of little help to whomever has not understood a sentence or paragraph if, in his conscientious belief that he may leave nothing behind uncomprehended, he reads it over and over again, or even starts once more from the beginning. Philosophical books defy the methodological *ancien régime* strategy that thinks it may not leave any unconquered fortresses in the rear; they want to be conquered in a Napoleonic manner, in a bold advance on the enemy's main force, after whose defeat the small border fortresses will fall on their own. Therefore, he who fails to understand something may expect enlightenment most certainly if he courageously reads on. The reason for this rule is that thinking and writing are not the same, which is difficult to accept for the beginner and, as the cases given above demonstrate, for some nonbeginners as well. In thinking, one blow actually strikes a thousand relations; in writing, these thousand relations must be neatly arranged on a string of a thousand lines. Schopenhauer said that his whole book

---

7. The first chapter of Volume 1, Book 1, Section 1 of Hegel's *Science of Logic* seeks to begin without any presuppositions whatsoever, by means of a "triple step" in which being is at first considered purely as that which is immediately before us when we begin our quest for purely logical knowledge; then being is acknowledged as the negation of nothing, which contradicts the immediacy assumed in the first moment and which seems to contradict the presuppositionlessness sought by Hegel; finally, the contradiction is overcome by positing becoming as logic's subject matter, of which being and nothing are abstractions, so that the beginning of logic is indeed mediated by its result but nevertheless succeeds in being mediated by no presupposition whatsoever. See Hegel, *Science of Logic*, trans. A. V. Miller (Atlantic Highlands, N. J.: Humanities Press, 1989), 67–105.

8. Baruch Spinoza (1632–1677) begins *The Ethics*, trans. Samuel Shirley (Indianapolis: Hackett, 1992) with a list of six definitions. Indeed, given his use of the synthetic, geometrical method, each of the five books of the *Ethics* begins with a set of definitions.

9. Rosenzweig uses the English phrase, "the general reader," in the original German text.

was meant to convey only a single thought, which, however, he could not convey more concisely than in the whole book.[10] Therefore, if any philosophical book is to be worth reading, it surely requires that one does not understand the beginning, or, at the very least, [that one] understands it wrongly. For otherwise the thought that it conveys will hardly be worth rethinking; since one already knows what "it is supposed to be driving at" at the beginning of its argument, one obviously already knows the thought. All this is valid for books only; they alone can be written and read without any concern for the time passing. Speaking and listening fall under different laws. Obviously only actual speaking and listening, not that which insults itself by calling itself [a] "lecture," where the listener must forget that he has a mouth and at best becomes a writing hand. But for books, it is valid indeed.

Consequently, where this main battle of understanding is fought, where the whole becomes surveyable at a glance, cannot be predicted; in general, already well before the last page, but scarcely before the middle of the book; and certainly hardly at exactly the same point for two readers. At least if they are independently minded readers [Selbstleser], and not readers who, from sheer learnedness, already know what is in a book before the first word and who, from sheer stupidity, still do not know [what it says] even after the last [word]. In the case of older books, the aforementioned reader-virtues were mostly distributed to two distinct types of men, say professors and students; in the case of newer books, they are happy to stand in personal union.

With this, we would be back at the *Star of Redemption* again. Everything just said about the reasonable way to read the beginnings of philosophical books is valid for its first volume. Above all, then: Hurry! No tarrying! The important [thing] comes first! And the difficult [thing], say the concept of nothingness, the "nothingnesses," which here seems to be only a methodological auxiliary concept, first reveals its contentful significance only in the short concluding paragraph of the volume, and its ultimate meaning only in the concluding book of the whole. What is said here is nothing other than a *reductio ad absurdum* and, at the same

---

10. In the preface to the first (1819) edition of *Die Welt als Wille und Vorstellung*, ed. Arthur Hübscher (Leipzig: F. A. Brockhaus, 1972), trans. E. F. J. Payne as *The World as Will and Representation* (Indian Hills, Colo.: Falcon's Wing Press, 1958), vol. I, xx, Arthur Schopenhauer (1788–1860) writes, "I propose to state here how this book is to read, in order that it may be thoroughly understood. What is to be imparted by it is a single thought. Yet in spite of all my efforts, I have not been able to find a shorter way of imparting that thought than the whole of this book."

time, a rescue of the old philosophy. Perhaps I [will] make what the first volume intends clearest to the reader if I attempt to explain this apparent paradox. All philosophy asked about "essence." It is by this question that it distinguishes itself from the unphilosophical thinking of healthy human understanding. For the latter does not ask about what a thing "really" [*eigentlich*] is. It is sufficient for it to know that a chair is a chair; it does not ask whether, say, it might really [*eigentlich*] be something entirely different. Philosophy asks exactly this when asking about essence. The world is by no means permitted to be the world, God by no means permitted to be God, man by no means permitted to be man, rather all must "really" be something totally different. If they were nothing else but actually only what they are, then philosophy—[heaven] forbid and forfend!—would ultimately be superfluous! At least a [kind of] philosophy which absolutely might ferret out something "entirely different."

Indeed, as far as my university knowledge suffices, this is what all previous philosophy wanted; and if I can trust my precise and self-sacrificing quarterly inspection of *Kant-Studien*,[11] then the ravens still fly around the mountain (still, unfortunately, finding young finches which, notwithstanding their beautiful bills, regrettably and successfully attempt to caw like them). As ever, the possibilities of the "reduction" of each one to the other are untiringly permutated, [possibilities] that, seen in large, seem to characterize the three epochs of European philosophy—cosmological antiquity, the theological Middle Ages, [and] anthropological modernity. In particular, of course, the darling idea of the modern era, the reduction to "the" I.[12] This reduction or "grounding" of experiences of the world and of God in the I that produces these

---

11. The philosophical journal *Kant-Studien* (Kant studies) was first published in 1897, edited by Hans Vaihinger (1852–1933), and is still published today. It became the official journal of the Kant-Gesellschaft (Kant Society), founded by Vaihinger in 1904. In a period when German philosophy was dominated by neo-Kantianism and was regarded as a central expression of German intellectual life, the society and its journal had a remarkable significance both within and beyond academic circles. According to Thomas E. Willey, *Back to Kant: The Revival of Kantianism in German Social and Historical Thought, 1860–1914* (Detroit: Wayne State University Press, 1978), 156: "Membership in the Kant Society included nearly all the Wilhelmine intellectual spectrum, from Ernst Cassirer to Elisabeth Förster-Nietzsche. Werner von Siemens, baron of Germany's electrical industry, held a lifetime membership."

12. Beginning with Gottfried Wilhelm Leibniz (1646–1716), German philosophers sought to philosophize about the occupier of the first-person perspective as such and thus found it necessary to depart from ordinary speech by speaking

experiences is even today so self-evident for scientific thought[13] that he who does not believe in this dogma, but rather prefers to reduce his experiences of the world—prefers to reduce the world and his experiences of God—to God, is simply not taken seriously. This philosophy takes reduction in general to be something so self-evident that if she takes the trouble to burn such a heretic, she accuses him only of a prohibited method of reduction, roasting him either as a "crass materialist" who has said: everything is world, or as an "ecstatic mystic" who has said: everything is God. That someone would not at all want to say: everything "is" . . ., does not enter her mind. But, in the "what-is?" question[14] directed at everything, lies the entire error of the answers. If an is-sentence is to be worthy of its utterance, then it must always introduce something new after the "is" which was not there before. Thus, if one asks such is-questions with respect to God and world, then one must not be surprised that the I shows up—what else is left over! Everything else, world and God, has already been introduced before the "is." And it is exactly the same if the pantheist and his associate, the mystic, discover that world and man are of divine "essence," or if the other firms, materialist and atheist, discover that man is only "nature's" product and God nothing but its reflection.

In truth, however, these three last and first objects of all philosophizing are onions that one may pare down as much as one wants—one will always encounter more onion skins and not something "entirely different." Only thinking necessarily falls into these errant ways by virtue of the altering force of the little word "is." Experience, no matter how deeply it may penetrate, discovers only the human in man, only worldliness in the

---

of "the I." This seemingly innocent — if awkward — move is sometimes said to be the first move down a slippery slope to a disastrously distorted conception of ordinary life.

13. The German word *Wissenschaft* denotes university-taught disciplines such as the humanities and philosophy and is not limited to those disciplines known in English as the natural and social sciences.

14. Socrates (c.470–399 B.C.E.) is sometimes said to have been the first to ask the question "What is *x*?" in the quest for a real definition or account of the essence of *x*. Certainly, Socrates' questions are portrayed by Plato (c.348–427 B.C.E.) as confusing his contemporaries, who often responded, like Euthyphro, not with a real definition but with an example or list of examples. Among other major philosophical developments, Plato's theory of ideas and Aristotle's (384–322 B.C.E.) theory of form and matter may be regarded as general attempts to answer the "What is *x*?" question. It is sometimes thought that Aristotle arrived at his list of categories by asking the "What is *x*?" question of an individual thing; its shape, color, location, and so forth.

world, only divinity in God. And only in God divinity, only in the world worldliness, and only in man the human. *Finis philosophiae?*[15] If it were, then so much the worse for philosophy! But I do not believe that it turns out so badly. Rather, at this point where philosophy would certainly be at an end with its thinking, experiential philosophy can begin.

In any case, that is the point of my first volume. The volume does not want to teach more than this: that none of the three great basic concepts of philosophical thinking can be reduced to another. In order to make this teaching have an impact, it is given in positive form: Thus it is not demonstrated that none of the concepts can be reduced to the two others, but rather, conversely, that each is to be reduced only to itself. Each is itself "essence," each itself substance, with all the metaphysical heaviness of this expression. If Spinoza, at the beginning of his work, passes on the scholastic concept of substance to the great Idealists of 1800— being in this respect the significant mediator between two epochs of European thought, precisely because he understood substance neither theologically like the epoch that had just passed by nor anthropologically like the coming epoch, but rather cosmologically-naturalistically, thereby rendering [substance] formal and also mutable—then he defines substance, famously (this impertinent word of the literati may stand here without the reader having to blush, for he usually knows the first sentences of philosophical books), as that which is in itself and is conceived through itself.[16] I could perhaps explain the intention of the difficult constructive parts of the three books of the first volume no better than if I say that there it is shown, for each of the three possible bearers of the "essence" concept, how it fulfills this definition in its special way. What I call "yes" corresponds to the *"in se esse"* ["being in itself"], what I call "no" to the *"per se percipi"* ["perceived in itself"] of the Spinozist definition.[17] Of course, not in such a way that it would now be roughly the same; in this entire essay, I give the reader of the book only pointers; if he wants to know what is in it, he must actually read it; that I cannot spare him.

---

15. Latin: The end of philosophy?

16. The definition of substance is the third definition at the beginning of Spinoza's *Ethics*, trans. Samuel Shirley (Indianapolis: Hackett, 1992), 31: "By substance I mean that which is in itself and is conceived through itself; that is, that the conception of which does not require the conception of another thing from which it has to be formed."

17. In fact, Spinoza defines "substance" as "that which is in itself and is conceived through itself [*per se concipi*]," not as that which is in itself and is perceived through itself (*per se percipi*). See previous note.

But in any case I believe that with what has just been said I have been able to describe the tendency of the first volume as well as one can if one is the author—i.e., certainly less well than a smart reader. To the question of essence there are only tautological answers. God is only divine, man only human, the world only worldly; one can drill shafts into them as deeply as one wants, one always finds the same again. And that holds for all three equally. The concept of God has no special status whatsoever. As *concept* of God, it is no more unattainable than the concepts of man and world. Conversely, the essence of man and the essence of the world—the essence!—are no more within reach than the essence—the essence!—of God. Of all of them we know equally much, and equally little: namely, everything and nothing. We know most precisely, know by the intuitive knowledge of experience, what God, what man, what world, taken for itself, is; if we did not know that, how could we talk about it, and, above all, how could we "reduce" some two of these to their respective other or deny the respective other two reductive possibilities! And we do not know at all and in any respect, by way of this deceptive, "transformative" knowledge of thinking, what else God is, the world is, and man is; if we knew that, how could that other intuitive knowledge persist over against such knowledge in such a way that it constantly coaxes us to ask this question and to engage in these reductions? Ghosts vanish at the cockcrow of knowledge; these ghosts never vanish. That we believe that one of these essentialities is closer to us, the other more remote, rests—like the connected misuse of the nonsensical words "immanent" and "transcendent"—on a confusion between the essentialities and the actualities of God, world, and man. Between those [actualities], there are closenesses and remotenesses, approaches and withdrawals; but these do not solidify into properties with substantial being, so that therefore God, for example, "would be" transcendent. No, rather, as essentialities, God, world, and man are equally transcendent in regard to each other and, as regards the actualities, we cannot say what they "are," but only that—however, this does not belong here.

But what do we know then about them besides and beyond this Everything and Nothing?[18] At least Something nevertheless, namely precisely what we mean by the words "divine," "human," and "worldly." To be sure, we mean thereby something entirely determinate, not interchangeable with one another. What then? Where do we find the three

---

18. Here Rosenzweig alludes to Friedrich Heinrich Jacobi's (1749–1814) argument that the rationalist philosopher's demand for an explanation of everything leads inexorably to Spinoza's monism, which leads in turn to nihilism. See Chapter 3.

essentialities, which are at the same time nonactual and intuitive, as these three adjectives separate them in their isolation from one another? Here, a second motif becomes visible, which is intertwined with the first, the logical-metaphysical, and which, in this interlinkage with the first motif, governs the structure of the first volume.

Where, then, are such essential forms, which indeed lack truth or vitality or actuality? A god who is not the true [God] and is not actual, a world which is not the vital [world] and is not true, humans who are not the actual [humans] and are not vital? [Forms] which know nothing and want nothing from one another, from both respective others? Shadows, then, which do not live in the same space with our actuality, our truth, and our lives, yet which haunt everything that happens in our space? The reader will find the answer if he consults his knowledge of Spengler.[19] Spengler's Apollonian culture comprises exactly the gods, worlds, and humans that are meant here. Spengler's concept of the Euclidean signifies exactly the essential separateness, the "transcendence" of one another, which has been described here. Except that, as always, Spengler interprets falsely what he has seen correctly. The mythical Olympus, the plastic cosmos, the tragic hero, are not done away with in virtue of [the fact] that they have been; they have not, in the strict sense of the word, "been" at all. When the actual [ancient] Greek prayed, he was certainly not heard by Zeus or Apollo but rather, of course, by God; nor did he live in the cosmos, but rather in the created world, whose sun, our sun, shone for Homer, too. And he was no hero of Attic tragedy, but rather a poor human like us. But although these three

19. Oswald Spengler (1880–1936) was the author of one of the most influential books of the post–First World War period, *Der Untergang des Abendlandes: Gestalt und Wirklichkeit* and *Der Untergang des Abendlandes: Welthistorischen Perspektiven* (München: C. H. Beck, 1918, 1922); trans. Charles Francis Atkinson as *The Decline of the West: Volume I: Form and Actuality* and *The Decline of the West: Volume II: Perspectives of World- History* (New York: Alfred A. Knopf, 1926, 1928). In Volume 1 (especially Chapters 2 and 6), Spengler distinguished between the Apollonian soul of Classical Culture, the Magian soul of Arabian Culture, and the Faustian soul of Modern Culture; and he interpreted these cultural differences as expressing themselves in different styles of mathematics, as well as in different aesthetic, cognitive, and religiophilosophical styles. Thus the Apollonian soul comprehended extension in terms of sensuously-present individual bodies, engaged in Euclidean geometry, and regarded mathematics as the theory of relations of the magnitudes, dimensions, and forms of bodies; whereas the Faustian soul comprehended extension in terms of abstract space, engaged in Cartesian geometry, and regarded mathematics as the theory of the limit.

forms were never actual, they are nonetheless the presupposition of all
our actuality. God is as alive as the gods of mythology; the created world
is as much actual, and as little mere "appearance," as the plastic, closed
finitudes in which the Greek believed himself to live, or [in which], as a
political creature, he wished to live, and which, as an artist, he created
around himself; the human to whom God speaks is as much the true
human and not at all or in any way a shell of ideals, like the hero of
tragedy in his rigid stubbornness. The spiritual forms which, in [all]
world history, were isolated and thus became visible only here, only in
Spengler's "Apollonian Culture," are contained in all life as its secret
and invisible presuppositions, regardless of whether this life is older or
younger, regardless of whether it itself has become historical form or
whether it has remained historically invisible life. This is the classical-
ness of classical antiquity—insofar as the first volume of the *Star* seeks
to set out the elemental contents of experience, purified from the ad-
mixtures with which thinking might occupy itself in them, it has to become, exactly in this, a philosophy of paganism. [The first volume] re-
constructs [paganism] itself out of historical forms, according to the
constructive derivation of the three "substances," whereby things go
badly for the favorites of modernity, the "spiritual religions of the Far
East."

Paganism is therefore in no way a mere religiophilosophical child's
bogyman for adults, as which it was employed by the orthodoxy of former centuries and, comically enough, again recently by Max Brod's
well-known book.[20] Rather, [paganism] is—no more and no less than
the truth. The truth, indeed, in its elemental, invisible, unrevealed
form. So that in general whenever it [paganism] wants to be not elemental, but rather the whole; not invisible, but rather form; not secret,
but rather revelation;—it then becomes a lie. But as element and mystery within the whole, the visible and the revealed, it is everlasting. Indeed, as everlasting as the great objects, the "substances" of thinking,
within the actual, nonobjective, and nonsubstantial experience.

For experience knows nothing of objects; it remembers, it lives, it
hopes and fears. At best, the content of memory could be understood as
an object; [but] then it would be precisely an understanding, and not
the content itself. For [the content] is not remembered as my object. It
is nothing but a prejudice of the last three hundred years that, in all
knowing, the "I" must be present; thus that I could not see a tree unless
"I" saw it. In truth, my I is only present if it—is present; for instance, if I

---

20. For Rosenzweig's view of Brod, see "Apologetic Thinking," translated in
this volume, Chapter 7.

have to emphasize that I see the tree because someone else does not see it, then, certainly, the tree is in connection with me in my knowing. But in all other cases I know only of the tree and nothing else; and the usual philosophical assertion of the I's omnipresence in all knowing distorts the content of this knowledge. Thus, experience does not experience the things, which certainly become visible as ultimate matters of fact[21] through thinking about experience; however, what it experiences, it experiences in [an] these matters of fact. And that is why it is so important for a clean and complete presentation of experience to have set out these matters of fact purely and to have opposed thinking's tendency to confuse [experience] in advance. These matters of fact are the cast list, the theater program, which, to be sure, is not a part of the drama itself, but which it does one good to have read in advance. Or, put differently: [they are like] the "once upon a time" with which all fairy tales begin; yet they only begin in that fashion, for in the course of the fairy tale and in the course of its narration, it can never happen again. The latter is indeed the more accurate simile. For if the first volume had answered the old question of philosophy: "what is?" and had done it in such a way that afterward the until-here-and-no-further of experience was called out to philosophical thinking's drive to unity, then experienced actuality itself could now be presented in the second volume. [But] not by means of the old philosophy, which does not reach beyond the usually false but, at best, correctly answered question concerning the "being"—and the actual "is" not. Thus, the second volume's method will have to be another, precisely the [method] of our recent simile: a method of narration. In his preface to his ingenious fragment *The Ages of the World*, Schelling prophesied a narrative philosophy.[22] The second volume attempts to provide it.

What, then, does it mean to narrate? He who tells something does not want to say how it "really" [*eigentlich*] was but, rather, how it actually

---

21. On "matters of fact," see Chapter 4, notes 45 and 47.

22. In the introductions to the 1811 and 1813 drafts of *Die Weltalter* (The world-ages), Schelling described the human as constituted by a silent dialogue between a supramundane principle that is original knowledge of creation and a lesser principle that yearns for knowledge, "Thus, according to its nature, everything known is narrated [*erzählt*]." When philosophy succeeds, it imitates the inner conversation or narrative constitutive of the human. See *Die Weltalter. Fragmente. In den Urfassungen von 1811 und 1813*, ed. Manfred Schröter (München: C. H. Beck, 1946; reprint, 1966), 4–5, 113–4, trans. Jason M. Wirth as *The Ages of the World* (Albany: SUNY Press, 2000), xxxvii.

came about. Even though in his well-known definition concerning his scientific intentions, the great German historian[23] used the former word rather than the latter word, he means it thus. The narrator never wants to show that it was really quite different—it is precisely the criterion of a bad, concept-obsessed or sensationalist historian to go for that—; rather, he wants to show how this and that—which is in every mouth as a concept or a name, such as the Thirty Years' War or the Reformation—really happened. For him too, something merely essential—a name or a concept—dissolves, but not into something equally only essential, rather into its own actuality, more precisely its own actualization. He will barely form is-sentences at all and, as already said, he will use even was-sentences at most at the beginning. Substantives, thus substance-words, occur in his narrative, it is true, but the interest does not lie in them, but rather in the verb, the time-word.[24]

That is to say, time becomes entirely actual to him. Not that what happens, happens in it, but rather that it, it itself happens. The sequence of the three books of the first volume was totally contingent; each of the other four possibilities [of arranging them] would have been equally possible. Essence wants to know nothing of time. Now, in the middle volume, the sequence becomes not merely important, but rather is the really important [matter] which is supposed to be communicated. It is already itself the new thinking of which I spoke at the beginning. If, say, the old [thinking] addressed the problem whether God is transcendent or immanent, then the new [thinking] attempts to show how and when He turns from the distant into the near God, and again from the near into the distant. Or, if the old philosophy establishes the determinism/ indeterminism alternative, then the new [philosophy] follows, say, the path of the act—out of the conditionedness of the character and the pulling underbrush of motives, by means of the one shining moment of grace of choice, toward a must which is beyond all freedom—and thus, overcomes the fluctuations of that alternative

---

23. Leopold von Ranke (1795–1886), the father of critical historical methodology in Germany, used this famous phrase in the preface to the first (1824) edition of his book, *Histories of the Latin and Germanic Nations*. See Ranke, *Sämmtliche Werke* (Leipzig, 1873–90), XXIII, v–viii; and the translation by Wilma A. Iggers in Georg Iggers and Konrad von Moltke, eds., *The Theory and Practice of History: Leopold von Ranke* (Indianapolis: Bobbs-Merrill, 1973), 135–38.

24. Rosenzweig's point is that the different tenses of verbs are the linguistic expressions of temporality in ordinary speech. In what follows, the German word *Zeit* is translated either as "tense" or as "time," depending on the context.

according to which man is compelled to view himself either as a dressed-up piece of the world or to "be" a disguised god. In effect, the new philosophy does nothing else but make the "method" of healthy human understanding into the method of scientific thinking. Wherein, then, lies the difference between healthy human understanding and sick human understanding which, exactly like the old philosophy, the philosophy of "philosophical astonishment"—astonishment means standstill[25]—sinks its teeth into something that it will not let go before it "has" it in its entirety? [Healthy human understanding] can wait, can keep on living, has no "idée fixe;" advice comes when the time comes. This secret is the whole wisdom of the new philosophy. It teaches, to speak with Goethe, the "understanding at the right time"—

Why is the truth so woefully
Removed? To the deepest ground banned?
None understands at the right time! If we
But understood at the right time, how near and broad
The truth would be, how lovely and mild![26]

The new thinking knows, just like the age-old thinking of healthy human understanding, that it cannot cognize independently of time—which until now has been the highest mantle of glory in which philosophy draped itself. As little as one can begin a conversation with the end, or a war with a peace treaty (which pacifists certainly might like), or life with death—but rather, for better or worse, one must learn to wait actively or passively until the time is ripe, and one is permitted to skip not a single moment—so knowledge too is, at every moment, bound to this very moment and cannot make [that moment's] past not past, or its future not future. This holds for everyday things, and everyone recognizes it. Everyone knows that, say, for a treating physician, the treatment is present, the illness past, and the death-certification future, and that it

---

25. "*Staunen heisst Stillsehen.*" According to *Grimms Wörterbuch* (Leipzig: S. Hirzel, 1854–1971; reprint, München: Deutscher Taschenbuch, 1984), XVII, 1177–78, the verb *staunen* was introduced into literary German from the Swiss by the poet Haller in 1730; in Swiss usage, *staunen* could mean "*still gedankensvoll oder gedankenslos dastehen*" (standing there still, either full or empty of thought). Similarly, in English, "to be astonished" may be related to "to be stunned," although the second edition of the *Oxford English Dictionary* (Oxford: Clarendon Press, 1989), 729, considers the connection "doubtful."

26. Johann Wolfgang von Goethe (1749–1832), "Hikmet Nameh," *West-östlicher Divan* (Western-eastern divan), *Werke*, II, 55.

would make no sense if, out of the whimsical idea of timeless knowledge, he wanted to try to eliminate knowledge and experience from the diagnosis, audacity and stubbornness from the therapy, and fear and hope from the prognosis. No one who is making a purchase seriously believes that what he sees before, colored by his desire to buy, will look the same to him later when he regrets having bought it. But this holds for the ultimate and highest [things] too, which are generally believed to be knowable only timelessly. What God has done, what He is doing, and what He will do; what has happened to the world, what will happen to it, what happens to man, what he will do—all this cannot be disconnected from its temporality, in such a way that one could know the coming kingdom of God as one knows the created creation, or that one might regard the creation as one may regard the kingdom of the future. Just as little may man have the lightning flash of always only present experience—which is always only present—carbonized into the past, and just as little [may man] expect [this lightning flash] from the future, since it is always only present, and to wait for it is the surest means to prevent its striking. And just as the human action is action only as long as it is still outstanding and, if executed, only a mere something that has happened, indistinguishable from anything else [that has happened].

Equally noninterchangeable are the tenses of actuality. Just as every single event has its present, its past, and its future, without which it is not understood at all or is understood only in a distorted way, actuality as a whole also has its past and its future, namely an everlasting past and an eternal future. To know God, world, and man means to know what in these tenses of actuality they do or what happens to them, what they do to each other and what occurs by one another. The separation of their "being" is here presupposed for, if they were not separated, they could not interact. If the other were "in its deepest ground" the same as I, as Schopenhauer wants it,[27] I could not love him to any degree, for I

---

27. See, e.g., *The World as Will and Representation*, 6, where Schopenhauer defends his idealism against the objection that, just as I know my existence to be independent of another's representation of me, so too the existence of objects in general is independent of their representation: "That other being, whose object I am now considering my person to be, is not absolutely *the subject* but is in the first instance a knowing individual. Therefore, if he too did *not* exist, in fact, even if there existed in general no other knowing being except myself, this would still by no means be the elimination of the *subject* in whose representation alone all objects exist. For I myself am in fact that *subject*, just as is every knowing being." Thus the deepest ground of reality is not a particular subject, but the subject that every knowing being is.

would be loving only myself. Or if God were "in me" or "merely my loftier self"—an assistant hairdresser's dogma, which must be subscribed to at admission into some youth groups, along with the other [dogma], namely that He is the magnificent All—this would constitute not merely an unnecessary linguistic obfuscation of an otherwise clear relation, but above all this God would hardly have anything to say to me, for what my loftier self has to say to me, I already know. And if there were a "godly" man—as an enthusiastic German professor under the impact of Rabindranath Tagore's teaching proclaimed[28]—then this man would actually find himself barred from the path to God, which is open to every human being who is human. So important is the presupposed separation of "being," of which, however, nothing further will be said in what follows. For, in the actuality which alone we experience, [the separation] is bridged, and all that we experience are experiences of such bridging blows. If we want to comprehend Him, God conceals Himself, the human, our self, closes itself up, and the world becomes a visible riddle. Only in their relations [to each other]—only as creation, revelation, and redemption—do they open themselves up.

And now this great world poem is retold in three tenses. However, it is really narrated in the first book alone, the book of the past. In the present, the narration gives way to immediate exchange of speech, because what is present, whether human beings or God, cannot be spoken of in the third person; they can only be listened to and addressed. And in the book of the future, the language of the chorus governs, for the future seizes even the individual only where and when it can say We.

Thus the new thinking's method originates out of its temporality. To be sure, this is the case in all three books, yet it is most visible in the core book of this volume and thus of the whole, in the second book, the book of the present revelation. Into the place of the method of thinking, as all previous philosophy developed it, steps the method of speaking. Thinking is timeless and wants to be; it wants to establish a thousand connections with one blow; the ultimate, the goal, is for it the first. Speaking is time-bound, time-nourished; it neither can nor will

---

28. Rabindranath Tagore (1861–1941) was a Bengali poet, dramatist, and novelist who became the first non-Westerner to win the Nobel Prize for Literature in 1913, after he had translated his poetry into English. Tagore's literature and his mystical worldview became enormously influential throughout Europe, including Germany. In 1920, in Darmstadt, Germany, a School of Wisdom, based on Tagore's educational ideas and patterned on a school he had founded in 1901, was established by Count Hermann Keyserling of Estonia (1880–1946).

abandon this, its nourishing environment; it does not know in advance where it will arrive; it lets its cues be given by others. It lives in general from the life of the other, whether the audience of the narration or the respondent in the dialogue or the cospeaker in a chorus; whereas thinking is always solitary, even if it is happening among several "symphilosophizing"[29] partners: even then, the other merely raises objections which I myself would really have to raise—which is the reason why most philosophical dialogues, including most of Plato's, are so boring. In actual conversation, something happens; I do not know in advance what the other will say to me because I myself do not even know what I am going to say; perhaps not even whether I am going to say anything at all; it could well be that the other begins, indeed, most often this is how it will be in genuine conversation, as one can easily be convinced by a comparative glance at the Gospels and the Socratic dialogues; Socrates is usually first to get the conversation on its way—that is, on the way of a philosophical discussion. The thinker knows exactly his thoughts in advance; that he "expresses" them is only a concession to the deficiency of our, as he calls it, communicative medium, which does not consist in the fact that we need language, but rather that we need time. To need time means: being able to anticipate nothing, having to wait for everything, being dependent on the other for one's own. All that is completely unthinkable to the thinking thinker, while it corresponds uniquely to the language thinker. Language thinker—for of course the new, speaking thinking is thinking, just as much as the old, thinking

---

29. In Critical Fragment 112, Friedrich Schlegel (1772–1829), a central figure in German Romanticism, wrote of a symphilosophical or sympoetical relationship between "the synthetic writer" and his or her reader, a relationship quite different from that between "the analytic writer" and his or her reader: "The analytic writer observes the reader as he is; and accordingly he makes his calculations and sets up his machines in order to make the proper impression on him. The synthetic writer constructs and creates a reader as he should be; he doesn't imagine him calm and dead, but alive and critical. He allows whatever he has created to take shape gradually before the reader's eyes, or else he tempts him to discover it himself. He doesn't try to make any particular impression on him but enters with him into the sacred relationship of symphilosophy or sympoetry." See Schlegel, *Philosophical Fragments*, trans. Peter Firchow (Minneapolis: University of Minnesota Press, 1991), 14. Schlegel's conception evidently anticipates Rosenzweig's intended relationship to his reader, yet Rosenzweig's point is that the old thinking is, as such, solitary, even if it is performed collaboratively; therefore, Schlegel's conception of the synthetic writer's relationship with his or her reader can only be fulfilled by a new thinking that is no longer philosophical in the old sense.

thinking did not occur without inner speech; the difference between old and new, logical and grammatical thinking does not rest on loud versus quiet, but rather on needing the other and, what amounts to the same, on taking time seriously. To think here means to think for no one and to speak to no one (for which one may substitute everyone, the famous "universality," if it sounds better to someone). But to speak means to speak to someone and to think for someone; and this Someone is always a quite definite Someone and has not only ears, like the universality, but also a mouth.

In this method is concentrated what the book can contribute to the renewal of thinking. Feuerbach[30] was the first to discover it, and it has been reintroduced into philosophy by Herman Cohen in [his] posthumous work, although the author was not aware of its revolutionizing force.[31] When I wrote [the *Star*], I was already familiar with those passages in Cohen. However, I am not indebted to them as the decisive influence for the realization of my book, but rather to Eugen Rosenstock, whose now published *Applied Psychology* had already been in my hands as a rough draft for a year and a half when I began to write.[32] Since then, and apart from the *Star*, the new science has appeared in another principal presentation, in the first volume of Hans Ehrenberg's work on idealism, *Fichte*, itself composed in the new form of genuine,

---

30. Ludwig Feuerbach (1804–72) was a student of Hegel, associated with the radical Young Hegelians. He developed an influential criticism of Hegel, focusing on the resolution of theology into anthropology and on the centrality of I-thou relationships to anthropology. See, e.g., sections 32–41 of his *Principles of the Philosophy of the Future*, trans. Thomas E. Wartenberg (Indianapolis: Hackett, 1996). In 1922, Hans Ehrenberg edited an edition of this work by Feuerbach, declaring him the discoverer of the I-thou concept.

31. In his introduction to Cohen's Jewish writings, Rosenzweig had developed the view that Cohen's later conception of human reason as created by and correlated with God is a significant departure from his earlier idealist conception of human reason as creative. For criticism of this interpretation, see Alexander Altmann, "Hermann Cohens Begriff der Korrelation" (Hermann Cohen's concept of correlation) in *Von der mittelalterlichen zur modernen Aufklärung: Studien zur jüdischen Geistesgeschichte* (From the medieval to the modern enlightenment: Studies in Jewish intellectual history) (Tübingen: J. C. B. Mohr, 1987), 300–17.

32. Eugen Rosenstock-Huessy (1888–1973), *Angewandte Seelenkunde* (Applied psychology), in *Die Sprache des Menschengeschlechts: Eine leibhaftige Grammatik in vier Teilen* (The language of the human race: An incarnate grammar) (Heidelberg: Lambert Schneider, 1963) I, 739–810, trans. Mark Huessy and Freya von Moltke as *Practical Knowledge of the Soul* (Norwich, Vt.: Argo Books, 1988), based on a letter from Rosenstock-Huessy to Rosenzweig.

time-consuming conversation.[33] Victor von Weizsäcker's *Philosophy of the Physician* will appear shortly.[34] Rudolf Ehrenberg's *Theoretical Biology* places the doctrine of organic nature for the first time under the law of real, irreversible time.[35] Independently of the aforementioned and of each other, the following authors penetrated to the focal point of the new idea, i.e., to what is dealt with in the central book of the *Star*, namely: Martin Buber in his *I and Thou*,[36] and Ferdinand Ebner's book *The Word and the Spiritual Realities*,[37] which latter was written at exactly the same time as my book. The notes to my *Jehuda Halevi*[38] contain instructive examples of the practical application of the new thinking. A precise and profound knowledge of all these things is contained in the basic foundation of the powerful, yet for the most part still unpublished, works of Florens Christian Rang.[39]

Theological interests helped the breakthrough to the new thinking in all those just mentioned. Nevertheless, it is no theological thinking. At

33. Hans Ehrenberg's (1883–1958) three volumes criticizing German Idealism, *Disputation* (München: Drei Masken Verlag, 1923–25), are written in dialogue form and deal with Fichte, Schelling, and Hegel, respectively.

34. Viktor von Weizsäcker (1886–1957) published numerous works on medicine and natural philosophy. See his *Gesammelte Schriften* (Collected works), ed. Peter Achilles (Frankfurt: Suhrkamp, 1988).

35. Rudolf Ehrenberg (1884–1969), *Theoretische Biologie vom Standpunkte der Irreversibilität* (Theoretical biology from the standpoint of irreversibility) (Berlin: Springer, 1923).

36. Martin Buber (1878–1965), *Ich und du* (Leipzig: Insel-Verlag, 1923), trans. Walter Kaufmann as *I and thou* (New York: Touchstone, 1996).

37. Ferdinand Ebner (1882–1931), *Das Wort und die geistige Realitäten: pneumatologische Fragmente* (The word and spiritual realities: Pneumatological fragments) (Frankfurt: Suhrkamp, 1980).

38. Rosenzweig, *Jehuda Halevi: Zweiundneuntzig Hymnen und Gedichte, Deutsch, mit einem Nachwort und mit Anmerkungen* (Jehuda Halevi: Ninety-two hymns and poets, German, with an afterword and with annotations) (Berlin: Verlag Lambert Schneider, 1927), trans. Barbara Ellen Galli in *Franz Rosenzweig and Jehuda Halevi: Translating, Translations, and Translators* (Montreal and Kingston: McGill-Queens University Press, 1995).

39. Florens Christian Rang (1864–1924) was already dead when Rosenzweig wrote "The New Thinking." Some of his writings have been published posthumously, such as *Shakepeare der Christ: eine Deutung der Sonette* (Shakespeare the Christian: An interpretation of the sonnets), ed. Bernhard Rang (Heidelberg: L. Schneider, 1954) and *Historische Psychologie des Karnevals* (Historical psychology of the carnival), ed. Lorenz Jager (Berlin: Brinckmann and Bose, 1983).

least absolutely and completely not what one had to understand by such a thing until now. Neither in the end nor in the means. It neither directs itself solely at so-called "religious problems" which it treats rather alongside or, rather, in the midst of logical, ethical, and aesthetic [problems], nor is it familiar with that attitude that is a mixture of attack and defense, never quietly concentrated on the matter in hand, which is characteristic of theological thinking. If that is theology, then it is, at any rate, as new a theology as it is a new philosophy. The introduction to the second volume deals with this question, just as overall the three introductions attempt to show the reader the paths which lead from the intellectual world familiar to him, to the world of the book. Theology may not debase philosophy to play the part of the handmaid, yet just as degrading is the role of charwoman which, in modern and in most recent times, philosophy has become accustomed to give theology. The true relationship between these two renewed sciences, as the aforementioned introduction develops it, is one of siblings, which must in fact lead to union [of the sciences] within the persons who maintain them. Theological problems want to be translated into human [problems], while human [problems] want to be driven into the theological. For instance, the problem of the name of God is only a part of the logical problems of the name in general, and an aesthetics which does not inquire into whether artists can attain bliss is a polite, but also an incomplete science.

Indeed, completeness is in general the proper verification of the new thinking. From the perspective of the old [thinking], [the new thinking's] problems are for the most part simply invisible and, if they push themselves into the field of vision, they are not recognized as scientific problems. This holds true not only of theological problems in the narrower sense, but also of the greater part of human [problems], which the grammatical method renders graspable for scientific comprehension, such as, for instance, the logic of the I and Thou or the already mentioned [logic] of the name. By contrast, from the position of the new thinking, the whole region of the old [thinking] remains accessible and intelligible. For instance, the problems of the old Aristotelean and Kantian logic remain problems for language thinking throughout, as problems of the It. As such they are dealt with in the first book of the volume, to be sure, only by way of a first orientation, but already dissociated from the wrong relation to the I and at least schematically prepared for the right relation to the He, to Him.

God created precisely not religion, but rather the world. And when He reveals himself, the world still remains in existence all around, indeed, is only afterward genuinely created for the first time. Not in the slightest does revelation destroy genuine paganism, the paganism of creation; it only lets the miracle of reversal and renewal occur within it. [Revelation] is always present and, if it is past, then [it is] out of that past which stands at the beginning of human history—revelation to Adam. [Revelation] as "renewed at every time" constitutes the content of the second volume, just as paganism as "everlasting" [constitutes] the content of the first. [The second] deals with the visible and audible, thus with revealed actuality, [while] its predecessor [deals] with its dark-mute, secret precondition. Here the historical shapes of revelation in their differentiation, Judaism and its antipodal offspring, Christianity, are still not under discussion at all. Only because and insofar as both renew the "revelation granted to Adam" is the new thinking Jewish or Christian thinking. And, on the other hand, because and insofar as paganism in its historical forms has either forgotten or renounced this revelation to Adam, who was as little a heathen as he was a Jew or a Christian—this historical paganism, on its own account paralyzed into a form, is not in the least everlasting. Precisely in its independence and in its having become form, it does not participate in actuality. By right have the temples of the gods crumbled, by right do their statues stand in museums, their service, insofar as they were ordered and regulated, may have been a singularly monstrous error—yet the prayers which rose to [these gods] from a tormented heart, and the tears shed by the Carthaginian father who led his son to Moloch-sacrifice—these cannot have been unheard and could not have remained unseen. Or should God have waited for Mount Sinai, or even Golgotha? No, as little as paths lead from Sinai or from Golgotha, on which He can be reached with certainty, so little can He have denied himself the [possibility of] encountering even the person who sought Him on the trails around Olympus. There is no temple built that would be so near to Him that man might take comfort from that proximity, nor is there one so distant from him that His arm could not easily reach even there. There is no direction from which He could not come and none from which He had to come; there is no block of wood in which He may not once take up his dwelling, and no psalm of David that always reaches His ear.

The special position of Judaism and Christianity consists precisely in this: that even if they have become religion, they find in themselves the impulses to free themselves from their religiosity and to leave the specialness and its surroundings in order to find their way back to the open field of actuality. All historical religion is from the beginning specialized, "instituted"; only Judaism and Christianity are at first specialized, and never for any length of time, and they have never been instituted. Originally, they were only something quite "irreligious," the one a matter of fact, the other an event. Religion and religions they saw

around themselves, but they themselves would have been most astonished to be identified as one. Only their parody, Islam, is religion from
the beginning and does not even wish to be anything else; it was "instituted" in full consciousness. The six passages in this volume where
[Islam] is dealt with therefore present the only parts of the book which,
strictly speaking, qualify as philosophy of religion.

But the "Jewish book"? as which it is already designated by means of
its cover page?[40] To be able to say with complete truthfulness what I
have to say now—I should like to speak as softly as the poet who ends his
powerfully wide-ranging fugue on the theme of cosmic beauty with the
unforgettable introduction: To me it appeared in the shape of a youth,
of a woman.[41] [Just as] I have received the new thinking in these old
words so, in them, have I given it back and passed it on. For a Christian,
as I know, words of the New Testament would have come to his lips instead of my words, [while] for a pagan, I think, not words from his sacred books [would have come to his lips]—for their ascent leads away
from the original language of mankind, not to it, like the earthly path of
revelation—but perhaps [words] wholly his own. But to me, these
[came]. And yet this is, to be sure, a Jewish book: not one that deals with
"Jewish things," for then the books of the Protestant Old Testament
scholar would be Jewish books; but rather one for which, to say what it
has to say, especially the new thing it has to say, the old Jewish words
come. Like things in general, Jewish things have always passed away; yet
Jewish words, even when old, share the eternal youth of the word, and if
the world is opened up to them, they will renew the world.

But the miracle thus remains that, nevertheless, there is now something with form, something imperishable. To be sure, not in the actual
world of ever renewed life, where only the present is present, while the
past only has been, and the future is only coming. But of these three,
time in the most temporal sense is, to be sure, the present alone. And as
the forms of paganism rise up into the present like something from creation's past, so too is redemption's future anticipated in eternal forms.
The stream of events casts brilliant figures onto the firmament above
the temporal world, and they remain. They are not archetypes; on the
contrary, they would not exist if they were not continuously brought
forth by the stream of actuality fed by its three invisible-secret sources.
Indeed, in these figures those invisible secrets become even figural, and
the constant course of life rounds itself off into recurrent form.

---

40. See note 1.
41. Goethe, "Pandora," 678, *Werke*, V, 354.

Judaism and Christianity are these clock-faces—both eternal—under the week-[hands] and year-hands of constantly renewed time. In them, [in] their year, the course of world-time, which cannot be copied but can only be lived and narrated, takes figural shape as a formed copy. In their God, their world, and their man, there becomes expressible the secret of God, of man, of world, which is only experienceable, but not expressible, in the course of life. What God, what the world, what man "is," we do not know, only what they do, or what is done to them; but how the Jewish or Christian God, the Jewish or Christian world, the Jewish and Christian man look, that we can know quite precisely. In place of the existing substances, which are everlasting only as secret preconditions of the ever renewed actuality, enter forms that eternally mirror this ever renewed actuality. The third volume deals with these.

The presentation of Judaism and Christianity that is given [in that volume] is thus not originally determined by interests [associated with the] study of religion, but rather, as should already be eminently clear from what was just be said, by general, systematic interests, in particular, by the question of an existing eternity, thus, by the task of overcoming the danger of interpreting the new thinking, say, in the sense or, better, the nonsense, of "life-philosophical" or other "irrationalist" tendencies.[42] Today, everyone who is clever enough to avoid the jaws of the idealistic Charybdis seems to be pulled down into the dark whirlpool of this Scylla. As a result of which, in both cases the presentation does not emerge from the consciousness appropriate to both, thus in the case of Judaism not from the law, and in the case of Christianity not from faith, but rather from the external, visible form, through which they wrest their eternity from time, thus in the case of Judaism from the matter of fact of the Jewish people, in the case of Christianity from the community grounding event; and the law and faith become visible here only out of these. Here then, on a sociological foundation, Judaism and Christianity are put next to one another and against one another. From this results a presentation, which does not do complete justice to the two but which, for this price, transcends, probably for the first time, the

---

42. A significant trend within late-19th- and early-20th-century philosophy was known as *Lebensphilosophie*, an approach to philosophy, influenced by Friedrich Nietzsche (1844–1900) and developed notably by Wilhelm Dilthey (1833–1911), that concerned itself with the practical demands of life, rather than with the theoretical demands of reason. Thinkers as diverse as Georg Simmel, Georg Lukács, and Martin Buber were attracted to it. Like Martin Heidegger (1885–1973), Rosenzweig is evidently aware that he might be taken for a *Lebensphilosoph* and rejects the identification.

apologetics and polemics usual in this field. I have said what is necessary about that elsewhere (in my essay "Apologetic Thinking"),[43] so I do not need to repeat myself here.

The sociological foundation on which the portrayal of Judaism and Christianity is built also plays a role in the sociological parts that are intertwined with that presentation. That the Jewish people rests on the matter of fact which it itself is, and the Christian community on the event around which it gathers itself, leads in the former case to a general sociology and in the latter case to a sociology of the arts. A messianic politics, thus a theory of war, concludes, then, the first book [of the volume], while a Christian aesthetic, thus a theory of suffering, concludes the second book of the volume.

Thus the treatment of ethical and aesthetic problems in relation to Judaism and Christianity comes to a conclusion in the first two books. Both [the ethical and aesthetical problems] pervade all three volumes, but [it is] here, in the third, [that] they are first laid out in the usual fashion, peacefully [and] separately in two books. However, [this is] due to the character of this volume, which overall in a certain sense returns to the waterway of the old thinking and its questions concerning being. That, for the rest, the peace is not yet so far along is shown precisely by the aesthetics in this volume. While the first volume deals only with the current basic concepts of aesthetics, and the second volume—both in its ultimate focus and indeed in its entire organization—liberated aesthetics from its connection—especially firm here because remaining unconscious—to the Idealist tradition, yet nevertheless, in the midst [of that liberation] developed the usual content of an aesthetics, the third volume lets [aesthetics] culminate in an applied aesthetic and, in this justification of art by means of craft, burns all ships which could ferry one back from this new land to the classical native land of the science of "purposeless pleasures."[44]

---

43. See Chapter 7.

44. Kant argues that judgments of taste make distinctive claims to universal validity because they express not some pleasure based on the attainment of a cognitive or practical purpose, but rather a pleasure based on the mere purposiveness of the object for human faculties. See, e.g., *Critique of Judgment*, trans. Werner Pluhar (Indianapolis: Hackett, 1987), Ak. 221: ". . . the liking that, without a concept, we judge to be universally communicable and hence to be the basis that determines a judgment of taste, can be nothing but the subjective purposiveness in the presentation of an object, without any purpose, (whether objective or subjective), and hence the mere form of purposiveness, insofar as we are conscious of it, in the presentation by which an object is *given* us."

I let myself linger relatively briefly over these things which, in their essentials, fill the first two books of the third volume. Indeed, these passages are held to be intelligible, to the degree that a critic has recommended the reader to begin with the introduction to this volume and to read on from there, backward and forward—against which advice I have no objection, on the assumption that it also eventually leads from the "backward and forward" [reading] to [a reading] from front to back. And I believe that, in what I have said above, I have administered several antidotes against [what there is] in the cited intelligibility [of those passages] that is likely to infect [the reader] with misunderstanding. All the same, in all that is understandable and misunderstandable [in the third book of the third volume], there still remains an entirely genuine unintelligibility. It is the same [unintelligibility] that must upset the simple soul by juxtaposing Judaism and Christianity, and that even disturbs the thinker who sees himself asked here with utter seriousness— not with that certain provisionality which could render the first volume bearable for him—"to multiply the existent."[45] Thus, truth is at stake in the concluding book of the volume and of the whole—truth, which can be but one.

With epistemological reflections—so one still believes today—all philosophizing must begin. In truth, philosophy will at most end with them. The author of this epistemological prejudice of our day, Kant, is himself, with his criticism, nothing but such an end. Namely [the end of] the historical epoch that began with the natural science of the Baroque. His criticism immediately applies only to the philosophy of this epoch. Copernicus's Copernican turn—which made man a speck of dust in the All—corresponds far more precisely than Kant thought to Kant's "Copernican turn," which, by way of compensation, placed man on the throne of the world. For the former excessive humiliation of man, at the cost of his humanity, the latter, likewise at the cost of his humanity, was the excessive correction. So all criticism comes only after the performance. As little as the drama critic has to say in advance, however clever he may be, because criticism is not supposed to testify to the cleverness he possessed before, but rather to the cleverness that first arose in him—so little does an epistemology that precedes knowing, that precedes this knowing, have a sense. For all knowing—if something is actually known—is a singular act and has its own method.

---

45. Rosenzweig is anticipating the inevitable objection that the *Star* violates the methodological stricture known — after the nominalist William of Ockham (1317–47), although he did not explicitly formulate it — as Ockham's razor: entities are not to be multiplied without necessity.

Methodological considerations about history in general substitute as little for a historical work grounded on the singular as a literary historian's treatment of a drama substitutes for the criticism of the newspaper reviewer that flows from the immediate impression of a performance—or, rather, even less, because in the case of drama and performance at least the book is the same, but "history in general"—fortunately—does not exist. Now, what is true for each singular work of a science—namely that it must approach its material with its own never before applied methods and instruments, if it wants to extract the secret of precisely this material, and that only the student lets his methods be prescribed by the teacher instead of by the material—holds exactly in the same way for philosophy as well. Except that, in virtue of the comical circumstance that philosophy is a university discipline, complete with professorships which have to be occupied, and freshmen who let "Philosophy Major" be printed on their calling cards, [it is the case] here that students who never get beyond the stage of being students are the norm to such an extent that they do not notice it, even to the point of their retirement at seventy and, as a result, they take the kind of epistemology that is certainly appropriate for school exercises to be the only one.

To knowing from which something comes out, just as with a cake, something must also have been put in. What was put into the *Star of Redemption* was, at the beginning, the experience of factuality prior to all of actual experience's matters of fact. [The experience] of factuality that forces upon thinking, instead of its favorite word "really," the little word "and," the basic word of all experience, to which its tongue is unaccustomed. God and the world and man. This "and" was the first of experience; so it must also recur in the ultimate of truth. Even in truth itself, the ultimate, which can only be one, an "and" must stick; otherwise than the truth of the philosophers, which may know only itself, it must be truth for someone. If it is nevertheless to be the one, then it can be only for the One. And it thereby becomes a necessity that our truth becomes manifold and that "the" truth transforms itself into our truth. Thus truth ceases to be what "is" true and becomes that which has to be *verified* as true. The concept of the verification of truth becomes the basic concept of this new epistemology, which takes the place of the old epistemology's noncontradictoriness-theory and object-theory, and introduces, instead of the old static concept of objectivity, a dynamic concept. The hopelessly static truths, like those of mathematics, which were made into the point of departure by the old epistemology, without ever getting beyond this point of departure, are to be conceived from this perspective as the—lower—limiting case, as rest is conceived as the limiting case of motion, while the higher and highest truths are only capable of being grasped as truths from this perspective, instead of having to be relabeled as fictions, postulates, and needs. From those most unimportant truths of the type "two times two is four," on which people easily agree, with no other expense than a little bit of brainpower—for the multiplication table a little less, for relativity theory a little more—the way leads, over those truths for which man is willing to pay, to those he cannot verify in any other way than with the sacrifice of his life, and finally to those whose truth can be verified only by risking the life of all generations.

This messianic theory of knowledge, however, which ranks truths according to the price of their verification and the bond which they found among men, cannot lead beyond both—ever irreconcilable—expectations of the Messiah: the expectation of the one to come and the expectation of the returning one—beyond the "and" of these ultimate risks for truth. There, verification stands only with God Himself, the truth is One only before Him. Hence earthly truth remains split—split in two as factuality outside the divine, as the original matters of fact: world and man. Together with their "and," they return in the final facts of Judaism and Christianity as world of law and faith of man, law of the world and man of faith.

But thus, in this return of the eternal-invisible presuppositions of this experience, in the final clarity of transexperienced truth, the true order of the three [volumes] now establishes itself, and, since God becomes the God of truth, the last book clarifies the confusion of the first, whose God had not merely no relation to world and man, but rather not even a firm place, so that he could signify not the God of truth, but rather only the false gods. There only the false gods had been able to appear as the fulfillment of the god-concept, of the question: what is God? Now, since every god-concept has long since darkened into the hidden God, and since God reveals Himself as creator, revealer, and redeemer, the First and Last and the Present-in-the-heart burns together in the God of truth, and of this God, in whom actual has-been and actual is and actual becoming shoot together, we may—now for the first time—say: He is.

Here the book concludes. For what now still comes is already beyond the book, a "gate" from it out into the No-longer-book. No-longer-book is the enraptured-startled knowledge that in this beholding the "world-likeness in the countenance of God," in this seizing of all being in the immediacy of a moment [*eines Augenblicks*] and blink of an eye [*Augen-blicks*], the limit of humanity is entered.[46] No-longer-book is

---

46. The term "moment" (*Augenblick*) shows the influence of Søren Kierkegaard (1813–1855), whose pseudonym, Vigilius Haufniensis, writes in *The*

also becoming aware that this step of the book toward the limit can only be atoned for by—ending the book. An ending which is also a beginning and a midpoint: stepping into the midst of the everyday of life. The problem of the philosopher is dealt with throughout the whole book, especially by the three introductions. Here for the first time does it find its definitive solution. Philosophizing should also continue in the future, precisely in the future. Everyone should philosophize once. Everyone should look all around once from his own standpoint and life perspective. But this view is not an end in itself. The book is no attained goal, not even a preliminary one. It must itself be taken responsibility for, rather than bearing itself or be being borne by others of its kind. This responsibility occurs in the everyday of life. Except that to know and live it as everyday, the day of the life of the All had to be traversed.

That it is difficult to speak about one's own book as the author, I have learned in writing these pages. The author may hardly claim to say something authentic. For precisely with respect to that which in his work is spirit and thus transplantable into other spirits, he himself stands no differently than anyone else. Indeed, the other, simply because he is another, may always undertake once again, with Kant's bold saying, which is therefore not so bold at all, "to understand Plato better than he understood himself."[47] I would not take this hope away from any of my readers. What the author himself has to say, even if he makes an honest effort to say it in the form of a commentary, will always easily turn into supplementary annotations. Which, in any case, with respect to what they underline and parenthesize in the book, become dependent on what has reached the author's ear as an echo. And which are therefore addressed only to the contemporary reader. And they will fail to satisfy even him, precisely in his contemporaneity. For what he asks for, and finally is also permitted to ask for, is precisely what is not given to him: a catchy characterization under which he could bury what has

---

Concept of Anxiety, trans. Reidar Thomte and Albert B. Anderson (Princeton: Princeton University Press, 1980), 88, that "the Moment is not properly an atom of time but an atom of eternity. It is the first reflection of eternity in time, its first attempt, as it were, at stopping time."

47. In his *Critique of Pure Reason*, A314/B370, Kant characterized the relationship between his use of Plato's term "idea" and Plato's own use by saying, ". . . when we compare the thoughts that an author expresses about a subject, in ordinary speech, as well as in writings, it is not at all unusual to find that we may understand him even better than he understood himself, since he may not have determined his own concept sufficiently and hence sometimes spoke, or even thought, contrary to his own intention."

perhaps been brought into experience regarding the new thinking, in the graveyard of his general education. That I did not give him this catchword was not ill will on my part; rather, I actually do not know any. To be sure, the work in which I have tried to expound the new thinking attacks certain catchwords with a special antagonism that goes far beyond the general antipathy to all isms, but should I, for that reason, let the book be pinned down to the usual opposites to those isms? Can I let it? The catchword I would soonest tolerate would be that of absolute empiricism;[48] this, at least, would cover the characteristic behavior of the new thinking in all three areas: the preworld of the concept, the world of actuality, the superworld of truth. That behavior, which knows [itself] to know nothing of the heavenly except what it has experienced—this, however, it actually [knows], no matter how philosophy may slander it as knowledge "beyond" all "possible" experience; and of the earthly too [it knows] nothing that it has not experienced—but about [what it has not experienced, it knows] absolutely nothing whatsoever, no matter how philosophy may praise it as knowledge "before" all "possible" experience. Such trust in experience might well constitute what is teachable and transmissible with respect to the new thinking, if it is not, as I feared above all, itself already precisely a sign of a renewed thinking—and if the catchword given above is not one of those remarks that, precisely because they come from the author himself, strike the reader, in part, not merely as easy, like many others on the preceding pages, certainly, but rather as all too easy and, in part, as more difficult than the book itself. Both are unavoidable. The greatest poet of the Jews knew the former when he let his heathen king be answered through the mouth of the sage: "My words are too difficult for you, for

---

48. Friedrich Wilhelm Joseph von Schelling (1775–1854) describes his mature philosophy as "metaphysical empiricism" in passages such as the following from Schelling, *Sämmtliche Werke* (Collected works), ed. K. F. A. Schelling (Stuttgart and Augsburg, 1856–61), II, 3:113–14: ". . . empiricism as such does not in any way exclude all knowledge of the supersensible, as is usually assumed and as even Hegel presupposes . . . there is also a metaphysical empiricism, as we wish to call it for the time being; under the *universal* concept of philosophical empiricism still other systems are therefore to be subsumed than those sensualistic ones which limit all knowledge to sense perception, or even deny the existence of everything supersensible." Similarly, by "absolute empricism," Rosenzweig means a philosophy that bases knowledge on experience but does not limit the objects of experience to the relative or conditioned objects of the senses, leaving room for the possibility of experience of the absolute, unconditioned, supersensible, or divine.

which reason they seem too simple to you."[49] And the latter [was known by] the greatest poet of the Germans, whose Mephistopheles, to Faust's impatient call, "many a riddle must be solved there," replies: "yet many a riddle is also propounded."[50]

49. Rosenzweig is certainly referring to Judah Halevi (c.1105–1141), *Kitāb al-Ḥujja waal-Dalil fī Naṣr al-Dīn al-Dhalīl* (Book of argument and proof in defense of the despised faith, completed in 1140), trans. by Hartwig Hirschfeld as *Book of Kuzari* (New York: Dutton, 1905; reprint, New York: Pardes, 1946) but the sentence quoted does not appear in any standard translation. According to Haggai Ben-Shammai, in correspondence with Diana Lobel, Rosenzweig may here be recalling Halevi's Kuzari I:29, of which the best English rendition is by Isaak Heinemann: "28. The Khazari: I see thee quite altered, O Jew, and thy words are poor after having been so rich. 29. The Rabbi: The poorest ones will become the richest, if thou givest me thy attention, until I have expressed myself more fully." Judah Halevi, *Kuzari: The Book of Proof and Argument*, abridged edition, by Isaak Heinemann (Oxford: East and West Library, 1947). We do know that Rosenzweig studied Arabic, which impressed Cohen, and this might account for his understanding of the text, which seems attuned to the Arabic original. (For the information on the Kuzari, we thank Diana Lobel and Haggai Ben-Shammai.)

50. Goethe, *Faust I*, 4040–41, *Werke*, III, 127.

IX
From 1925 to 1929

In 1925 Rosenzweig began work with Buber translating the Bible. By the time Rosenzweig died in December of 1929, they had completed the Torah (the Pentateuch), Joshua, Judges, Samuel, Kings, and the book of Isaiah, together with various essays on translation and the Bible.[1] "The New Thinking," as we indicated above, was written in 1925, and a collection of his shorter writings was published in 1926 as *Zweistromland*.[2] The little piece "Transposed Fronts" was written in May 1929 as a review of the recently published second edition of Hermann Cohen's *Religion der Vernunft*. Rosenzweig died of pneumonia on December 10, 1929, at the age of forty-two.

Rosenzweig's participation in the translation project with Buber can be understood, like the translation and commentary of Halevi's poems, as an application of his system and views about Jewish life and its historical task. To Rosenzweig, biblical translation was part of a nexus that involved speakers, listeners, the address of God, and the hearing, the responding of Jews. The biblical text carried within it an oral, resonant quality that translation needed to capture and convey; reading the Bible should involve a listening, to the words, the sounds, the voices, and ultimately to the Voice.[3] For Rosenzweig, both study of texts and actions can be vehicles of return to an intimacy with God.

In 1923 Rosenzweig had published an introduction to the *Collected Jewish Writings* of Hermann Cohen. His brief review of the second edition of Cohen's last work, *Religion der Vernunft aus die Quellen des Judentums*, refers back to that introduction and to the recent debate at Davos between Cohen's foremost student, Ernst Cassirer, and Martin Heidegger, at that time the holder of the chair of philosophy at Marburg. This review, too, reflects Rosenzweig's commitment to the "new thinking" and to his system.

Heidegger had published *Sein und Zeit* in 1927, and in 1929, the year of the confrontation, Cassirer had published the final volume of his *Philosophy of Symbolic Forms*. The two met at Davos in Switzerland from March 17 to April 6 as part of the second annual Davos conference, attended by 200 students and 30 faculty. As one commentator has put it, the debate occurred at three levels, dealing with their differing views on the interpretation and significance of Kant, on the understanding of man and human existence, and on political and ideological issues.[4] Rosenzweig seems to have heard about the debate from Leo Strauss and from a newspaper report by Hermann Herrigel in the evening edition of the *Frankfurter Zeitung* on April 22, 1929. "Transposed Fronts" praises the new, second edition of Cohen's last book. Rosenzweig takes the opportunity to note that the actual title, as Cohen intended it, means to point to the one religion of reason which is common to all but which is conveyed to Cohen and other Jews through the sources of Judaism, while it is conveyed to others in other ways. He also notes that Cohen has two legacies, one that follows the tradition of the old thinking, the other that of the new. Here is where Rosenzweig refers to the Davos debate and calls attention to its significance for understanding that twofold legacy.

The new thinking is that mode of philosophical thinking that deals with the particularity of human existence and the embeddedness of the individual subject in the world, history, and living experience. It also philosophizes from the point of view of that subject, that I. In "Transposed Fronts" Rosenzweig associates Heidegger's treatment of human existence as *Dasein* with his own appropriation of the new thinking in the second and third parts of the *Star* and with Cohen's appreciation for the particular I in the religious life described in *Religion of Reason*. Rosenzweig does not go so far as to characterize Cohen's thinking in his last work as an example of the new thinking, but it does, on his view, point in the direction of the new thinking by distinguishing the abstract individual from the concrete, particular subject and by describing how that particular I comes to self-recognition through the encounter with God in the dialectic of guilt, remorse, atonement, and forgiveness. It is both provocative and ironic for Rosenzweig to associate Cassirer, the Jew, with the legacy of Cohen that perpetuates the old thinking and Heidegger, by this time the nonbeliever and later the Nazi party member, with the legacy of Cohen that perpetuates the new thinking and the legacy with which Rosenzweig himself identifies.

Rosenzweig's response to the Davos debate, his interpretation of Cohen, and especially his understanding of Heidegger and his own affinity with Heidegger deserve careful consideration, much more than we can give it here. Rosenzweig seems unaware of the moral and political implications of Heidegger's thinking, at least some of which emerged at Davos with Cassirer's critique of Heidegger regarding human freedom. As one commentator puts it, "in Cassirer's view, when philosophy makes freedom a contingency, history and culture are no longer understood as activities of self-understanding, and man is robbed of the basis for self-respect. Cassirer never gives up this objection to Heidegger, and it becomes the basis of his criticism of later years, when he connects Heidegger's thought with the intellectual climate of National Socialism."[5] Heidegger's active participation in and support of Hitler and Nazism only became clear in 1933 and in subsequent years. There is now an enormous literature tracing his actions, statements, and inaction regarding Nazism and the genocidal extermination of Jews and others in the death camps; the question of the relationship between Heidegger's philosophy, both early and late, and his political views and conduct has been widely debated. It appears, at any rate, that in 1929, when Rosenzweig called attention to Heidegger's portrayal of *Dasein* as an expression of the new thinking, he was not aware of the right-wing, conservative, *völkish*, and antisemitic side of Heidegger's thinking and of the possibility that his analysis of *Dasein* might be implicated with such a political ideology.[6] If he had, one can only wonder why he would associate himself with Heidegger and align both of them with that legacy of Cohen that he especially revered.

Rosenzweig and Heidegger differed in many ways. Cassirer had objected to the way in which situation and contingency swallow up human freedom on Heidegger's view of the human condition or *Dasein*, thereby undermining the grounds for meaning and dignity. With regard to Rosenzweig's thinking, the differences have to do with eternity and God. Certainly Rosenzweig and Heidegger did not understand temporality and eternity in the same way, and they diverged dramatically over the role of God in human existence, history, and life. Heidegger took human existence to be wholly situated in the world and in time; hence, the role of meaning, interpretation, and understanding for human life is also wholly situated, limited, contingent, and conditional. In a sense, Rosenzweig's most dramatic difference with Heidegger comes here, for while he admits that from the point of view of human living and human existence in the world and history, meaning and understanding are situated, bounded, and shaped by one's community, traditions, and memory, there is nonetheless another point of view from which the meaning of history and human life is unified, precise, clear, and permanent. It is this point of view with which Rosenzweig associates the notion of eternity, which is in one way distinct from human life and history and in another linked to it. In other words, as Rosenzweig sees it, the meaning of human historical existence is at the same time grounded in eternity and conditioned in time; the event of revelation calls forth a human response that takes shape as a life lived toward redemption. Prior to redemption, human historical existence is linked to a transcendent ground but determined in content and shape by its historical, human, limited matrix. After redemption, the two would become one. For Heidegger, either there is no such redemption or, if there is, it is wholly dependent upon the achievement of the finite, human disclosure of that which seeks expression in existence. In *Sein und Zeit* in 1927, and by 1929, when the debate in Davos took place, the very special role of Being in Heidegger's thinking would have been, in Rosenzweig's view, occluded by the centrality of *Dasein* as human existence that is a being-in-the-world. Hence, if Rosenzweig knew very much at all about Heidegger, he should have known that his own acknowledgment of eternity and Heidegger's rejection of it, of the complimentary role of time and history in his own thought, and of the preeminent role of time and history for Heidegger, amounted to a momentous difference and one that most likely would register in political and moral views on a large scale. One can only wonder why Rosenzweig did not see, that is, that Heidegger's response to historicism and relativism was utterly different from his own and why he was not deeply worried, if not genuinely frightened, by it.[7]

Neither Heidegger's nor Rosenzweig's views about human historicity and the situated character of human existence were, in the decades of the war and of Weimar, unique. They shared a good deal with the thinking of others, among them Georg Lukács, Georg Simmel, Max Weber, Wilhelm Dilthey, Karl Barth, Rudolph Bultmann, Ludwig Wittgenstein, and Edmund Husserl. It was a period of restless, dramatic wrestling with the very notion of philosophy and with the implications of one's conception of philosophy for moral and political issues. How one understood philosophy's relation with ethics, ontology, politics, religion, and art was of momentous significance. Rosenzweig began his lifelong wrestling with these issues in Freiburg and with his studies with Meinecke; he ended them in Frankfurt with his translation of the Bible together with Buber. It was a struggle never completed, rudely cut short by illness at a time when forces were seething within Germany that would transform and deepen the very problems with which Rosenzweig had engaged. It is tantalizing to imagine how Rosenzweig himself, had he survived the atrocities and horror of the years following his death, would have responded.

Endnotes

1. These essays include: "Scripture and the Spoken Word," "Scripture and Luther's Translation," "The Secret of Form in the Biblical Tales," "On the Significance of the Bible," and "The Eternal (Mendelssohn and the Name of God)." Rosenzweig's and Buber's essays on the Bible and translation were published in 1936 as *Die Schrift und ihre Verdeutschung*. An English translation, *Scripture and Translation*, was published in 1994 (Bloomington, Ind.: Indiana University Press).

2. Buber and Rosenzweig had completed the first four books of the Torah and were working on Deuteronomy. *Zweistromland* included "The Oldest System Program of German Idealism," "The New Thinking," "Introduction to the Academy Edition of *Hermann Cohen's Jewish Writings*," "On Hermann Cohen's *Religion of Reason*," "A Memorial Page," "It Is Time," "*Bildung* and No End," "A Rabbinic Book," "Apologetic Thinking," "The Builders: On the Law," and "New Hebrew?"

3. The best place to explore Rosenzweig's views on translation and on the Bible and its role in Jewish experience is *Die Schrift und ihre Verdeutschung*, now available in English translation, *Scripture and Translation*. Michael Fishbane has an excellent essay on Rosenzweig, translation, and the Bible, "Speech and Scripture: The Grammatical Thinking and Theology of Franz Rosenzweig," in *The Garments of Torah: Essays in Biblical Hermeneutics* (Bloomington, Ind.: Indiana University Press, 1989), 99–111.

4. See David R. Lipton, *Ernst Cassirer: The Dilemma of a Liberal Intellectual in Germany 1914–1933* (University of Toronto Press, 1978), 155–59, especially 156. Also, John Michael Krois, *Cassirer: Symbolic Forms and History* (New Haven: Yale University Press, 1987), 42–44. Krois, in an informative footnote, explains that there is a protocol of the debate, written by Joachim Ritter, a student of Cassirer, and Otto Friedrich Bullnow, a student of Georg Misch invited by Heidegger. This protocol is not a transcript, but Heidegger seems to have trusted it since he allowed it to be published as an appendix to the 4th edition of his book *Kant und das Problem der Metaphysik*. There is an abbreviated version of the protocol, translated in Carl H. Hamburg, "A Cassirer-Heidegger Seminar," *Philosophy and Phenomenological Research* 25 (1964–65), 213–22, with Hamburg's comments on 208–13, and in Francis Slade, "A Discussion between Ernst Cassirer and Martin Heidegger," in *The Existentialist Tradition*, Nino Langiulli, ed., (New York: Doubleday Anchor, 1971), 192–203, see 225–26, note 26. For a discussion of Cassirer's defense of freedom against Heidegger, see Donald Phillip Verene's introduction to *Symbol, Myth, and Culture: Essays and Lectures of Ernst Cassirer, 1935–1945* (New Haven: Yale University Press, 1979), 36–42. See below, Chapter 10, notes 8, 10, 13.

5. Verene, 40–41.

6. The moral and political differences between Cassirer and Heidegger, present in the Davos debate, are not at all clear from Herrigel's report in the *Frankfurter Zeitung*. Herrigel's account focuses on their Kant interpretations and their differing approaches to a philosophical anthropology. He notes that Heidegger emphasizes what happens and not human freedom, the relation of human *Dasein* to the totality of being rather than the preeminence of human freedom for human dignity and self-respect. Herrigel also emphasizes how revolutionary Heidegger takes his thinking to be, to the degree that his philosophy cannot be articulated in Cassirer's terms.

7. An excellent and widely cited essay is Karl Löwith, "M. Heidegger and F. Rosenzweig: A Postscript to *Being and Time*," in *Nature, History, and Existentialism*, ed. Arnold Levison (Evanston, Ill.: Northwestern University Press, 1966), 51–79. The essay originally appeared in *Philosophy and Phenomenological Research* 3 (1) (1942). Löwith, of course, is fully aware of Heidegger's commitment to Nazism and refers to it explicitly in his essay (76). Moreover, he notes its connection with Heidegger's thought: "This political 'engagement' [Heidegger's rectorship in Freiburg] in the factual events of the time . . . was not a deviation from *Being and Time*, as the naive suppose. It was a consequence of Heidegger's concept of human *Dasein* as a temporal and historical existence that only recognizes temporal truths relative to its own *Dasein* and its potential being" (76). Löwith goes on to associate this deficiency with Heidegger's lack of openness to eternity or truth; basically the comments in the text articulate a similar point in slightly different terms.

X

"Transposed Fronts"
(1929)

Ten years after Hermann Cohen's death, the first edition of his posthumous religio-philosophical work[1] was out of print. That first edition had been under an unlucky star. Here and there its text—even in those first two-thirds whose printing Cohen himself had supervised—resembled the haphazard reproduction of some manuscript of an old work more than a modern book, let alone one by Cohen. Cohen always put special care into establishing the texts of his works, faithful to his maxim, transmitted by Robert Fritzsche: "The philological must always be in order."[2] In this second edition, Bruno Strauss has indeed made up for the neglect of these "philological [matters]" in the first. With [the] most beautiful critical reflection and the most pious empathy, he produced the most reliable text [possible] under the circumstances, from a collection of samples of possible textual corruptions—even long marginal notes by others, e.g., by the great Frankfurt Rabbi Nobel,[3] who assisted [his]

---

1. After Hermann Cohen's death in 1918, his major work on religion was first published as *Die Religion der Vernunft aus den Quellen des Judentums* (The religion of reason out of the sources of Judaism) (Leipzig: G. Fock, 1919). It was republished in a second edition as *Religion der Vernunft aus den Quellen des Judentums. Nach dem Manuskript des Verfassers neu durchgearbeitet und mit einem Vorwort versehen von Bruno Strauss* (Religion of reason out of the sources of Judaism. Reworked anew in accordance with the author's manuscript and provided with a foreword by Bruno Strauss) (Frankfurt am Main: Kaufmann, 1929; reprint, Wiesbaden: Fourier, 1988). Rosenzweig addresses the significance of the change of title below. For an English translation, see *Religion of Reason out of the Sources of Judaism*, trans. Simon Kaplan (New York: Frederick Ungar, 1972; 2nd enl. ed., Atlanta: Scholars Press, 1995).

2. R. A. Fritzsche, *Hermann Cohen aus persönlicher Erinnerung* (Hermann Cohen from personal recollection) (Berlin: Cassirer, 1922), 10.

3. Nehemiah Anton Nobel (1871–1922), was an influential Orthodox rabbi, around whom gathered a circle of intellectuals (including Rosenzweig) during his years as rabbi at Frankfurt am Main (1910–22). In rabbinics, Nobel was a

friend and teacher, had slipped into the text, as in works from the time before the invention of the printing press!

The book even went under a false title for the nine years of its first run! It was called: *The Religion of Reason out of the Sources of Judaism;* in truth it is called: *Religion of Reason out of the Sources of Judaism* without the aggressively and intolerantly definite—here, indeed, all too definite—article. Not meant either, of course, is the opposite, the indefinite article, which would actually be too indefinite here. Cohen means rather, equally far from both haughty exclusivity and comfortable letting-anything-go [*Allesgeltenlassen*], the share in the one and universal religion of reason, which the sources of Judaism, arising upon his own inheritance, supply to him. For him, these [sources], for others, others. But for him, these. And to be sure: the sources are primordial sources, from which humankind has drunk. However, just this historical consciousness mixes, into the pious modesty of being permitted to participate, a little humble but joyful pride.

Thus the Jewish side of the work, the task of a "Jewish ethics and philosophy of religion," which it undertook to accomplish within the compass of a comprehensive study, and to which—this much one can say already today—it has provided one of the few classical solutions for Judaism, is not the most important one; at any rate, at this moment and in the current philosophical situation, it is not the most important aspect. Today, at least, the work's classical character is overshadowed by its current significance.

Just as this current significance could become visible only after Cohen's death, so it also lies beyond Cohen's own intention and insight. Indeed, overall he has had a strange fate as a thinker. The works of his journeyman years, which he produced in Kant's workshop, and in particular the first work,[4] the work of a twenty-eight-year-old, then

---

student of Rabbi Azriel Hildesheimer (1820–99), founder of the Orthodox rabbinical seminary at Berlin and leader of the centrist wing of German Orthodoxy, in contrast to the separatist wing led by Rabbi Samson Raphael Hirsch (1808–88). Nobel resigned his first rabbinic position at Königsberg in order to study at Marburg under Cohen, whose close associate he remained when he returned to the rabbinate at Leipzig, Hamburg, and Frankfurt. Rosenzweig expressed his appreciation for Nobel's profound preaching and teaching in his memorial essay of 1922, "Der Denker: Nachruf auf A. N. Nobel" (The thinker: Obituary for A. N. Nobel), *Der Mensch und sein Werk: Gesammelte Schriften III: Zweistromland* (The man and his work: Collected writings III: Land of Two Streams) (The Hague: Martinus Nijhoff, 1984), 667–69.

4. *Kants Theorie der Erfahrung* (Kant's theory of experience) (Berlin: Dümmler, 1871).

revolutionized the philosophical science of the time and, at least in their negative effect, in the antipsychologistic interpretation of Kant, they are generally accepted and have retained their unchanged validity until today, hence after almost sixty years. The works of his master years did not fare that well: his own system did not gain recognition outside the narrower school,[5] and even there it stood in the shadow of his earlier Kant interpretations. Thus, the great comprehensive system,[6] for which the time supposedly longed, appeared not in step with the time, but next to it, the remote work of a mind very much moved by his time, yet alienated from it. And finally, the seventy-year-old graybeard sketched the originally unforeseen, even directly foreclosed, extension and addition [of his system], and with this completion, he did not, to be sure, stride into his own time but strode over it into ours.

For what may have appeared only five years ago, when I expressed it in an introduction to Cohen's Jewish writings,[7] as my personal opinion about the philosophical tendency of the present time has now become common knowledge. Just recently at Davos,[8] in front of a European

5. The "Marburg School," generally distinguished from the "Heidelberg School" of neo-Kantianism associated with Heinrich Rickert (1863–1936) and Wilhelm Windelband (1848–1915).

6. Hermann Cohen, *System der Philosophie. Erster Teil: Logik der reinen Erkenntnis* (System of philosophy. First part: Logic of pure cognition); *System der Philosophie. Zweiter Teil: Ethik des reinen Willens* (System of philosophy. Second part: Ethics of the pure will); *System der Philosophie. Dritter Teil: Ästhetik des reinen Gefühls* (System of philosophy. Third part: Aesthetics of pure feeling) (Berlin: Cassirer, 1902–12).

7. Rosenzweig's introduction to Hermann Cohen, *Jüdische Schriften* (Jewish writings), ed. Bruno Strauss, vol. 1 (Berlin: C. A. Schwetske, 1924; reprint, New York: Arno Press, 1980), xiii–lxiv; also printed in Rosenzweig, 177–223.

8. In 1929, a three-week course at Davos, Switzerland, was attended by approximately thirty professors and over two hundred students, culminating in a debate between Ernst Cassirer (1874–1945) and Martin Heidegger (1889–1976). Cassirer was a leading pupil of Cohen who, because of antisemitism and despite his important publications, was able to secure a professorship only in 1919 at the University of Hamburg, after thirteen years as a *Privatdozent* (unsalaried lecturer) at the University of Berlin. Heidegger's position, associated first with Catholic scholasticism and then with phenomenology and life-philosophy, was explicitly hostile to neo-Kantianism, although he had written his dissertation under Rickert. By 1929, Heidegger had developed an interpretation of Kant's philosophy as an ontology of human finitude anticipating his own work, an interpretation overtly opposed to Cohen's neo-Kantian interpretation of Kant's

forum, there took place that debate between Cassirer, Cohen's most distinguished disciple, and Heidegger, the current holder of Cohen's Marburg chair, which Hermann Herrigel[9] reported in detail in the university column of the *Frankfurter Zeitung* of April 22, 1929, as a representative confrontation between the old and the new thinking.[10] And here, Heidegger, the Husserl disciple and Aristotelian scholastic — whose holding of Cohen's lectern all the "old" Marburg school

---

philosophy as analysis of the necessary conditions for the possibility of science. However, Heidegger regarded the reformation of neo-Kantianism by Paul Natorp (1854–1924), Nicolai Hartmann (1882–1950), and, to some extent, Cassirer, as eliminating the methodological priority of natural science central to Cohen's view and as moving in directions similar to those of his own work. See Heidegger, "Zur Geschichte des philosophischen Lehrstuhls seit 1866" in *Die Philipps Universität zu Marburg 1527–1927* (The Philipps University at Marburg, 1527–1927) ed. H. Hermelink and S.A. Kaehler (Marburg: N.G. Elwert'sche Verlagsbuchhandlung, 1927), 681–87, translated by Richard Taft as "Appendix VI: On the History of the Philosophical Chair since 1866" in Heidegger, *Kant and the Problem of Metaphysics*, 5th ed., enl. (Bloomington, Ind.: Indiana University Press, 1997), 213–17.

9. Hermann Herrigel was the author of *Das neue Denken* (The new thinking) (Berlin: L. Schneider, 1928). Ingo Farin has located a copy of Herrigel's article on the Davos debate.

10. Rosenzweig's view of the debate may have been colored not only by Herrigel's article, but also by the report of Leo Strauss, who visited Rosenzweig on the way back from Davos, according to Steven Schwarzschild. See Karfried Gründer, "Cassirer und Heidegger in Davos 1929" in *Über Ernst Cassirers Philosophie der symbolischen Formen* (On Ernst Cassirer's philosophy of symbolic forms), ed. Hans-Jürg Braun, Helmut Holzhey, and Ernst Wolfgang Orth (Frankfurt: Suhrkamp, 1988), 301. For Strauss's impression, see Strauss, "An Introduction to Heideggerian Existentialism" in *The Rebirth of Classical Political Rationalism: An Introduction to the Thought of Leo Strauss*, ed. Thomas L. Pangle (Chicago: Chicago University Press, 1989), 28: "There was a famous discussion between Heidegger and Ernst Cassirer in Davos which revealed the lostness and emptiness of this remarkable representative of established academic philosophy to everyone who had eyes. Cassirer had been a pupil of Hermann Cohen, the founder of the neo-Kantian school. Cohen had elaborated a system of philosophy whose center was ethics. Cassirer had transformed Cohen's system into a new system of philosophy in which ethics had completely disappeared. It had been silently dropped: he had not faced the problem. Heidegger did face the problem." The information in this note is due to the research of Ingo Farin.

philosophers could only feel to be an irony of intellectual history[11] — advocated against Cassirer a philosophical position [that is] precisely our position,[12] that of the new thinking, which falls entirely into line with what starts from that "last" Cohen.

For what else is it when, against Cassirer, Heidegger gives philosophy the task of revealing to man, the "specifically finite being," his own "nothingness in all freedom," and of calling him back "to the harshness of destiny, from the lazy aspect of a man who only utilizes the works of the spirit"?[13] How is this concluding formulation of the philosophical

---

11. In 1923, Heidegger had begun teaching at the University of Marburg, from which Cohen had retired in 1912. However, Heidegger did not occupy the chair previously occupied by Cohen, although he might be said to have occupied the position of pedagogical prominence once held by Cohen at Marburg. In fact, Heidegger replaced Nicolai Hartmann, who had replaced Paul Natorp. When Heidegger was shown a copy of Rosenzweig's comments on Davos, he responded only that the inaccuracies concerning his position at Marburg should be corrected. See Gründer, "Cassirer und Heidegger in Davos 1929," 290–302. The information in this note is due to the research of Ingo Farin.

12. On the relationship between the philosophies of Heidegger and Rosenzweig, see Karl Löwith, "M. Heidegger and F. Rosenzweig or Temporality and Eternity," *Philosophy and Phenomenological Research* 3 (1942): 53–77; "M. Heidegger and F. Rosenzweig: A Postscript to Being and Time" in *Nature, History, and Existentialism*, ed. Arnold Levison (Evanston, Ill.: Northwestern University Press, 1966), 51–78.

13. Rosenzweig's account is based on that of Herrigel, according to whom Heidegger said at Davos that the central problematic of philosophy "has to lead man back beyond himself into the whole of beings, in order to make the *nothingness of his Dasein* evident to himself in all his freedom," and that philosophy has the task of "calling man back to the harshness of destiny, from the lazy aspect of a man who only utilizes the works of the spirit." Herrigel's account should be compared with the account published in Heidegger, *Kant und das Problem der Metaphysik*, Fünfte vermehrte Auflage (Frankfurt am Main: Vittorio Klostermann, 1990) on the basis of notes made by Otto Friedrich Bollnow and Joachim Ritter, supplemented by Heidegger's typewritten text. For an English translation, see "Appendix IV: Davos Disputation between Ernst Cassirer and Martin Heidegger" in Heidegger, *Kant and the Problem of Metaphysics*, 204: ". . . philosophy's central problematic . . . leads man back beyond himself into the totality of beings in order to make manifest to him there, with all his freedom, the nothingness of his *Dasein*. This nothingness is not the occasion for pessimism and melancholy. Instead, it is the occasion for understanding that authentic activity takes place only where there is opposition and that philosophy has the task of throwing man back, so to speak, into the hardness of his fate from the shallow aspect of a man who merely uses the work of the spirit."

task different from that passionate advocacy of "the individual *quand même*"[14] against the "intellectual-bourgeois-thoughts" [that] one should "honor the thinker in his soul and, therefore, regard the poor individual's intellectual contribution toward the eternity of culture as his main strength and authentic worth" (Cohen's letter to Stadler after Gottfried Keller's death),[15] the vital and personal source of those insights of the "last Cohen" that ripened into philosophy only after a quarter century? If, at Davos, Heidegger said that what he called *Dasein*[16] could not be expressed by a term in Cassirer,[17] the aforementioned introduction[18] has already shown how the run-up to the "leap into *Dasein*"[19]—to express it in Heideggerian terms—leads from precisely the basic concept

---

14. *Quand même* often means "nonetheless" or "all the same," as in *merçi quand même*, "thanks all the same." It is sometimes used to mean "without reservation" or "unqualified," as in *il est un crétin quand même*, "he is an unqualified idiot."

15. Cohen's letter, written in July 1890, was published in *Gabe, Herrn Rabbiner Dr. Nobel zum 50. Geburtstag dargebracht* (Gift presented to Rabbi Dr. Nobel on his 50th birthday) (Frankfurt am Main: J. Kauffmann, 5682/1921), 10. Gottfried Keller (1819–90) was a poet and novelist, while August Stadler (1850–1910) was a philosopher and Kant scholar.

16. The German word *Dasein*, ordinarily used to mean "existence," is used by Heidegger to designate the being that each human being is. He avoids words such as "human being" and "subject," since they are fraught with traditional philosophical meaning, and his goal is to uncover the meaning covered over by the philosophical tradition.

17. Herrigel reported that, although his brief report could not do Heidegger justice, "At least this much has thereby become clear: that in this philosophy, contrasted with Cassirer, every word receives another sense and stands in other relationships, as even Heidegger himself said, that what he signifies with [the word] '*Dasein*' does not allow itself to be expressed with Cassirer's concept." See *Kant and the Problem of Metaphysics*, 203: "I believe that what I describe by *Dasein* does not allow translation into a concept of Cassirer's."

18. See note 7.

19. According to Herrigel, Heidegger said at Davos that the task of philosophy was "to create the preparedness for man's leap into *Dasein*." No such phrase is ascribed to Heidegger in the notes referred to in note 12. However, in that report, Cassirer is reported to have replied to Heidegger's question, "What path does man have to infinitude? And what is the manner in which man can participate in infinity?" by saying, "Man cannot make the leap from his own proper finitude into a realistic infinitude. He can and must have, however, the metabasis which leads him from the immediacy of his existence into the region of pure form. And he possesses his infinity solely in this form." See *Kant and the Problem of Metaphysics*, 200–1.

of Cohen's later philosophy, the "correlation," taken in the sense given to it by Cohen. Not for nothing does the work of old age contain an ingenious chapter that, leaving all that is "Marburg" far behind, replaces Idealism's "creative" reason with that created by God, reason as creature.[20]

The survivors of the "school" —not Cassirer!—would like to turn the dead master into a schoolmaster. The living, progressing history of the spirit thwarts any such disciple-like undertaking; it does not bother itself with such claims, and, since the dead Cid is now riding out again, transposes the fronts. The school with its schoolmaster dies; the master lives.

---

20. See chapter 5 of Cohen, *Religion of Reason,* "Creation of Man in Reason." In his introduction to Cohen's Jewish writings, Rosenzweig had developed the view that Cohen's later conception of human reason as created by and correlated with God is a significant departure from his earlier Idealist conception of human reason as creative. For criticism of this interpretation, see Alexander Altmann, "Hermann Cohens Begriff der Korrelation" (Hermann Cohen's concept of correlation) in *Von der mittelalterlichen zur modernen Aufklärung: Studien zur jüdischen Geistesgeschichte* (From the Medieval to the Modern Enlightenment: Studies in Jewish Intellectual History) (Tübingen: J. C. B. Mohr, 1987), 300–17.

Bibliography

Works by Franz Rosenzweig

Hegel und der Staat. Aalen: Scientia, 1962.

Der Mensch und sein Werk: Gesammelte Schriften III: Zweistromland: Kleinere Schriften zu Glauben und Denken. Ed. Reinhold and Annemarie Mayer. Dordrecht: Martinus Nijhoff, 1984.

Der Mensch und sein Werk: Gesammelte Schriften I.1 and I.2: Briefe und Tagebücher 1909–1918 and 1918–1929. Ed. Rachel Rosenzweig and Edith Rosenzweig-Scheinmann, in collaboration with B. Casper. The Hague: Martinus Nijhoff, 1979.

Der Mensch und sein Werk: Gesammelte Schriften II: Der Stern der Erlösung. Ed. R. Mayer. 4th ed. The Hague: Martinus Nijhoff, 1976.

Die Schrift. Aufsätze, Übertrágungen und Briefe. Ed. K. Thieme. Frankfurt am Main: Europäische Verlagsanstalt, 1964.

English Translations

"Apologetic Thinking." Trans. Joachim Neugroschel. In *The Jew: Essays from Martin Buber's Journal*, ed. Arthur A. Cohen. University, Ala.: University of Alabama Press, 1980.

"Atheistic Theology." Trans. R. Goldy and F. Hoch. *Canadian Journal of Theology* 14 (2) (1968): 79–88.

Franz Rosenzweig and Jehuda Halevi: Translating, Translations, and Translators. Ed. and trans. Barbara E. Galli. Montreal and Kingston: McGill-Queen's University Press, 1995.

Franz Rosenzweig: The New Thinking. Ed. and trans. Alan Udoff and Barbara Galli. Syracuse: Syracuse University Press, 1998.

Franz Rosenzweig: God, Man, and the World. Lectures and Essays. Ed. and trans. Barbara E. Galli. Syracuse: Syracuse University Press, 1998.

Judaism Despite Christianity: The Letters on Christianity and Judaism between Eugen Rosenstock-Huessy and Franz Rosenzweig. University of Alabama Press, 1969; Schocken, 1971. Includes: A. Altmann, "Franz Rosenzweig and Eugen Rosenstock: An Introduction to Their Letters on Judaism and

Christianity" and Dorothy M. Emmet, "The Letters of Franz Rosenzweig and Eugen Rosenstock-Huessy."

On Jewish Learning. Trans. N. N. Glatzer. New York: Schocken Books, 1955.

Scripture and Translation. With Martin Buber. Trans. Lawrence Rosenwald and Everett Fox. Bloomington, Ind.: Indiana University Press, 1994.

The Star of Redemption. Trans. William W. Hallo from the 2nd ed. of 1930. New York: Holt Rhinehart & Winston, 1970. Reprint, University of Notre Dame Press, 1985.

Understanding the Sick and the Healthy: A View of World, Man and God. Trans. N. N. Glatzer. New York: Noonday Press, 1954. Reprint, with new introduction by Hilary Putnam, Cambridge, Mass.: Harvard University Press, 1999.

On Franz Rosenzweig

Altmann, A. "Franz Rosenzweig on History." In *Between East and West: Essays Dedicated to the Memory of Bela Horovitz,* ed. A. Altmann, 194–214. London: East and West Library, 1958. Reprint, in Altmann, *Studies in Religious Philosophy and Mysticism,* 275–291. Ithaca: Cornell University Press, 1969, and in *The Philosophy of Franz Rosenzweig,* ed. P. Mendes-Flohr, 124–137. Hanover, N.H.: University Press of New England, 1988.

_____. "Theology in Twentieth-Century German Judaism." *Leo Baeck Institute Yearbook* 1 (1956): 193–213.

Avineri, Shlomo. "Rosenzweig's Hegel Interpretation: Its Relationship to the Development of his Jewish Reawakening." In *Der Philosoph Franz Rosenzweig,* ed. Schmied-Kowarzik. Munich: Verlag Karl Alber, 1988. Vol. 2, 831–38.

Batnitzky, Leora. *Idolatry and Representation: The Philosophy of Franz Rosenzweig Reconsidered.* Princeton: Princeton University Press, 2000.

Bergman, Samuel Hugo. "Franz Rosenzweig: Beyond Liberalism and Orthodoxy." In *Faith and Reason: An Introduction to Modern Jewish Thought.* 55–80. New York: B'nai B'rith Hillel Foundations, 1961.

Berkovits, Eliezer. *Major Themes in Modern Philosophies of Judaism.* 37–67. New York: Ktav Publishing House, 1974.

Brenner, Michael. *The Renaissance of Jewish Culture in Weimar Germany.* New Haven: Yale University Press, 1996.

Buber, Martin. "Franz Rosenzweig." In *Pointing the Way.* 87–92. New York: Harper and Brothers, 1957.

Cahnman, Werner J. "Friedrich Wilhelm Schelling and the New Thinking of Judaism." In *German Jewry: Its History and Sociology,* ed. Joseph B. Maier, Judith Marcus, and Zoltan Tarr, 209–48. New Brunswick, 1989.

Casper, Bernhard. *Das dialogische Denken: Eine Untersuchung der Religionphilosophischen Bedeutung Franz Rosenzweigs, Ferdinand Ebners, und Martin Bubers.* Freiburg: Herder, 1967.

_____. "Responsibility Rescued." In *The Philosophy of Franz Rosenzweig*, ed. Mendes-Flohr, 89–106.

Cohen, Arthur A. *The Natural and Supernatural Jew: An Historical and Theological Introduction.* 149–78. New York: Pantheon Books, 1962.

Cohen, Richard A. *Elevations: The Height of the Good in Rosenzweig and Levinas.* Chicago: University of Chicago Press, 1994.

Derrida, Jacques. "Interpretations at War: Kant, the Jew, the German." *New Literary History* 22 (1) (1987): 39–95.

Dietrich, Wendell S. "The Character and Status of the Concept of History in Three Twentieth-Century Systems of Judaic Thought: Cohen, Rosenzweig, Levinas." In *From Ancient Israel to Modern Judaism: Intellect in Quest of Understanding.* Ed. Jacob Neusner, Ernest S. Frerichs, and Nahum Sarna. Atlanta, 1989.

Fackenheim, Emil L. Review of Glatzer, N. N. *Franz Rosenzweig: His Life and Thought. Judaism* 2 (4) (1953): 367–72. Reprint, in *The Jewish Thought of Emil Fackenheim*, ed. M. L. Morgan. Detroit: Wayne State University Press, 1987.

_____. "The Systematic Role of the Matrix (Existence) and Apex (Yom Kippur) of Jewish Religious Life in Rosenzweig's *Star of Redemption.*" In *Der Philosoph Franz Rosenzweig*, ed. Schmied-Kowarzik, Vol. 2, 567–75.

_____. *To Mend the World.* 58–100. New York: Schocken Books, 1982; 3rd ed., Indiana University Press, 1994.

Fishbane, Michael. "Speech and Scripture: The Grammatical Thinking and Theology of Franz Rosenzweig." In *Garments of Torah*, 99–111. Bloomington, Ind.: Indiana University Press, 1989.

Franks, Paul. "All or Nothing: Systematicity and Nihilism in Jacobi, Reinhold, and Maimon." In *The Cambridge Companion to German Idealism*, ed. Karl Ameriks. Forthcoming.

Freund, Else Rahel. *Franz Rosenzweig's Philosophy of Existence: An Analysis of the "Star of Redemption."* The Hague: Martinus Nijhoff, 1979; originally published as *Die Existenzphilosophie Franz Rosenzweigs: Ein Beitrag zur Analyse seines Werkes "Der Stern der Erlösung."* Berlin: Felix Meiner Verlag, 1933.

Friedman, Michael. *A Turning Point in Philosophy: Heidegger-Cassirer-Carnap* (forthcoming).

Funkenstein, Amos. "An Escape from History: Rosenzweig on the Destiny of Judaism." *History and Memory* 2 (2) (1990): 117–35.

_____. "The Genesis of Rosenzweig's *Stern der Erlösung.*" *Jahrbuch des Instituts fur Deutsche Geschichte, Beiheft* 4 (1982): 17–29.

Gadamer, H. G. "Die Philosophie und die Religion des Judentums." In *Kleine Schriften I: Philosophie-Hermeneutik*, 201–10. Tübingen: J. C. B. Mohr/Paul Siebeck, 1967.

Gibbs, Robert. *Correlations in Rosenzweig and Levinas.* Princeton: Princeton University Press, 1992.

Glatzer, Nahum N. *Essays in Jewish Thought.* University, Ala.: University of Alabama Press, 1978. Includes: "Franz Rosenzweig in His Student Years," "Franz Rosenzweig: The Story of a Conversion," "Introduction to Rosenzweig's *Little Book of Common Sense and Sick Reason,*" "The Frankfort Lehrhaus," and "Shenato ha-Aharona shel Franz Rosenzweig."

––––––. *Franz Rosenzweig: His Life and Thought.* New York: Farrar, Straus and Young, 1953; reprint, 2nd ed., Schocken Books, 1961; Hackett, 1998.

Greenberg, Yudit Kornberg. *Better Than Wine: Love, Poetry, and Prayer in the Thought of Franz Rosenzweig.* Atlanta: Scholars Press, 1996.

Guttmann, J. *Philosophies of Judaism. The History of Jewish Philosophy from Biblical Times to Franz Rosenzweig.* 367–398. New York: Holt, Rinehart and Winston, 1964.

Haberman, J. "Franz Rosenweig's Doctrine of Revelation." *Judaism* 18 (3) (1969): 320–36.

Hansen, Frank-Peter. *"Das ältestes Systemprogramm des deutschen Idealismus": Rezeptionsgeschichte und Interpretation.* Berlin: Walter de Gruyter, 1989.

Harvey, Warren Zev. "How Much Kabbalah in *The Star of Redemption.*" *Immanuel* 1 (summer 1987): 128–34.

Herrigel, H. *Das neue Denken.* Berlin: Verlag Lambert Schneider, 1928.

Horwitz, Rivka. *Buber's Way to I and Thou: An Historical Analysis and the First Publication of Martin Buber's Lectures: "Religion als Gegenwart."* Heidelberg, 1978.

––––––. "Franz Rosenzweig on Language." *Judaism* 13 (4) (1964): 393–406.

––––––. "Franz Rosenzweig's Unpublished Writings." *The Journal of Jewish Studies* 20 (1969): 57–80.

Idel, Moshe. "Franz Rosenzweig and the Kabbalah." In *The Philosophy of Franz Rosenzweig,* ed. Mendes-Flohr, 162–71.

Jay, Martin. "Politics of Translation. Siegfried Kracauer and Walter Benjamin on the Buber-Rosenzweig Bible." *Leo Baeck Institute Yearbook* 21 (1976): 3–24. Reprint, in *Permanent Exiles,* chap. 12. New York: Columbia University Press, 1985.

Kluback, William. "Time and History: The Conflict between Hermann Cohen and Franz Rosenzweig." In *Der Philosoph Franz Rosenzweig,* ed. Schmied-Kowarzik, Vol. 2, 801–13.

Kroner, Richard. "The Year 1800 in the Development of German Idealism." *The Review of Metaphysics* 1 (4) (1948): 1–31.

Levinas, Emmanuel. "Franz Rosenzweig." *Midstream* 29 (9) (1983): 33–40.

––––––. "Franz Rosenzweig: A Modern Jewish Thinker." In *Outside the Subject.* 49–66. Stanford: Stanford University Press, 1994.

Löwith, K. "Heidegger and F. Rosenzweig or Temporality and Eternity." *Philosophy and Phenomenological Research* 3 (1942): 53–77. Reprint, in *Nature,*

History, and Existentialism. Chap. 4: "M. Heidegger and F. Rosenzweig: A Postscript to Being and Time." Evanston, Ill.: Northwestern University Press, 1966.

Meinecke, Stefan. "A Life of Contradiction: The Philosopher Franz Rosenzweig and his Relation to History and Politics." *Leo Baeck Institute Yearbook* 36 (1991): 461–89.

Mendes-Flohr, Paul. "Franz Rosenzweig and the Crisis of Historicism." In *The Philosophy of Franz Rosenzweig*, ed. Mendes-Flohr, 138–61. Reprinted in Mendes-Flohr. *Divided Passions*, 311–37. Detroit: Wayne State University Press, 1991.

_____. "Franz Rosenzweig and the German Philosophical Tradition." Introduction to *The Philosophy of Franz Rosenzweig*, 1–19.

_____. "Franz Rosenzweig's Concept of Philosophical Faith." *Leo Baeck Institute Yearbook* 34 (1989): 357–69.

_____. "Mendelssohn and Rosenzweig." *Journal of Jewish Studies* 38 (autumn 1987): 203–11.

_____. "1914: Franz Rosenzweig writes the essay 'Atheistic Theology.'" In *Yale Companion to Jewish Writing and Thought in German Culture*, ed. Sander L. Gilman and Jack Zipes, 322–26. New Haven: Yale University Press, 1997.

_____. "Rosenzweig and Kant: Two Views of Ritual and Religion." In *Philosophers and Politicians: Essays in Jewish Intellectual History in Honor of Alexander Altmann*, ed. Jehuda Reinharz and Daniel Swetschinski, 315–341. Durham, N.C.: Duke University Press, 1982. Reprint, in *Divided Passions*, Mendes-Flohr. 283–310.

_____. "The Spiritual Legacy of Franz Rosenzweig." *Tikkun* 2 (1) (1987): 99–101.

_____. *The Philosophy of Franz Rosenzweig*. Hanover, N.H.: University Press of New England, 1988.

Mendes-Flohr, P. and J. Reinharz. "From Relativism to Religious Faith. The Testimony of Franz Rosenzweig's Unpublished Diaries." *Leo Baeck Institute Yearbook* 22 (1977): 161–74.

Morgan, Michael L. "The Curse of Historicity: The Role of History in Leo Strauss's Jewish Thought." *Journal of Religion* 61 (October 1981): 345–63. Reprint, in *Dilemmas in Modern Jewish Thought*. Bloomington, Ind.: Indiana University Press, 1992.

_____. "Franz Rosenzweig, Objective Truth and the Personal Standpoint." *Judaism* 40 (1991): 521–30. Reprint, in *Dilemmas in Modern Jewish Thought*.

_____. "Jewish Philosophy and Historical Self-Consciousness." *Journal of Religion* 71 (1991): 36–49. Reprint, in *Dilemmas in Modern Jewish Thought*.

Mosès, Stéphane. "Franz Rosenzweig in Perspective: Reflections on his Last Diaries." In *The Philosophy of Franz Rosenzweig*, ed. Mendes-Flohr, 185–201.

_____. *System and Revelation: The Philosophy of Franz Rosenzweig*. Detroit: Wayne State University Press, 1992.

_____. "Walter Benjamin and Franz Rosenzweig." *Philosophical Forum* 15 (1984), 188–205. Reprint in *Benjamin: Philosophy, Aesthetics, History*, ed. Gary Smith. Chicago: University of Chicago Press, 1989.

Pöggeler, Otto. "Between Enlightenment and Romanticism: Rosenzweig and Hegel." In *The Philosophy of Franz Rosenzweig*, ed. Mendes-Flohr, 107–23.

Putnam, Hilary. Introduction to *Understanding the Sick and the Healthy*, trans. Nahum Glatzer, 1–20. Cambridge, Mass.: Harvard University Press, 1999.

Rose, Gillian. "Franz Rosenzweig—From Hegel to Yom Kippur." In *Judaism and Modernity: Philosophical Essays*, 127–54. Oxford: Blackwells, 1993. 127–54.

Rotenstreich, N. "Common Sense and Theological Experience on the Basis of Franz Rosenzweig's Philosophy." *Journal of the History of Philosophy* 5 (4) (1967): 353–60.

Schmied-Kowarzik, Wolfdietrich. *Der Philosoph Franz Rosenzweig*. 2 vols. Munich: Verlag Karl Alber, 1988.

Scholem, Gershom. "At the Completion of Buber's Translation of the Bible." In *The Messianic Idea in Judaism and Other Essays in Jewish Spirituality*. 314–19. New York: Schocken Books, 1971.

_____. "On the 1930 Edition of Rosenzweig's *Star of Redemption*." In *The Messianic Idea in Judaism*, 320–24.

Schwarzschild, S. S. *Franz Rosenzweig: Guide of Reversioners*. London: The Education Committee of the Hillel Foundation, 1960.

_____. "Franz Rosenzweig's Anecdotes about Hermann Cohen." In *Gegenwart im Ruckblick*, ed. H. A. Strauss and K. R. Grossmann. Heidelberg: Stiehm, 1970.

_____. "Rosenzweig on Judaism and Christianity." *Conservative Judaism* 10 (2) (1957): 41–48.

Stahmer, H. M. *"Speak That I May See Thee": The Religious Significance of Language*. New York: Macmillan, 1968.

Theunissen, M. *Der Andere. Studien zur Sozialontologie der Gegenwart*. Berlin: Walter de Gruyter, 1965; second edition, 1977. Trans. as *The Other*. Cambridge, Mass.: MIT Press, 1984.

Wiehl, Reiner. "Experience in Rosenzweig's New Thinking." In *The Philosophy of Franz Rosenzweig*, ed. Mendes-Flohr, 42–68.

Wolfson, Eliott R. "Facing the Effaced: Mystical Eschatology and the Idealistic Orientation in the Thought of Franz Rosenzweig." *Zeitschrift für Neuere Theologische Geschichte/ Journal for the History of Modern Theology* 4 (1997): 39–81.

Index of Names

Adret, Solomon ben: 98 n. 8
Altmann, Alexander: 2; 3; 7 n. 2; 7 n. 4;
 7 n. 7; 152 n. 20
Aquinas, Thomas: 97; 97 n. 6
Archimedes: 33
Aristotle: 54 n. 16; 116 n. 14; 129; 149
Augustine: 97; 97 n. 5
Avineri, Shlomo: 86; 93 n. 11

Bacher, Wilhelm: 22 n. 20
Baeck, Leo: 4; 90; 99 n. 10; 104–7
Barth, Karl: 7 n. 2; 88–89; 92 n. 3; 143
Below, Georg von: 7 n. 3
Benjamin, Walter: viii
Ben-Shammai, Haggai: 139 n. 49
Bismarck, Otto von: 74; 74 n. 5; 75; 76;
 77; 80; 80 n. 20; 81; 82; 86
Bloch, Ernst: 44 n. 9
Böhme, Jakob: 57 n. 23
Boyle, Robert: 68 n. 45
Breysig, Kurt: 7 n. 5
Brod, Max: 90; 99 n. 10; 101–4; 105;
 106; 107; 120; 120 n. 20
Buber, Martin: vii; 3; 4; 5-6; 9 n. 18; 10
 n. 1; 73 n. 1; 84; 86; 89; 91; 109–10 n.
 1; 128; 128 n. 36; 132 n. 42; 140; 143;
 144 n. 1; 144 n. 2
 I and Thou: 86; 112; 112 n. 6; 128;
  128 n. 36
 Three Addresses: 5–6; 9 n. 18; 10 n. 1
Bullnow, Otto Friedrich: 144 n. 4; 150
 n. 13
Bultmann, Rudolf: 92 n. 3; 143
Butler, Bishop Joseph: 67 n. 45

Casper, Bernhard: 7 n. 3
Cassirer, Ernst: 115 n. 11; 140–43; 144
 n. 4, 145 n. 6; 148–49 n. 8; 149–52
Cohen, Hermann: 3; 4; 8 n. 6; 15; 15 n.
 13; 22 n. 20; 28; 37; 78 n. 17; 84-85;

89; 90; 105; 105 n. 23; 111–12 n. 5;
127; 127 n. 31; 139 n. 49; 140–43;
146–52
 Religion of Reason out of the Sources
  of Judaism: ix; 84–85; 140–43;
  146–52
Cohn, Jonas: 7 n. 3; 28; 30
Copernicus, Nicholas: 110–11 n. 2; 134
Curtius, Ernst Robert: 7 n. 7

Dahlmann, Friedrich Christoph: 77; 77
 n. 14; 78; 79
Dante Alighieri: 48 n. 2; 101
David, Abraham ben (of Posquiéres):
 21–22 n. 19
Derrida, Jacques: vii
Descartes, René: 33; 39
Dilthey, Wilhelm: 4; 26; 132 n. 42; 143
Dinter, Arthur: 100 n. 14
Drews, Arthur: 10; 10 n. 3

Ebner, Ferdinand: 128; 128 n. 37
Eckermann, Johann Peter: 50; 50 n. 10
Ehrenberg, Hans: 2; 7 n. 5; 30; 38; 39;
 41; 44 n. 9; 45 n. 13; 56; 56 n. 21; 60;
 69; 69 n. 48; 109 n. 1; 127; 127 n. 30;
 138 n. 33
Ehrenberg, Rudolf: 1; 2; 25; 26; 36; 39;
 41; 43; 48 n. 1; 51–52 n. 11; 56 n. 21;
 72 n. 53; 84; 85; 128; 128 n. 35
Eisenmenger, Johann Andreas: 100; 100
 n. 13
Elbogen, Ismar: 4

Fackenheim, Emil: vii
Farin, Ingo: ix; 149 n. 9; 149 n. 10; 150
 n. 11
Feuerbach, Ludwig: 6; 127; 127 n. 30
Fichte, Johann Gottlieb: 16; 16 n. 15;
 29; 33; 39; 55 n. 19; 73 n. 1

Index of Subjects

1800: x; 1–2; 3; 7 n. 6; 27–43; 46 n. 25; 50; 69; 74; 81; 117. *See also* Fichte; German Idealism; Goethe; Hegel; Kant; Schelling

absolute: 32; 34; 38; 40; 41; 42; 50; 53; 54; 56 n. 21; 57; 58; 69
actuality: 16; 17; 18; 19; 30; 36; 49–50; 52; 56; 56 n. 21; 66; 69 n. 48; 70; 71; 79; 96; 99; 118; 119–20; 122; 124–25; 131–32; 136. *See also* Ehrenberg, Hans; Schelling
   of reason: 54–57; 60; 60 n. 29
   of God: 36; 56
aesthetics: vii; 111–12; 111–12 n. 5; 119 n. 19; 120; 129; 133; 133 n. 44; 143
aggadah: 5; 102–3; 102 n. 18
art: *See* aesthetics
atheism: 10–24; 32–34; 116

Baden-Baden: 1; 7 n. 5; 10 n. 2; 44 n. 11; 44 n. 12; 45 n. 13; 78 n. 7
Berlin: 3–4; 77 n. 12; 84; 85; 90; 146–47 n. 3
Bible: vii; viii; 5; 18 n. 17; 22 n. 20; 23 n. 21; 23 n. 22; 23 n. 24; 42; 53 n. 13; 61 n. 34; 91; 101 n. 15; 131; 140; 144 n. 1; 144 n. 2; 144 n. 3

Cassel: 1; 25; 85
Catholicism: *See* Christianity
chosen people: *See* people
Christianity: 1–2; 3; 11–13; 36; 39–41; 50; 50 n. 10; 52 n. 11; 71 n. 51; 88; 90; 96–97; 100; 101; 103–4. *See also* theology
   Catholicism: 39
   neo-Protestantism: 21
   Protestantism: 11; 39; 89
Copernican revolution: *See* revolution

correlation: 127 n. 31; 152; 152 n. 20. *See also* Cohen
creation: 2; 34; 55; 59; 63; 120; 124; 130; 136

dark ground: *See* ground
Davos: 140–43; 145 n. 6; 148–52; 148–49 n. 8; 149 n. 10; 150 n. 13; 151 n. 17; 151 n. 19

enlightenment: 11–12
epistemology: 52; 52–53 n. 12; 134–36
ethics: 22; 45 n. 13; 64; 78; 80; 111–12; 111–12 n. 5; 129; 133; 143; 147; 149 n. 10
essence: 17; 19; 20; 21; 35; 63; 102; 106; 108; 115–21
eternity: *See* time
existentialism: vii; 2; 7 n. 2; 35
experience: 36; 87; 115; 116; 120–21; 124; 135; 138
   empiricism: 36; 138; 138 n. 48. *See also* Schelling
   experiential philosophy: 117

factuality: 67; 67–68 n. 45; 69; 70. *See also Faktum*; matter of fact
Faktum: 41; 68; 68–69 n. 47; 69; 70. *See also* factuality; matter of fact
First World War: viii; 5; 25; 41–43; 73 n. 2; 74; 74 n. 3; 82–83; 84; 85; 86; 92 n. 1; 92 n. 8
Franco-Prussian War: 74; 76 n. 10; 81–82
Frankfurt: 77 n. 12; 84; 86
freedom: 33–34; 59; 63; 69 n. 47; 106; 122–23; 142; 145 n. 6
Freemasonry: 40; 46 n. 25
Freiburg: 1; 28; 44 n. 12; 145 n. 7
Freies Jüdisches Lehrhaus (Free Jewish Study House): 84; 86; 91; 93 n. 11
French revolution: *See* revolution